Mother Elmer and I
to the N.W.T. from Toronto
gust 1903. in a Colonist Car.

ONE CANADA

MEMOIRS OF THE RIGHT HONOURABLE

JOHN G. DIEFENBAKER

ONE CANADA

MEMOIRS OF THE RIGHT HONOURABLE

JOHN G. DIEFENBAKER

THE CRUSADING YEARS 1895-1956

MACMILLAN OF CANADA

TORONTO

ISBN 0-7705-1331-X

Printed and bound in Canada by Hunter Rose
for The Macmillan Company of Canada Limited
70 Bond Street, Toronto M5B 1X3

First Printing, October 1975
Second Printing, October 1975
Third Printing, November 1975

To Olive

LIST OF ILLUSTRATIONS

*Photographs not otherwise credited are from
Mr. Diefenbaker's personal collection.*

(BETWEEN PAGES 80 AND 81)

1. John and Elmer Diefenbaker, about 1902
2. William Thomas Diefenbaker and Mary Florence Bannerman on their wedding day
3. William Diefenbaker and his pupils from Greenwood School, 1899
4. Grandfather George Diefenbacker, 1905
5. The homestead house near Borden, Saskatchewan
6. William Diefenbaker and the pupils at Hoffnungsfeld School
7. Uncle Ed Diefenbaker
8. John G. Diefenbaker in 1915
9. Lieutenant Diefenbaker and friends, November 1916
10. The young lawyer, 1919
11. The house in Wakaw
12. Mrs. Florence Diefenbaker, 1920

(BETWEEN PAGES 144 AND 145)

13. The Conservative candidate, 1925
14. July 1 celebration at Macdowell, Saskatchewan
15. The Prince Albert courthouse
    (Saskatchewan Archives: Star-Phoenix Collection)

16. With party colleagues, 1929
17. Leader of the Saskatchewan Conservative Party, 1936
   (Saskatchewan Archives)
18. Mr. Diefenbaker with his parents and brother Elmer
19. The House of Commons, 24 June 1940
   (Public Archives of Canada)
20. With his law partners
   (Saskatchewan Archives: Star-Phoenix Collection)
21. A pointed comment, 1948
   (Louis Jaques–Canada Wide)
22. Mr. and Mrs. Diefenbaker at home
   (Saskatchewan Archives: Star-Phoenix Collection)
23. Visiting supporters at the Carle and Brownlee Livery
   Stable
   (Saskatchewan Archives: Star-Phoenix Collection)
24 & 25. With friends and admirers at Glenside
   (Saskatchewan Archives: Star-Phoenix Collection)

(BETWEEN PAGES 208 AND 209)

26. Chatting with a delegate, October 1948 *(Canada Wide)*
27. John Bracken and George Drew*(Canada Pictures Ltd.)*
28. The candidates and their wives
   (Andrews-Newton Photographers, Ottawa)
29. Addressing the delegates   *(Canada Wide)*
30. Two seasoned campaigners
   (Public Archives of Canada)
31. "Chief Eagle"
   (Saskatchewan Archives: Star-Phoenix Collection)
32. A reception in honour of John and Olive Diefenbaker
   following their marriage
   (Saskatchewan Archives: Star-Phoenix Collection)
33. The three candidates at the Leadership Convention,
   December 1956   *(Canada Wide)*
34. Supporters marching around the convention hall
   (Wide World Photos)
35. Acknowledging the cheers of supporters
   (Canada Wide)

36. Congratulating the newly elected Leader
(Wide World Photos)
37. Mr. and Mrs. Diefenbaker   *(Canada Wide)*
38. Mr. Diefenbaker with his mother
   (Saskatchewan Archives: Star-Phoenix Collection)

The publishers are indebted to Rolly Productions, Ottawa, Ontario, for permission to use the two coloured lithographs by Eleanor Kish and Rachel H. Beaulieu reproduced as endpapers in this book.

PREFACE

This is the first of three proposed volumes of my Memoirs. The second and third volumes to be published will follow apace.

For the past several years I have been collecting and dictating material for my Memoirs. It has proven a more complicated task than I first imagined. The many duties incumbent upon a Member of Parliament, to say nothing of three intervening general elections since I ceased to be Leader of the Progressive Conservative Party of Canada, often had to take precedence over this work.

Having a mass of material on hand, what I needed most was the assistance of a writer-historian to collate and structure my material into book form. For this purpose I enlisted the experience and the research and narrative skills of John A. Munro, M.A., who, with the able assistance of Dr. John H. Archer, President of the University of Regina, has been responsible for the preparation of the literary side of my Memoirs. They, in turn, had the advice and counsel of my long-time friends Mr. Thomas Van Dusen and Mr. Gregor Guthrie.

To each and all of them I extend my heartfelt thanks, and as well my gratitude to the Canada Council for the financial support provided to Mr. Munro and Dr. Archer in their work.

FOREWORD

It is difficult to imagine two historians engaged in a more
superfluous task than that of introducing the Right Honourable John George Diefenbaker, the man and his memoirs, to the reading public. Canadians have lived their
lives in the shadow of his political presence. Consider
that John Diefenbaker has been on the political stump
since 1917; consider also that over eighty per cent of Canada's population has been born since he made his political debut in support of Sir Robert Borden's Unionist Government. Still, we cannot be other than impressed by the
uniqueness of this so long awaited opportunity to examine with Mr. Diefenbaker the forces and circumstances
that shaped, not simply the character of a single individual, but an important part of the country as a whole. It
may be contended that never before have Canadians
been presented with so complete a Western overview of
their nation's political history. And, perhaps more important in reading this first volume of the Diefenbaker story,
if we think ahead upon the events and achievements that
surrounded his tenure as Prime Minister of Canada and
as national Leader of the Progressive Conservative Party,
we may then see the past revealed, visiting itself upon the
present to lend shape to the future. The Canada that
shaped John Diefenbaker would through his agency help
determine our future as a nation.

John Diefenbaker's is a life that began in 1895, a year not otherwise distinguished for events of moment in Canadian history. How many readers, for example, will remember that Canada's Prime Minister in 1895 was Sir Mackenzie Bowell? This was the Victorian era, settled and sane, and its designation alone seemed sufficient to ensure an orderly and British advance of time and circumstance. Yet, 1895 was to be the last full year of a Conservative ascendancy in Canadian federal politics that had begun with Sir John Macdonald and Confederation. Macdonald was now three years dead. Canada's seventh Prime Minister, Wilfrid Laurier, was in the wings. Canada's thirteenth Prime Minister was born that 18 September.

John George Diefenbaker was born in Ontario but reared in the pioneer West. It is not, however, just his environs which fascinate, but the portrait of the man himself: his framework of convictions, ideals, biases, concepts; the pattern of personal experience—the prairie boy with his longings and his dreams, the young officer invalided home launched into politics, the lawyer catapulted into national prominence in criminal and civil law, the political hopeful vetted in the realities of Saskatchewan politics. As the Member from Lake Centre, he entered the national arena. The Man from Prince Albert became Prime Minister of Canada. John Diefenbaker tells in his own words of those things that compelled him to champion their change: the helplessness of farmers caught up in market forces beyond their control, the plight of native Canadians, the evils of discrimination affecting those of other than English or French antecedents, the northern frontier hobbled through lack of vision, the subordination of our cultural identity in the shadow of the United States. Here is the public and the private man. If this first volume seems to make his private convictions and his public life explainable, there are also disclosures that seem to make more complex the diverse forces conflicting on the broad stage of this remarkable man's career. This must be so. His is no simple personality content and at ease with his times.

The title of this work is *One Canada*. John Diefenbaker's is a dream we have long known: a Canada in which no man can be discriminated against or demeaned because of his racial origin, his colour, or his creed. He learned early that he could not legislate "goodness" into the hearts of men. Despite this, he hoped that a Canadian Bill of Rights would ensure each Canadian man and woman the fundamental freedoms that were theirs by birth or by adoption. That he would have no second-class citizenship, no hyphenated Canadianism, he conveys to his readers with telling conviction. Nor would he have a balkanized Canada.

Eighty years old this September, 1975, he is Canada's, if not the Commonwealth's, grand old Chief. Of course, the term "old" is no more than a chronological distinction, for his power in the House and on the stump, now legendary, seems unabated. To many he has long seemed a touchstone of consistency in a world fraught with uncertainty. He stands foursquare as the guardian of our institutional heritage, at times a lone voice protesting the senseless assault on the signs and symbols of our national ethos. He has become an institution, although probably not a benign one to those who sit opposite him in the House. So much of the aura remains. So much of the record is high drama.

It has been a privilege to have had an opportunity to play some part in bringing Canadians this authentic voice of one of the makers of modern Canada.

John A. Munro
John H. Archer

ONE CANADA
MEMOIRS OF THE RIGHT HONOURABLE
JOHN G. DIEFENBAKER

CHAPTER ONE

WHAT DETERMINES THE CHARACTER OF A MAN? Whence does he get his strength to endure, to abide by his principles, and to reject the concept of the impossible in human affairs? It is my conviction that a man is the end product of his ancestors, proximate and remote, that he is endowed at birth with a heritage of character, but that this character may be influenced by fortuitous circumstances. The roots of my immediate forebears were deeply imbedded in pioneer Canada. Dispossessed Scottish Highlanders and discontented Palatine Germans were regenerated in the New World. The union of their children's children produced yet another generation of Canadian pioneers.

My father's parents were born in Upper Canada and lived in the hamlet of Hawkesville in Waterloo County. Their parents, in turn, had emigrated from Baden in the first part of the nineteenth century. Grandfather Diefenbacker (a spelling he used until his death in 1907) was a highly skilled wagon- and sleigh-maker. When he was some seventy-eight years of age, he made us a magnificent wagon of oak and maple to use on the homestead. Unfortunately, he had no knowledge of Western roads, and the wheels were too low and the gauge too narrow to be of any use over prairie trails. But it was a fine piece of work. We never let him know that we could not use it except around the homestead. My only encounter with him was in 1902 when we spent about three weeks at my grandparents' place at Hawkesville. The cottage is still there, attractive even today. Grandmother, whose maiden name was Lackner, was a typical housewife, a dutiful rather than an affectionate person when dealing with young people. Grandfather held strong opinions and was of independent mind. I remember him saying, when someone suggested that Grandfather might do something for a particular person in expectation that he would benefit in the long run: "I won't do it; I don't like him!"

On my mother's side, my great-grandfather Campbell, from Argyll, Scotland, a blacksmith, settled in what is now the King City area near Toronto in 1825 or 1826. My mother's mother, Flora Campbell, was born on board ship, just off Newfoundland. The other side of Mother's family, the Bannermans, kindled my early interest in the North with their stories of travel and adventure. They had seen the North as few others had or, indeed, would wish to.

The name Bannerman originated in the hereditary duty of bearing in battle the standard of the Scottish clan. My great-grandfather, George Bannerman, came from the Kildonan strath in Sutherland in the Highlands. Culloden in 1746 and the final defeat there of the Young Pretender, Prince Charles Edward, saw most of the Bannermans killed. (The Bannermans, a sept of the Clan Forbes, were not numerous enough to rate a separate grave and had to share a common one.) The break-up of the clan system followed the disaster of Culloden. Then came the notorious closures at the turn of the nineteenth century which drove the Scottish crofter from his land. Landed lords decided that there was more profit in wool and mutton than in tenant farmers; and there was no power to say them nay. Everywhere, poor Scots were evicted from their cottages, displaced by the hundreds and thousands so that large districts might be converted into extensive sheepwalks. Some went south, either to Edinburgh or Glasgow, or on to England. Others came to America. My great-grandfather and great-grandmother Bannerman were among the victims of the Sutherland clearances of 1811 and 1812. The Countess of Sutherland had decided that she needed the land for her own purposes.

The ruin of my great-grandfather's cottage is still to be seen in the Kildonan strath. I saw it, or what was left of it, for myself in 1968, when I unveiled a cairn to the memory of Sir John A. Macdonald's mother and father, who had lived at Rogart, fifteen miles or so from Kildonan. Later, they moved to Glasgow, where Sir John was born, and then migrated to Kingston in Upper Canada. When I was Prime Minister, during a visit to Scotland in 1958 we attended church in Helmsdale. Of course, our retinue was fairly large what with our staff and the pressmen. The minister made no reference to our presence except in the last minute or so when he said that the Highlands are forever in the hearts of the descendants.

Homeless, the Bannermans were fortunate to be among the hundred selected from some seven hundred applicants to form the third party of settlers destined for Canada's Red River in 1813. Upright, hardy, Gaelic-speaking Presbyterian folk, with a love for the land, they were attracted by the settlement scheme of that great Scottish philanthropist, Thomas, fifth Earl of Selkirk. A man in advance of his times, Lord Selkirk devoted his fortune and his life to establishing new settlements in British North America for those of his countrymen who had been forced to leave their ancestral homes.

What feeling must have gripped the hearts of George Bannerman, his brothers and sisters, and, of course, my great-grandmother as they left their beloved Scotland for a perilous crossing of the North Atlantic into Hudson Bay. Certainly, their voyage was hard, for in the cramped quarters of that sailing ship typhoid broke out. They were to be disembarked at York Factory, from where they would make their arduous way to the colony by river, portage, and lake. Instead, they were dumped off at Churchill in the late fall of 1813 by their captain who, apparently terrified by the prospect of the typhoid's spreading, refused to take them farther. Thus, adding to their miseries, they were compelled to spend their first winter in Canada on the cruel Arctic banks of the Churchill River. Two Bannermans were among the dead, one at sea, the other marked by a board in the graveyard at Churchill. It was in the early spring of 1814 when they made their way overland to York Factory and the Hayes River which would provide them with a water route to the site of their new homes. According to my great-grandfather, they were forced to leave Churchill before the snow had gone because the English Governor of the fort was irritated by their shooting too many ptarmigan. The distance to be covered was some one hundred and ten or twenty miles, with the added hazard of late blizzards. There was another loss of life. To keep their spirits up, the procession was led by two pipers: one, my great-grandfather's brother, and the other a member of the Gunn family. Finally they arrived. But not until 21 June 1814 did the York boats carrying them from Hudson Bay reach Lord Selkirk's river settlement, just above the forks where the Assiniboine meets the Red.

They could not have known that after all they had suffered, privations almost beyond understanding today, they would find themselves caught up in battles waged between two competing fur-trade empires, the North West and the Hudson's Bay companies. For many, this was too much to bear. What they sought was simply the chance to build anew, not to be pawns in a struggle remote from their understanding or interest. This situation prompted one hundred and thirty-three of them, after enduring yet another hard winter, to leave the Red River for Upper Canada, where they had been promised aid in resettlement and where they might live their lives in peace. This time they travelled in canoe brigades by way of Fort William to the East. Their route had been long and arduous, from Kildonan in the Highlands to where finally my great-grandfather settled, first in what is now Elgin County, and later in what was called the Scotch Settlement, near Holland Landing.

To complete the background on my mother's side, during the time of the Crimean War the Bannermans moved to Bruce County, to the Tenth Concession of Bruce Township, where my mother, Mary Florence Bannerman, was born. Their house, brick and stone, was the first to be built in that region. It would appear that they had prospered. When they began their move to Bruce, Great-grandfather had five thousand dollars in gold. This they carried in the feed bag under the wagon, a place thieves were not likely to search. I never knew my grandparents on my mother's side; they died when I was only two or three years old.

The Bannermans, as I have mentioned, were Presbyterians. My maternal grandmother was a Baptist, and when finally she was able to persuade her husband to join her church, their home became the centre for Baptist itinerant ministers in that part of Ontario. My grandfather, John Bannerman, became a Deacon of the Baptist Church. In their home there were no activities on Sunday apart from attendance at church services. It would be unusual, so I was told, if the sermon was limited to less than two hours. Sometimes there were two services on the same Sunday of equally generous length. These were a deeply religious people who took little interest in public affairs.

I might add from what my mother told me that despite this general lack of interest in public affairs, there arose considerable division within the Bannerman family over the Rebellion of 1837. My great-grandfather, no lover of the Family Compact, bore arms to follow William Lyon Mackenzie. In fact, he followed him as far as the United States border, which Mackenzie reached in fast retreat. Great-grandfather could go no farther because he was bearing arms on behalf of the Crown; he had in conscience rejected Mackenzie's rebellion as a solution to Upper Canada's problems. Over a hundred years after the event of which I am writing, I had gentle sport in recounting this story in the House of Commons to the outrage of the then Prime Minister, Mr. Mackenzie King, who took an overweening pride in the achievements of his maternal grandfather.

Great-grandfather told my mother a story of life in the early 1830s which I have always found instructive. The greatest celebration of all in Upper Canada, one that brought all the people together within reasonable distance, was a public execution. He himself had been present at one. The pioneers arrived a day ahead for the festivities. With whiskey selling at less than a dollar a gallon, liquor became a source not only of exhilaration but of inspiration for the assembled, enabling them the more to enjoy the spectacle. The condemned man was a teenager whose offence had been pickpocketing. The death penalty was then imposed for some fifty or sixty offences. The law was less harsh than it had been; no longer were prisoners drawn and quartered. But the theory was that punishment must be imposed so that the criminal would understand the gravity of the sin he had committed. Also, deterrence was then the argument and still is among those who advocate capital punishment. On this occasion, the young man made a speech in the traditional style of condemned criminals in Upper Canada: he admitted his guilt and asked for forgiveness. He was not restricted to a fixed length of time, since time really meant nothing. While he was making his testimony of guilt, four of the assembled pioneers found that their pockets had been picked.

My father, William Thomas Diefenbaker, was born 6 April 1868, the day before the assassination of Thomas D'Arcy McGee, of whose life and works Father was later to become an enthusiastic student. He looked upon McGee as the philosopher and orator of Confederation. Father attended high school in Berlin (now Kitchener), finishing his grade eleven at Collingwood Collegiate. He then taught school on a temporary certificate at a couple of schools before taking his Model or Normal School course in 1890-91 at the Model School in Ottawa.

I am not certain how Father got through his courses because it appears that during his year in Ottawa he spent most of his time sitting in the Gallery of the House of Commons. Those were formative years in the history of Canada. Sir John A. was in the last year of his life. Laurier was the rising star. Father did not like Sir John A. because of his legendary capacity for drinking and because of his reputation for wiliness, although he had a considerable regard for Macdonald's capacity as a leader in Parliament. Father's unstinting admiration was for Laurier and he remained a follower until 1917 when, because of the conscription issue, and along with thousands and thousands of others, he left the Liberal Party, first to become a Unionist and then, like most of those who left, to become a Conservative. Father acquired a wide knowledge of the mechanics of Parliament. He knew the rules inside and out. Indeed, he virtually memorized Bourinot's book on parliamentary procedure. The House of Commons lived for him, and it lived for me when I heard him recount the events he had witnessed and stories of the parliamentary personalities he had seen. If he had ever had the opportunity of becoming a Member, this would have crowned his highest, although never voiced, ambition.

Father was an unusually good student. He belonged to a farming family that had a high regard for education. His brothers, with two exceptions, were teachers. Among his cousins were doctors and bank managers. There were certain fields of study that particularly interested Father. He had an unusual command of language, an addiction for etymology, the history of words and their origins. He also had a capacity for learning languages (which he could not pass on to me). He spoke French well. But I think that his greatest affection was for Shakespeare (*Coriolanus* was his favourite play). He was a thoroughly well-versed student of Gibbon. His knowledge of British history was phenomenal, with particular emphasis, as I recall, on the manner in which freedom had been established; he had a deep respect for the law. He did not take the same interest in Canadian history, beyond the Rebellion of 1837. He was to remain a student throughout his life. Indeed, when we were on the homestead, he took up astronomy and became quite expert in it. Always interested in mathematics, he regretted that he had been unable to go to university. So, at the age of sixty he decided he must study calculus.

Father was an unusual person. He was not a driver in any sense of the word, but a dreamer who loved books. He was an excellent teacher. It is of interest to note that he is the only teacher to have had two future Canadian Prime Ministers as pupils. Father was not Mackenzie King's professional teacher, but when he took his Normal School year one of the requirements was that the student teacher would teach for two or three weeks in some schoolroom. Father was assigned to the primary school in Berlin in which Mackenzie King was a pupil, already designated by his mother as a Prime Minister-to-be, with a mission, as he told Father, to carry out what his mother's father, William Lyon Mackenzie, had been unable to do in Upper Canada and restore the name of Mackenzie to its proper calibration. Father was one of the two or three people to call Mackenzie King "Willie" in later years, and at Mr. King's request. I might add that Mr. King's esteem for my father did not carry over to the son.

Father had an affection for all who were in difficulty, no matter what the cost or how little money he had. Regardless of who came along, whether they were worthy or unworthy, if they asked for assistance, Father would give it. When it was pointed out to him that he had given money to a worthless character, his answer always was, "One is bound to make a mistake now and then, but I would sooner make the mistake of giving than of not giving." His philosophy of life: do unto others as you would they do unto you.

Mother was an unusual woman, deeply proud of her Highland ancestry, canny and "a wee bit fey". She was careful, and determined never to spend a dollar that could be saved. Both my parents were devout Christians. But Mother's was the much more determined personality. I don't think she ever knew the meaning of defeat. She would say: "If we help others, we help ourselves." When I look back over my life, Mother gave me drive, Father gave me the vision to see what could be done.

My father and mother were married in May 1894, in the village of Underwood, near Tiverton in Bruce County, Ontario. They had met while Father was teaching school there. When a better position was offered him in a school in Normanby Township in Grey County, just out of the village of Neustadt, he took it. They moved from Underwood a few weeks before my birth on 18 September 1895. The only recollection I have of our life in Neustadt is one concerning my dog. I have always been fond of dogs and as a little fellow I was determined to have one. Finally I got my wish, a mongrel puppy named Tip. I loved him. But my joy was short-lived. Some people near by gave him meat with strychnine in it. I buried him in front of the shed at the back of our house. It was a sad ceremony. I do not recollect this, but Mother told me that as Tip was laid to rest I said, "Now I know what it means to die."

We stayed in Neustadt until 1897. My brother Elmer was born there. As brothers, our relationship over the years approached that often described but seldom encountered ideal. I am sorry, though, that there were to be no more of us and, in retrospect, particularly sorry that Elmer and I were to grow up without sisters. Given our later isolation on the homestead, our separation from other boys and girls, it became natural to think of women as a species apart, an experience destined to leave a permanent mark on one's attitude towards them.

Father in 1897 got a school in Greenwood, a most beautiful part of Ontario. There, I have more in the way of recollections. Times were hard but not desperate. A look at the minutes of the school trustee meetings indicates that the very small salary paid to Father was often long overdue (firewood being supplied on occasion as part of the salary). Sometimes credit for the purchase of groceries would be provided at the local store by resolution of the school board. There were, however, many things to sustain us in the more difficult period of our life. In our home in Greenwood, and in all our subsequent homes, Bible reading and family prayer were daily and rewarding experiences. No meal was ever begun until grace had been said. On Sundays we went to church and Sunday School at Uxbridge. Although I was only four, I was allowed to go to school in Greenwood. I objected to staying home; I knew how to read, having learned in order to understand the thermometer on page one of the *Globe*, which gave the weather forecast each day.

Music was also a part of our lives. We always had a

Thomas organ in our home. Father was an accomplished player; Mother played reasonably well. When we later moved to Todmorden, Father played the organ in the Methodist Church and frequently sang solos. He taught a music class after school hours and spent many hours composing songs and hymns. When living in Ottawa in 1890-91, he had been a tenor in the choir of the Dominion Methodist Church. For myself, except for an occasional march or Handel's *Messiah*, I have no emotional response to music. All I can muster in song is a rather dreary monotone hum.

Our place in Greenwood had a tremendous growth of lilacs and was most attractive every spring. I remember also that there was a hill by our house. It must have been a quarter of a mile long with a very sharp gradient. In winter, older boys went down it on double-decked sleds. I thought I could do this too. Down I went. All at once there loomed in front of me a team of horses pulling a milk cart. I passed between their front and hind legs, scraping the top of my head on the cart tongue. Had I raised my head, I could have been decapitated. Another recollection is that we children were very frightened of a most distinguished man, the greatest criminal lawyer of his time, T. C. Robinette. He came out on Sundays to visit his girl friend, Miss Green, whose father ran the store at the foot of the hill. We were very frightened of him because we had heard that he defended men who had killed others. We thought he must be very wicked to do this. When, many years later, I was honoured by being called to the bar of Upper Canada, his son, the distinguished counsel, J. J. Robinette, Q.C., was Treasurer of the Upper Canada Law Society. I might add that I have raised strong objection to the Government of Canada taking over the fine agricultural land and magnificent old homes of the Greenwood area for a new airport. The face of this countryside deserves to remain unspoiled.

Small-town Ontario at the turn of the century, as I recall it, was completely detached. Each village and town lived to itself. People developed a deep loyalty for their particular locality and were not much interested in the rest of the province. Curiously enough, though, when the migration took place from Eastern Canada to the Prairies, you might ask someone, "You came from Ontario. What part?" Never would they say, "I lived at Greenwood" — or Brougham or Uxbridge or Whitby — but, "Near Toronto".

Father's ambition was to teach in Toronto and in the summer of 1900 he made a number of applications to the city's schools. As a step in that direction, Dr. Fotheringham, the Superintendent of Schools, suggested that he apply to the School Board of Plains Road District in the eastern suburbs of the city. He did so and was accepted.

In 1900, we moved to Todmorden. The whole area there, which would be two miles and a half from the centre of Toronto, was a vast market-garden area; on the site of our cottage there is today a drugstore and I think a two- or three-storey building. We lived a year on the northwest corner of what is now the intersection between Don Mills Road and O'Connor Drive. The school where Father taught and which I attended was several blocks to the east. Our home then was on the highway taken by the aristocrats of Toronto in their newfangled electric carriages when out for a spin on a Sunday. I saw practically the beginnings of this new traffic: how they travelled, looking neither to right nor left, the cynosure of all eyes, the women in big hats, with a kind of handkerchief around their chins, and the men wearing dusters. Sometimes these cars ran and sometimes not. When they broke down they afforded me a great deal of enjoyment. I would ask the drivers such helpful questions as, "Do you think it will ever start again?" This, I found, having done it once, practically assured sharp ejaculations of annoyance, so I invariably raised the question at every opportunity, just to test the reaction. Needless to say, none of these people offered me a ride, however much I might secretly have wished for one. Not until 1907, when on the homestead, did we get our first ride in an automobile, in the back of a Brush one-seater, owned by a real estate man in Radisson, Saskatchewan.

The first time I attended any great national event was on the return of the Canadian Contingent from the Boer War. They were to parade passing Toronto's City Hall. Mother had me dolled up, a sight to behold. She had always been a skilful seamstress, and I had on a Fauntleroy collar and a blue velvet sailor suit, trousers with two buttons, and a little Scotch Balmoral. The scavenger in East Toronto was a good-hearted man called Skelhorn. He used to go around on a horse-drawn wagon with a big tank on it to collect the garbage or the slops and swill, which he then sold for hog feed. I had become attached to Skelhorn and he offered to drive me into town for the event. (Why I didn't go with my parents, I can't remember.) Mr. Skelhorn had removed the pump and the handle from the top of the tank, leaving the opening uncovered. I was sitting atop the wagon as we moved on to Danforth Avenue off Don Mills Road. There was a depression in the road and a bump. The team staggered, there was a jerk, and I fell into the tank. The swill had been removed but there were several inches of grease at the bottom of the tank. I was unhurt but I was the filthiest mess that anyone could imagine. I left Skelhorn at the Toronto market and against his advice headed for the parade. At City Hall everything was roped off to keep the crowds back. That did not stop me. There was Mayor Urquhart of Toronto along with all the other political and military celebrities on the steps of the City Hall, and four or five feet away that urchin covered with grease. I was such a fright that nobody dared touch me. There I watched with wonder the returning soldiers and joined in the cheers for the Highlanders. When my mother heard what I had done, she was shocked. "We'll be disgraced," she said, "for all time to come." We were not disgraced. I could not have been recognized no matter what.

I was extraordinarily fond of fishing as a boy; I still am, as was my father before me. There is a pleasure and, above all, a peace to be enjoyed in fishing beyond anything else I know; it is as if the outside world were forbidden to intrude upon a fisherman's thoughts. In the summer of 1902, we spent some three weeks tenting on Stoney Lake, near Lakefield, Ontario. We were accompanied by my mother's sister Sadie and her husband, the Reverend E. J. Bridgeman, the Baptist minister at Lakefield. Father was out fishing for most of the daylight hours and kept us fully supplied with bass. Once he hooked on to a muskellunge, which, after a few minutes, got away. Since then, although I have fished successfully from British Columbia to New Brunswick and in the Northwest Territories for salmon, steelheads, trout, grayling, sturgeon, goldeyes, and whitefish, the one fish that has eluded me is the muskellunge. Father's greatest catch was in the Prince Albert National Park, where, in 1938, he boated six lake trout weighing a total of ninety-four pounds.

At school, however, things were sometimes unpleasant. The Plains Road School had only one room in use, with twenty-eight students in all grades. Father was the teacher. It is unfortunate for a son to go to his father's school because the other pupils are very quick to resent any suggestion of allegedly preferential or differential treatment. Father was sensitive to this situation. One result was that I was not allowed to have children from the school over to play. Another was that I suffered a discipline that was harder than for other pupils. This does not mean that Father discriminated against me; far from it, for his devotion knew no bounds. But when there was some mischief in the class and I was blamed whether rightly or wrongly by the other students, their word was accepted. I remember discussions among the boys on how, while accepting the punishment, one might escape the pain of strapping. One of the older pupils—he was about fourteen—claimed that the solution lay in rubbing poison ivy into your hands and face. This I did, and I do not need to tell you the results. Also, I was forbidden to take part in fights. It would not have served my family well had I entered into battle with the son of a school trustee. The consequence of this was that I was the loser whenever I was attacked or challenged. I suppose that I was a fairly sensitive boy but do not think unnaturally so. I used to get quite upset when my schoolmates teased me about my name. I felt that my forebears' having been in Canada for so long a time made me a Canadian. I was just seven years old, but my ideas on that subject have not changed with the passage of time. One must remember, however, that in those days Toronto was ninety-eight per cent British. The Toronto of that day would not recognize the Toronto of today.

Financially, times continued to be difficult. The salary received by Father was, as I recall it, four hundred dollars a year and it was hard for Mother to make ends meet. Father had bought things on credit and owed some three hundred dollars. The debt was not easily cleared away. As a direct result of this experience, it became a fixed rule in our family that never again would we buy anything on credit. This self-imposed ban was temporarily lifted when we moved onto the homestead, but was renewed when we moved into the city of Saskatoon in February 1910. To add to his small income as a teacher, Father taught after hours, tutoring in bookkeeping. In 1901, we moved into a duplex, about a mile closer to the city down Don Mills Road. The Ashes who lived in the other section of the duplex lived well. Among other things they had Quaker Oats in five-pound paper boxes. We had oatmeal for breakfast, but in bulk. Elmer and I always hoped for the day when we would have boxed oatmeal, but that day never came.

At an early age I developed a consciousness of injustice which has never left me. The idea of the poor being treated differently, the working man being looked down upon as a digit, filled me with revulsion. I was beginning to add to my Highland inheritance an acquired distrust of powerful forces and a concern over their overwhelming impact on the helpless. I formed a friendship with two or three Negro boys in our area who, in my opinion, were being badly treated. I must admit, however, that when I was five or six years old I called out a term of derision to a Negro groom riding one of the Robert Davies thoroughbreds past our house; it was not "fuddle duddle"! I will never forget the castigation I got from my father, or my promise to him that as long as I should live I would never use that expression again.

Robert Davies had a racing stable near by, and from day to day his horses would pass by on the way to or returning from the race track. I have always been fond of horses, and it may be that this dates back to experiences at Todmorden. Mr. Davies' trainer, Mr. Jenkins, occasionally would give me a ride on the sulky, to my great joy. How different was my experience with the young lads of the Davies family. They had everything that money could buy. They had Shetland ponies and two-wheel carts in which the poor were not allowed even the shortest ride.

Father took me wherever he went. Elmer was too young, being but three or four years of age, to go along to the city. Almost every Saturday Father would get a ride into Toronto's downtown areas. The prize of all trips was to be taken to the tower of the City Hall, or to Queen's Park. On a few occasions we went over to Upper Canada

College, which was almost directly west of our home on Don Mills Road. It was natural for Father, who was deeply devoted to the Monarchy throughout his life and defended it strongly against all comers, to take the family to see the Duke and Duchess of Cornwall and York, when they visited Toronto in 1901. It was a great day. Mother, however, did not share Father's devotion to the Crown, having inherited the memories of the slaughter of the clans at Culloden. Bonnie Prince Charlie was to her a living, not an historical, figure. She had a feeling toward the English that was not one of complete adulation, and she could not take the same pride as Father in being a part of an Empire on which the sun never set. When Queen Victoria died, Father regarded it as one of the most calamitous events of all time. Would the world ever be the same? I can see him now. When he came home to tell us the news, he broke down and cried.

Although their attitude fell far short of pacifism or conscientious objection, my parents shared a deep hatred of war. No doubt Mother derived her perspective on war from the way in which her parents and grandparents had interpreted the Highland experience. Father's related experiences went back to the Napoleonic wars, or at least I presume so, to when Father's grandfather was knocked down by a French soldier, his pig stolen, and his leg broken when he resisted. It was an ancestral experience that never was entirely forgotten.

Father, as I have mentioned, had a more than ordinary appreciation of the meaning of Parliament and of public service. He was able to convey to his pupils and to anyone in conversation with him his belief that only in individual service is it possible to make that contribution to Canada that each of us, according to his talents, should make. He had a persuasive way about him. There can be no other explanation for the fact that, when I came into the House of Commons in 1940, of the twenty-eight pupils who had been in the Plains Road School in Todmorden in 1903, four were Members: Joe Harris, George Tustin, Bob (R.H.) McGregor, and myself (Conservatives all). When later a celebration was planned to honour my father at the Plains Road School, each of us wrote and said that it was due to him that we had gone into public life. Father did not live to receive these tributes. He regarded politics as the highest of callings. Certainly, he was enthusiastic at the thought that Elmer and I might become interested in public life. For himself, for reasons that he best understood, he was content to serve the public weal through his church, his schools, and his lodge, the Independent Order of Foresters. He was interested, he always cast his vote, but he never sought political or elective office. More devoted to his duties in my opinion than was necessary, Father suffered a breakdown in health in the spring of 1903. The doctors considered that he was on the verge of developing what was then described as galloping consumption. Their advice was that he leave Toronto and seek the benefits of a prairie climate. Consequently, Father placed his name with an agency that handled teaching vacancies. He soon received, and accepted, an offer from a school in the Fort Carlton area in the Northwest Territories.

CHAPTER TWO

ALL OUR RELATIVES were strongly opposed to our leaving Ontario. It seemed to them that we were going to the uttermost ends of the earth, into territories virtually unknown. Only eighteen years earlier, rebellion had flared, and the Northwest was no place for civilized people. Life there, they felt, would be rough and unrewarding. So strong was their protest that Father began to doubt the wisdom of accepting the school. During our last three weeks in Toronto, we were staying with Mother's brother, Duncan Bannerman, a grocer and dairyman on Davenport Road. I remember one particular conversation between my parents. Father said, "Mary, do you really think we should go? Your brother Duncan says 'no' and my brothers say 'no'." Mother's response was, "We're going. Once you put your hand to the plough, you don't turn back." Father, however, continued to have second thoughts.

Furniture, dishes, bedding, clothing, all were packed and sent on by freight on the CPR to Regina, thence through Saskatoon to Rosthern on the Regina–Prince Albert branch line. Of course, we did not have the money to travel in style, to sleep in elegant, comfortable carriages, or to eat in luxurious dining cars with damask curtains and gleaming silverware. We were to travel colonist class, a very basic third-class accommodation used mainly for transporting immigrants to the Prairies. Realizing that there would be no sleeping accommodation and no meals served, Mother prepared and carefully packed lunches to carry us through to Winnipeg, and put together two rolls of quilts, blankets, and pillows. This was 15 August 1903. The train was to leave Toronto in the late afternoon. Father went down early to put our supplies on board. Misdirected by a railway official, he placed our food and bedding on a car whose destination was *not* Winnipeg. We arrived shortly before departure time to find, too late, what had taken place. Thus, we began our journey. Could there have been a more inauspicious launching into a new country?

The colonist cars were filled with immigrants in search of new homes and with field workers going West to work on the harvest. The immigrants were a medley of different races, their hearts filled with hope that Western Canada would be their land of promise. They had endured the discomforts of a steerage-class ocean crossing and now were enduring the equal discomforts of the train. Wonderful people, they provided Elmer and me with blankets and shared some of their food with us; but the first real meal we had after leaving Toronto was at Fort William. I shall never forget that ride. Pairs of hard wooden seats facing each other looked as though they had been removed from some abandoned railway station. Above, a hard wooden shelf swung down from the wall, a sort of primitive upper berth, without curtains, where Elmer and I slept, tied in so that we would not fall. Mother and Father sat up on the seats below. At one end of the car there was a wood-burning kitchen range, a water barrel, a few cups, and a wash basin. Mile after mile after endless mile, Elmer and I learned something of the meaning of eternity.

As for Father, he saw in our predicament a

confirmation that he had been right in doubting the wisdom of our leaving Toronto. At Fort William, he proposed that we turn back. Mother said, "We started out and we're going on." Father was quite set and replied that no matter what, he was returning. Mother would have none of this. She told him, "If you do, the rest of us will carry on and you'll come out sooner or later." That was the difference in their spirits. Father used to say, "Well, you know, Mary is always right. Sometimes I don't think so at the time, but it always turns out to be the proper course to take." How different would have been our lives, and mine in particular, had we turned back. Such are the "ifs" of life.

Winnipeg station was the funnel into a new world for the prairie colonists. I remember Winnipeg, however, for a restaurant just outside the station on Main Street where for thirty-five cents I had the most enjoyable meal of my life. After an hour or two we were back on the train to Regina, the centre of the New West. Father still felt that we should go back. Mother stood firm.

At Regina, we began the final leg of our journey. By the time we arrived in Saskatoon, Father's total ready cash amounted to one dollar and seventy-five cents. Time meant nothing to the railway crews. From Craik to Dundurn with sloughs alive with ducks, ducks in the thousands, the train stopped three times as the crew went out to shoot. The passengers knew better than to complain. According to the wits of that day CNR (the Canadian Northern Railway) stood for "Can Not Run". It might well have applied to the CPR. There was the story of the chap who rushed in to the station and said, "Am I in time?" "Oh, yes," was the reply. "It's the first time I've ever seen this train on time," the passenger commented. They told him, "This is yesterday's train." Finally we arrived.

Father decided to write to his brother Ed and to Uncle

Duncan to inform them of our safe arrival. We went to the little Post Office on First Avenue for stamps. They were sold out because of the demand created by the large number of immigrants passing through. The Post Office, however, was generally well run in those days. There have been changes since! The population of Saskatoon was then only about five hundred. On the West Side there were still some of the tents of the Barr colonists, Englishmen who came over under the leadership of the Reverend Isaac Barr and who established themselves ultimately at Lloydminster. They were full of courage, but knew little of the pioneering trials that were to be their daily lot; and they were often "taken in" by the locals because they didn't know the ways of Canada.

Then aboard for the town of Rosthern, some forty miles north of Saskatoon. It was dark when we arrived. Everyone was out to meet the train, perhaps a couple of hundred people speaking languages we did not understand: Ukrainian, Hungarian, Polish. Many spoke in German and a few in French, both of which languages Father could speak very well. Mother, who could only speak English, described the scene as a modern Tower of Babel. The Ukrainians were dressed in fall and winter sheepskin coats. I might mention that I have never quarrelled with the view that Clifford Sifton, Laurier's Minister of the Interior, did an amazing job in bringing in the new multitudes to Western Canada. These settlers and their descendants have made great contributions to Canada.

Rosthern was a booming town. In the part of the Territories to become Saskatchewan, it was second in grain elevators only to Indian Head. There were nine, and pioneer farmers brought wheat there for market from as far away as seventy-five miles. It was so prosperous that one street was popularly known as "Millionaire Avenue", and was further distinguished by having a Hungarian Count as a restaurant keeper, Count von Racjcs.

We stayed for two nights at the Queen's Hotel, a welcome relief after a train ride of about seventeen hundred
and fifty miles. Mr. Joe Zimmerman who ran the hotel
was a splendid host. His son, young Joe, five or six years
old, was even better. He used to collect the remnants of
hard liquor and beer from the bar glasses and pour them
into a single container. This he highly recommended. "It's
wonderful how you feel," he said. There was some consternation when he got caught trying to introduce Elmer
and me to the demon drink; the very thought of intemper-
ance was anathema in our family. Later, when we were
on the homestead, Mr. Zimmerman owned and operated
the hotel at Radisson. Occasionally, Elmer and I would
be treated to a meal there. It hardly seems possible today
but there was an excellent meal for twenty-five cents.

After two days' rest, we started out on a double box
wagon for Father's school near Carlton, seventeen miles
across country. There were no roads, only trails. The hurricane deck of a Bain wagon with no springs under the
board seats does not give one of the world's most comfortable rides. Our driver, Mr. Dyck, lived about a half-
mile from the schoolhouse. The school district bore the
name of "Tiefengrund" (Deep Ground), derived from the
fact that the topsoil was deep and fertile. Wheat was the
main farm product. The district was inhabited generally
by German Mennonites who had migrated in the late
nineties from East Prussia. They differed from the Mennonites whom we later knew in the Borden district in that
they spoke High German and not the "plat deutsch". Also
in the neighbourhood were three or four old-country
French farmers, and, of course, there were Indians and
Métis in close proximity.

The schoolhouse was the community centre, the place
of meeting. The schoolroom and the teacher's living quarters were contained in one building. There were three
rooms and the kitchen in our quarters, and at the back of

the premises, in a separate building, a summer kitchen. Mother made curtains, and with Father's help papered the walls and made the place comfortable and attractive. Soon we had a cow, some chickens, and three pigs located out back in a small barn with a thatched roof.

We lived in an area in which we walked with history. Dr. Cheadle and his party had hunted buffalo there in 1862. I once met two old Indians who claimed to speak with first-hand knowledge of the expedition which took Cheadle and his associate, Viscount Milton, from the Red River to the Pacific Coast, the first successful overland expedition. Captain John Palliser wintered at Carlton in 1857. The Earl of Southesk was there in 1859 and recorded this description in his diary as he proceeded north and west from Fort Carlton, across the North Saskatchewan River, on 26 July:

Looking back towards the Fort, the opposite banks of the river seemed like an English park, rising after the first steep ascent in gradual slopes luxuriantly clothed with wood, disposed by nature in groups and gladed masses, as if some skilful hand had been cutting the forest into forms of symmetry.

First established in 1795, Carlton House was a major Hudson's Bay Company centre for most of its ninety years. (Its name was probably taken from the Prince of Wales' residence in England.) It also became an important point of call for explorers and traders travelling the Carlton or Saskatchewan Trail, linking Fort Garry and Edmonton. Great numbers of Red River carts over the years had screeched their way along this famous highway. There were few such carts when we arrived, but I once saw four or five in a convoy, spread across the prairie, the front cart taking the lead, the left wheel of each succeeding cart following in the track made by the right wheel of the cart preceding it. They needed no horns to announce their presence. Without axle grease, their approach was known when half a mile distant. It was said by a constable of the North West Mounted Police that they should have been used for religious purposes because they would shake the devil right out of you.

The first battle in the 1885 Rebellion took place at Duck Lake, only a few miles from our schoolhouse. It was there that Gabriel Dumont, the superb leader of the Riel forces, lost his brother. How it began has never been made quite clear to me, but it was generally accepted that Gentleman Joe McKay fired the first shot during a scuffle with one of Gabriel Dumont's followers. I later came to know Gentleman Joe very well. He lived in Prince Albert until a great old age. McKay, of part Indian origin himself (his paternal grandfather had been a Hudson's Bay Company official), was a member of one of Saskatchewan's most distinguished families. (Two of the McKays became Conservative Members of Parliament for Prince Albert, one later becoming a Justice of the Court of Appeal in Saskatchewan.)

Members of the North West Mounted Police often passed by our place. No doubt it was coincidence but they usually arrived at mealtime. Those who had fought in the Rebellion fired my boyhood imagination by the recital of the events as they recalled them. They gave me a pride in the Mounted Police that has never dimmed through the years. One I particularly remember was Sergeant Pook. I would listen to him by the hour as he told of the battles of Fish Creek and Batoche, and of how twice a bullet passed through his clothing without wounding him, once through his left epaulet, and once through his right sleeve. It was the Sergeant who first told me about Gabriel Dumont. Pook had lost comrades in the fighting but this did not stop him from paying tribute to the greatest guerrilla fighter of them all. I might add that the Mounted Policemen that I knew did not share the same admiration for Riel.

Gabriel Dumont was a military genius. As a young teenager he was selected by the chiefs and leaders of his Métis people to lead the buffalo hunt from the Red River which, in reality, was a paramilitary exercise, requiring more than considerable skill. He was known to have killed more buffalo in one year than Buffalo Bill in a lifetime. He would have wiped out the loyalist troops at Fish Creek if it had not been for Riel, who rushed in shouting, "Enough blood today. God says no more." He was a military strategist of the highest quality. He used to come by our place now and then. He could speak no English, but he could shoot, and he gave us some examples of his marksmanship. On one occasion, through an interpreter, he told us that at the battle at Fish Creek he was within a hundred and fifty yards of Middleton, the British general commanding the Canadian troops, and that he could have shot him, "But I never shoot a dead moose."

We were rather afraid of Dumont, and I, at least initially, thought of him as the enemy. He was known to have personally killed a dozen men during the events of '85. When I met him, he was sixty-eight years old. He was an imposing figure, his hair still jet black, with the most unusual part in it that I have ever seen. In 1949, when his field notes were finally published (they had been written by an amanuensis when he was in exile in Montana, for Dumont could not write), I found an explanation for his hair part: a bullet had grazed the top of his head during the battle of Duck Lake. Dumont was a legitimate hero and deserves a better place in history than he has received. So far as I have been able, I have tried over the years to see that justice has been done to him.

I have never had the same regard for Riel. I do not consider Riel a martyr. He has been built up as a hero in consequence of publicity and politics. Many who have united behind Riel have failed to recall that he regarded the Pope as anti-Christ and himself as the true viceroy of the Almighty on earth. Now there was every reason for the Métis to become aroused over what was happening on the banks of the South Saskatchewan in 1884 and 1885. They had sought refuge from the onrush of European civilization by trailing to Batoche, St. Laurent, and that area. Their just claims were ignored and there were great injustices done. Riel was in exile in Montana as a consequence of the Red River Rebellion of 1870-71; Dumont and three companions brought him back. In July and August of 1884, Riel was quite reasonable and knew what he wanted. Only later did a mania strike him. Just before the Christmas of 1884, he said that if Macdonald would give him thirty-five thousand dollars (as opposed to the one hundred thousand dollars Riel claimed he was worth), he would go back to Montana and the devil take the Indians and Métis. If a man has principles he does not put them up for barter on the auction block. As for Riel's trial, he hanged himself. He had the best of lawyers. Both Charles Fitzpatrick and F.-X. Lemieux afterwards held the highest of judicial positions. Riel was insane. Even within the McNaghten Rules, there is no question about it. If I had a case in which the evidence of insanity was as clear, I would not have to submit any further evidence, I feel sure. If he had allowed his lawyers to carry the defence as they wanted to, he would have been found "not guilty" by reason of insanity. He voiced objections to the defence of insanity when raised by his counsel, and his own speech at the end of the trial, which he had no business delivering from the dock, was a brilliant effort when read, but the most powerful refutation of his insanity. That he had a "recommendation to mercy" indicates that the jury was divided, in spite of a lingering public outrage over his murder of Scott in the Red River in 1870. Scott had been noisy, truculent, offensive, and fanatically opposed to Riel and all his work, religion, and race. But Scott's death was murder. It may be that Riel was hanged

in 1885 because of Scott's murder, although the offence
with which he was charged was treason. Riel's death resulted in serious damage to the fortunes of the Conservative Party in Quebec, and even today is referred to in criticism of Conservative candidates. Men who would never
have given Riel a thought became attached to his cause
by instant ties of race and brotherhood. Laurier was able
to make political capital out of the bitter resentment en-
gendered by Riel's hanging. The Conservative Party, on
the other hand, has had this millstone around its neck in
Quebec ever since.

In 1904, Indians in the Carlton and Duck Lake areas
were aroused and there were rumours of a threatened
outbreak over basically the same issues as those leading
to the Rebellion of 1885. The indifference of the federal
government to Indian rights and problems, however, was
compounded by a continuing and deep resentment
among the Indians over the fate of Almighty Voice, killed
some seven years earlier by shell splinters from a NWMP
nine-pounder gun. This gun had been brought up from
Regina when police and a posse of local citizens failed in
two gun battles to dislodge Almighty Voice from a copse
of poplars, some miles east of Domremy, in which he and
two companions had taken refuge. I heard the story told
and retold by members of the NWMP as they sat in our
kitchen. Almighty Voice's career of crime had had its beginnings in the NWMP lock-up at Duck Lake. He was arrested in October 1895 for cattle rustling, a charge which
he strongly denied. A police officer allegedly told him he
would be hanged for his offence. Indians regarded hanging with almost superstitious horror. He escaped custody.
In eluding capture, he killed three Mounties and the postmaster at Duck Lake before his final destruction. His
bravery and boldness in defying what was considered an
oppressive white society and the heroic circumstances of
his death made him a legendary figure to Indians and

Métis, who regarded him as a heroic victim, not a criminal.

I recall one Sunday morning in 1904, very early, hearing loud noises outside our place—the sound of voices and of horses moving about. Our school-home was surrounded by mounted Indians in war paint. We wondered, had the threatened outbreak begun? Father went into the yard to ask what they wanted. It was explained that they were looking for an Indian from the reserve adjoining Duck Lake who had become insane and was dangerous. They wanted to know if we had seen him. We had not. But I saw something that day that I had never seen before. It was getting on into the morning by this time, and our unexpected guests were hungry. We were asked for nothing but the kitchen utensils. Rabbits were everywhere; and to watch an Indian, with no weapon but his hands, catch a rabbit was not an ordinary sight. Caught, skinned, and cleaned, it was ready for the pot in a matter of minutes.

Indians frequently called in, had tea with us, and went their way. Often, Father would give them clothing. We liked them. But one day, an Indian called Aaron Buffalo hit the jackpot. Father gave him the Prince Albert coat that he had worn at his wedding. Aaron pridefully wore it and outshone the chiefs of the nearby reserves with sartorial distinction.

Indian lore and Indian history, just as the story of the opening of the West, have always fascinated me. Over the years, I think that the Indians have understood my feelings for them, and they have shown their reaction by making me a chief of five or six tribes in Saskatchewan and Alberta. I felt it most unjust that they were treated as less than full citizens of Canada, that they did not have the vote. I promised that if I ever had the power to do so, they would be given that right. This I carried out when I was Prime Minister. Believing, as I did, that it would be a long time, if ever, before an Indian could be elected to the House of Commons because of their numerical minority in any one constituency, I appointed Chief James Gladstone, an outstanding and devoted servant of his people, to the Senate. How wrong I was; Leonard Marchand was elected in 1968 and Wally Firth in 1972, both capable Members of Parliament.

Apart from a few incidents, the lawlessness the United States experienced from the time it started its Indian wars right through to 1900 did not exist on the Canadian Prairies because of the vigilance of the Mounted Police. One story oft told, whether factual or not, relates to one of these rare incidents. American thugs used to slip over the border to Fort Walsh and terrorize the area. One of these bandits rode into the fort one day, and was, to say the least, trigger-happy. There were four or five people standing outside to whom he was demonstrating his marksmanship in a rather personal way by showing them how close he could shoot without hitting them. Just then, along came a whiskered, hoary old chap riding a mule. As he stepped down, the American said to him, "Do you dance?" "No," was the reply. "Well, you're sure going to learn now, and as long as you keep dancing, you won't get shot." With that, the thug began to shoot near the old man's feet. Around and around the old man went. Finally, the six-guns were empty. Much amused, the American said, "Well, you can dance now, can't you?" The old man said, "Sure can," and walked over to his mule, put his hand under the saddle blanket and pulled out a vicious-looking buffalo gun. Showing that it was loaded, he pointed it to the nose of the American gunman, and said, "You ever kiss a mule?" "No," was the reply, "but I've sure been waitin' to do so all these years."

In those early days, various members of the NWMP were the younger sons of the British aristocracy. Some came to Canada for adventure and some because their families wished them to be abroad. During stopovers at our home I heard, on more than one occasion, discussions between police officers concerning the origins of their family titles. One went back to Bosworth Field in 1485, and he cast aspersions on the other whose ancestral nobility began during the reign of Charles II. From the youngest recruit, however, to the veteran members there was a deep regard for justice and its maintenance. The settlers believed in the integrity of the Force and wrong-doers respected it. Justice was not only done, it was believed to have been done, even though when a crime was committed the investigation was done by a member of the Force and, if a charge was laid, the prosecuting officer would be a member of the Force; oftentimes, too, the presiding magistrate was a commissioned officer of the Force. On the lighter side, while great judges have left their imprint in the annals of history by the wisdom of their judgments, few could surpass that of my good friend, NWMP Superintendent P. W. Pennefather. When the courtroom over which he was presiding turned into pandemonium, he uttered these immortal words: "As long as I preside over this blankety-blank court, no blank, blank, blank is going to make a blank, blank of this great and historic institution." The first two blanks were ordinary profanity. The next three dealt with canine ancestry, and the last two dealt with a horse's anatomy.

With our arrival in the West, we lived in a new world. The skies at night were ablaze with Northern Lights, which seemed to whisper and swish. In September 1903 we heard for the first time what became familiar to us for the next seven years, the howl of coyotes. Two of these animals can terrify with their howls as though they were a pack. Here there was none of the loneliness of a big city, however. Everyone tried to make us know that we were under their constant care, and this was always true as the old-timers welcomed the newly arrived. We had food in abundance, wildfowl, jack rabbits, and tame chickens. Vegetables were brought to our door. The Mennonites in the district made pork sausages and cured hams for us. In that first fall, the ratepayers brought us loads of fire-wood and helped us cut it into stove lengths. Everyone shared in the business of everyone. Where illness struck or a family was in need, the neighbours helped. Most children came into the world with the aid of older women as midwives. The nearest medical doctor was in Rosthern, some seventeen miles distant.

Every two weeks Father would catch a ride to Rosthern to get supplies and to hear the local news and gossip. For newspapers we had the *Rosthern Enterprise*, a weekly, the *Globe* from Toronto, and the *Waterloo Chronicle*, a weekly of Father's boyhood. And we always had books to read. My love of history began with the reading of a broken set of *Ridpath's History of the World*. G. A. Henty's novels were an inspiration to me; I loved the way he wove adventure and history together. (Very few people know that Henty covered the Battle of Batoche for a London newspaper.) I never had the same interest in the Horatio Alger stories; each was too much like the other. We also had a large single-volume encyclopedia, which I read and re-read. The Bible was an open book. Shakespeare, Gibbon, and Macaulay were our familiars.

Our home and hospitality were open to all visitors. Mother was a good cook. The Mounted Police, as I have mentioned, were regular visitors. School inspectors stayed with us while they conducted inspection of Father's and neighbouring schools. Travellers, salesmen, immigrants en route farther west would be invited for meals. Often offered, payment was always refused; this was the rule and it continued later throughout the years on the homestead, although the number of visitors was then greatly reduced as we were no longer on the main route. On Sunday, church service was held at the school.

The people in our immediate area, as I have observed, were mainly Prussian Mennonites—excellent farmers, well-to-do, law-abiding, and pacifist. They followed the principles of Menno Simons, who lived in the sixteenth century, their Luther. Their services were held in German. They were fond of music and it pleased them greatly when Father agreed to play the organ and act as choir leader for their services.

On Christmas eve, 1903, Father arranged a concert at the school. Elmer and I were to sing a duet, "It is Christmas in the city, It is Christmas on the farm." When our turn came to perform, Elmer sang well; my voice cracked, and that was the last time I tried to sing in public.

Later that night, Santa Claus brought both Elmer and me repeater air guns with nickel-plated barrels and a supply of BB pellets. We tried these guns out on Christmas morning and found that a constant pull on the trigger would empty fifty BB pellets from the magazine in a few seconds. That morning, Elmer and I went to the church service. Elmer brought his gun. When Mother saw us, she motioned to him to get the gun out of the room. In his haste to do so, Elmer pressed the trigger. The Bishop trembled with indignation; we were sent outside and not allowed to return. From then on the Bishop described us as "unredeemable rascals".

New Year's Day, 1904, was spent by us with the family of Joe Samletski, one of the few non-French Roman Catholic families for many miles around. While we were there, a large covey of prairie chickens flew into the yard where the granary was located. Mr. Samletski decided to shoot a few for the noon meal, only to find that he had no powder for his muzzle-loader. That did not deter him. He set three gopher traps in the yard and we had a feed of chickens for lunch.

Father was always fond of hunting, and within a week or so of arriving at Carlton my brother and I went out with him for prairie chicken. When we stopped by a creek a pheasant appeared. Father shot it. Where it came from is a mystery, for it was not until thirty-five years later that I saw pheasants again on the Prairies and they were imports from the United States. Father had quite a strong sense of humour. When he was seventy-six years old, I took him duck hunting some fifty miles northeast of Saskatoon. We were on a slough surrounded by willows. Father was perched on a large rock about fifteen feet out, concealed by a blind. I was about a hundred yards away on the shore. I had given him a double-barrelled gun that was very touchy. Too often, when you pulled one trigger both barrels went off. As the ducks came in, I heard a shot, and down came three. But that was not the biggest splash. Both barrels had gone off, and Father was knocked into the slough by the recoil. I rushed over and up he came. The water was not deep (only about five feet), but he was an awful mess, spitting and sputtering and covered with filthy algae. As I got him into the punt, Father looked at me and said, "John, if I were a swearing man this is one time I would say 'damn'." That was the most profane I had ever known him to be.

As I have mentioned, our home and the school at Carlton were all in one building. The school portion of the building had just one room. Our desks were made of rough two-inch lumber. Our books and supplies were generally purchased from a school supply house in Brandon, Manitoba. And, of course, no schoolroom was complete without a series of charts, held together in a case on the wall. The most prominently displayed dealt with the evils of drink. Another illustrated the dangers of smoking, showing the physiological results certain to follow. I did not care for that one, as I found viewing the human innards disturbing.

During our residence at Carlton, Hague, and on the homestead, serious illness struck members of the family only once. Mother was never strong but she kept going until the summer of 1904. She was then directed by her physician to have surgery. He suggested that she should go to hospital in Winnipeg. She went by train, sitting up both going there and returning at the end of five weeks. On her return, the wagon ride home from Rosthern put her in bed for another two weeks.

While she was away, Father, Elmer, and I batched it. Mother had a beautiful set of china which even today would be highly regarded. I think only two or three dishes survived our batching. After every meal we piled them up. After ten days, the whole thing fell down and the breakage was almost total. Needless to add, Mother was less than pleased.

In the summer of 1905, Father decided that he would like to become a landowner. As I recall the sequence of events, one of the school inspectors had filed on a homestead in the district and it was suggested that, since the entry was not to be retained, Father might file on the quarter section. We felt it wise to see the land before deciding whether to file or not. In addition, Father wanted to look at some of the unsettled Doukhobor land which the Department of the Interior was opening up for general settlement. (Doukhobor immigration to Canada had slowed to a trickle, with the result that tens of thousands of acres originally set aside for the sect lay unclaimed.)

Father and I set out in an old buggy drawn by a lazy broncho. We crossed the North Saskatchewan River at the Petrofka ferry and went in search of land. There were very few settlers in the eastern and northern parts of the area. What interested me was the number of wolves and foxes everywhere. Finally, we saw a town ahead and wondered what it was. We drove and drove and still the town seemed no closer. It was a mirage. We went west as far as Maymount looking over various quarter sections, all soil that had never known the cut of the plough. Finally, after four days, we came to the quarter section of which we had been told, just north of Borden. There was the iron survey post and the four diamond-shaped excavations which surrounded every post. The inscription showed it to be on the S.E. Quarter of Section 8, Township 41-8-West 3rd. Our home to be.

To feed us on this trip, Mother had made up an ample lunch basket. Somehow we managed to eat it all by the second day. Hence, we had little or nothing on the third and fourth days. Worn out by hunger and thirst, we found a hospice, a homesteader's sod shack. Our host was a Swede, a bachelor, and he gave us a royal welcome. "I'll take you right in and, by yee, I'm sure glad to meet you boys. I haven't seen anybody for weeks." And he added, "I've got some wonderful flapjacks for you," reaching up to the top shelf and bringing down three or four. They were covered with fly dirt. I did not eat any. Father did, because he felt that hospitality cannot be rewarded by ingratitude. Then the Swede said, "By yee, you oughta have something fresh and I'll get you some wild ducks and cook them." There was no refusing him. He went out, but instead of shooting wild ducks, he shot a couple of mud hens, birds virtually inedible. He fried them, and I started in with gusto. It was indescribably awful. But, the unforgettable taste experience apart, his was a typical example of prairie hospitality. He gave us his best.

Another experience occurred at the Doukhobor village of Petrofka. This was a communal village, the farmer residents working their several farms, with the production becoming the property of all the residents. (Before many years, the hard workers decided that they would rather be on their own.) We walked up a street where a number of women were dumping beets and cabbage into a very large barrel some six feet in height and in diameter. They were preparing borsch. Father asked for tea; it was agreed that we should have tea if I would get into the barrel and tramp the vegetables. I agreed, taking the place of a lad of about my age, Peter Makaroff, who eleven years later graduated with a B.A. degree from the University of Saskatchewan, a member of my year and class. He went on to become a distinguished counsel in the courts of the province of Saskatchewan. It was not uncommon in the early days to see a dozen Doukhobor women pulling a single share plough. They had the finest horses, but "saved" them by keeping them in the stable.

Father and I returned to Carlton and shortly after went to the city of Prince Albert to make entry for the homestead. As it was expected that there would be quite a large number of prospective homesteaders, we went there two days in advance of the opening day for filing. Father had taken a milking stool with him and sat thereon in front of the office for two days and nights while I slept on the floor of the pool hall. I brought him tea and sandwiches two or three times a day. He was second in line on the opening day; he signed the application, paid the ten-dollar fee, and was granted his entry for the homestead. We were all proud to know that in three years Father would be a landed plutocrat.

CHAPTER THREE

THE LAW REQUIRED that a homestead be occupied within six months, and be lived on for at least six months each year for three years. Failure to move onto the homestead within the stated period would permit the entry to be cancelled. Father believed that there was not much danger that our entry would be cancelled for a year or more since there was so much land available for settlement. In any case, he had no money to build a shack-home and barn, or to purchase a team of horses or machinery. The Land Registry officials had the right to grant relief against cancellation, and Father judged that his grounds for inability to move onto the homestead would be good enough to protect him against loss of his entry. He next decided to try to secure a school which would give him a better salary, so that he would be able to save the money needed for moving onto the land.

He was successful, hence our move to Hague, some thirty miles southeast of Carlton, in August 1905. Hague was a village with a population of between two and three hundred. It had a railway station, four grain elevators, three stores, a lumber yard, and a blacksmith shop. Rather than rent a house, Father decided to purchase a one-and-a-half-storey cottage. The purchase price was seven hundred and seventy-five dollars, the monthly payments seven dollars and seventy-five cents. He thought this a good investment, and so it proved. He had the rental for twenty-eight years and then sold the house and property at about the amount of the original purchase price. We built a "barnlet", about ten feet by twelve by six, out of shiplap. It was so warm that the chickens laid eggs all winter long. The chicken feed cost nothing since Elmer and I gathered up the wheat spillings at the elevators. It was a beautiful steading, since torn down and replaced by a modern dwelling. Only the maple trees we planted remain.

In addition to his teaching, Father took on the jobs of Secretary of the Village and Assessment Clerk. I might add that in the preparation of assessment notices, I did a share of the work. It was while doing this that Father decided to teach me bookkeeping. After six weeks or so of intensive training, he decided that "Cash Dr. to Merchandise" and things of that nature were not for me. That decision, however, did not cause him to release me from filling in assessment forms, addressing envelopes, and the like. I began to make my first money in Hague doing farm work for fifty cents a day, and selling the *Saskatoon Phoenix* newspaper.

On 1 September 1905, Saskatchewan and Alberta became provinces. I was ten years old. Father decided there should be a celebration of the event and took over its organization in Hague. There were few flags to borrow from the villagers, so he went to Saskatoon and bought a couple of dozen small Union Jacks and had them put up. A town meeting was held at the schoolhouse. Father was chairman and spoke feelingly of Confederation and of what it meant. The school choir sang "The Maple Leaf Forever", "Rule Britannia", and "God Save the King". It was a red-letter occasion for all.

During the summer vacation in July and August 1905, we moved onto the homestead temporarily. We built a shack some twelve by eighteen feet. In addition, Father had ten acres of land broken. To protect our property from cancellation, we moved to the farm permanently in August of 1906. Gerhard Derksen, whose house and barns adjoined the west boundary of Father's land, provided us with transport. This consisted of a team and a hayrack. It was loaded up with our Thomas organ, furniture and trunks, and all manner of household possessions. Lily, our cow, was tied to the rear axle, and the chickens, in cages, were piled on top of the load. Away we went across some forty miles of prairie trails to Borden and to yet another experience.

Our first stop on the trip was again at the Doukhobor community of Petrofka on the west bank of the North Saskatchewan River. In later years we got to know these people well. Their spiritual leader was Peter Verigin, known as "Lordly". He was an impressive-looking man. I saw him on one occasion seated in a democrat hitched to two spirited stallions. If he exercised many of the prerogatives of a lord of the manor which were hardly of a spiritual nature, he nevertheless showed deep concern for his followers and was regarded by his people as the possessor of supernatural powers.

We travelled for two days and one night, sleeping in the open. It was after dark on the second day before we arrived at Derksen's. The next morning, we saw across his fields the tall poplar surrounded by willows that marked our home. Before leaving Hague, Father had arranged for a teaching position at a salary of six hundred dollars a year when a new school district was opened in a Mennonite district some three miles northeast of the homestead bearing the name of Hoffnungsfeld (in English, Hopefield). At the same time as we took up our land, Father's brother Ed secured a school in the Halcyonia district some three miles southeast of the homestead. The people there were old-country English and Ontario-born.

Ed took a homestead diagonally across from Father's and there built a one-room shack.

I should say something now about Father's youngest brother, Edward L. Diefenbaker. He was a born teacher and a most successful one. He taught school in Saskatchewan for many years. In retirement he lived in Regina. He never ceased his quest for knowledge, and when he died in the 1960s at the age of eighty-six, he was still wrestling with the philosophy of Kant and Schopenhauer. He was my teacher from grades seven to ten.

Habitations in our area varied considerably. The Mennonites had lumber buildings, as did farmers in the Halcyonia district. The Ukrainian immigrants had houses constructed of small logs, the spaces between caulked with mud and lime. The Doukhobors had much the same type of construction and in both types of houses the rooms were spotlessly clean. Not a few of the old-country English immigrants built sod shacks, much less costly to construct and quite comfortable. I recall one bachelor who had over the entrance to his shack a board on which there was a never-to-be-forgotten inscription: "This is the domicile edifice of Edwin Baker—son of the Lord Mayor of Birmingham". For our house, it was decided that there should be three rooms, the largest of which would be divided into a living room and a bedroom for our parents. Elmer would bunk in the kitchen, while the third room was for storage, and was often to be used by overnight visitors. (I was to sleep in Uncle Ed's shack.) Father wanted Mother's kitchen to be the most attractive room. In consequence, it was lined with "V"-joint boards, which took varnish well. (This lumber cost one hundred and twenty-five dollars a thousand, compared with shiplap at less than fifty dollars.)

Father had never built anything before, except for the "barnlet" in Hague, but after talking over the matter with a neighbour, he proceeded to finish not only our home but Ed's shack as well. The heavy beams were laid on the ground, and the scantlings were raised on them. The roof supports were placed on the top cross-bars, all of this done before the walls were closed in. Every nail in these buildings, and the one-and-one-half-storey barn which was built after the house was completed, was driven by either Father, Elmer, or me. The shingling was done almost entirely by my brother and me, and nearly ended in disaster when on the first day a board which we believed was securely nailed gave way.

The first year Father planted a small vegetable garden. It produced sufficient potatoes and garden stuff to meet our needs. Mother planted a flower garden. To brighten it, she put in some sunflowers. The Mennonite people were fond of sunflower seeds, and had a skill all their own. They would put a handful in their mouths and shell them, the hulls coming out in a steady flow. I never ceased to marvel at their ability; it was done so fast that it seemed a special kind of perpetual motion.

We were happy and, although urban dwellers might judge otherwise, we were content. When things were bad, and that was frequently, it was taken as something to be expected. We always had plenty of wholesome food. Our meals were mainly of home produce, with occasional groceries obtained in trade for Mother's premium-quality butter. On two successive years, Uncle Duncan in Toronto shipped us barrels of apples. There were no insulated freight cars, and when brought out by neighbours from Borden station they were frozen. We had plenty of milk, bread, and butter. Mother and Father took turns with the milking. Elmer and I were in charge of the hand churn. Buttermilk became a favourite drink for me and remains so. A basic food was prunes. For protein we had poultry, pork, wildfowl in season, and, occasionally, fresh beef. In the spring, after the June rains, we picked buckets of mushrooms which flourished in the old buffalo wallows. Chickens and turkeys, wildfowl, prairie chickens and ducks were in abundance, as were wild geese. We soon learned not to kill Sand Hill cranes. Father came home one day with one, but it proved so tough you could not have split the gravy with an axe. Of wild fruits and berries, there were always scores of quarts in the store room; Mother's target in the growing season was some thirty quarts of strawberries, fifty quarts of Saskatoon berries, and up to one hundred quarts of raspberries. Our major problem was the well. The water was not potable; strongly alkaline, it had a pronounced cathartic effect on anyone who drank it. We tried several locations for a well without success, and, as a result, for the entire period we were on the homestead, twice a week we would have to haul a barrel of water on a stoneboat from the Derksen farm half a mile away.

There were few trees near our land. We got firewood from the Ukrainians to the north of us. It came in long pole lengths. It was a mark of distinction to have those twenty-, thirty-, or forty-foot poles put up tepee fashion. A good settler was identified on the basis of his tepee. The English-speaking people on the Prairies (that is, British, Canadian, and American) went mainly into southern Saskatchewan, where the land was free from trees or rocks. The Ukrainians did not do that. They took up what others thought was the worst land. From their experience in the steppes of the Ukraine, they chose the park land. To open it for farming, settlers had first to grub out the trees and rocks by hand, a toil I am thankful we were spared in large degree. Father, Elmer, and I grubbed about four acres; this took weeks and weeks. At least the Ukrainian settler did not encounter the enmity of some of the old-timers, who were anything but favourable to the invasion of what they called "foreigners" coming in and taking the best land. Generally, however, the newly opened land tended to be a great social leveller, where each helped anyone in need, regardless of racial origin.

As I have mentioned, ours was a Christian family. There was no severity or stuffiness or stiffness about it, no super-sanctimonious attitude of trying to force others to follow our same course; but there was a clear distinction between what was right and what was wrong. Crime resulted in an outcasting of the offender. If a thing was wrong, it could not be justified, and there was no more to say. Although we were in no way permitted the luxury of believing that some parts of the Old Testament might be simply allegorical, I think that my father and mother were New Testament people. Their lives were centred in the New Testament. However trying the circumstances, there was a simple acceptance of the fact that all things worked together for good for those who loved the Lord. This attitude may never be recovered, but some of it would do today's society no harm.

I was eleven years old and in grade seven when we first moved to the homestead. It was arranged when the school terms began in the fall of 1906 that I should go to Halcyonia School with Uncle Ed, and Elmer would go with Father to Hoffnungsfeld School. Each school was some three miles distant from the homestead. Spring, summer, and fall, until Uncle Ed was able to afford a buggy, we walked to and from school each day. In the winter, we rode on an open, horse-drawn cutter, made of two-by-fours and heavy planks. The pupils at Halcyonia School were mainly old-country English, from around Birmingham. The school where Father taught and which Elmer attended was in a Mennonite district. For my part, I got to play a little soccer and cricket at recess and lunch hour. Elmer had none of that at his school, despite the fact that Father had been an outstanding soccer player in his younger days. For Mother the days were incredibly long. Father and Elmer and Uncle Ed and I went our separate ways at eight o'clock in the morning and did not return until five-thirty in late afternoon. Mother was completely alone during the day. The closest neighbours were half a mile away and they spoke only German. Of course, she was an excellent housekeeper but, more important, she was a tremendous inspiration to my brother and me. Our isolation seemed to bring us together as a family, engendering a close relationship that was to be a source of strength through life.

Elmer and I had little time or opportunity for play. In the early morning, before school, we had our chores. Our principal job in the evening, apart from helping Mother at mealtime, was to keep the wood-box filled, both at home and at Uncle Ed's. Until we were able to get coal, during our third year on the land, it was not unusual for the wash basin to be partly frozen over when we arose. My evenings were normally filled with lessons and reading. However, I do remember that we made kites now and then, and that usually they did not fly. We also ran a small trapline for weasels (ermine) each year in the late fall and early winter. That, however, was for profit; one year we had a harvest of ninety pelts, which brought us over sixty dollars. I have indicated that Mother kept down the grocery bills by selling butter to the local merchant in Radisson. To help further, she began to raise turkeys on a larger scale than any of our neighbours. She made money in one year only, however, and then the total return was less than forty dollars. In the two other years misfortune struck. One summer was wet and her eighty turkey chicks contracted a disease known as pip; they were a total loss. In the next, Mother carefully nursed her turkey flock of fifty through the summer. In October, when she was about to market them, they disappeared. One night the turkeys were as usual around the barn; the next morning they were gone. We found their carcasses in badger holes.

One enjoyable pastime for Elmer and me was to spend

many hours riding the bronchos. Having no saddles, we rode bareback and became fair horsemen. Father and Uncle Ed never rode and therefore had no personal knowledge of the extent to which one's posterior gave raw and painful evidence of having ridden without a saddle! I often went out on horseback hunting for prairie chicken. I was thrown several times when the broncho stepped into a badger hole, a fact that in no way led to my parents' purchasing a saddle for us—they just couldn't afford it. We also attempted one day in early May 1907 to teach ourselves how to swim. Our parents had gone into Borden for the day. There was an almost circular slough, about fifty feet in diameter, near by. There had been some thaw and there was about a two-foot depth of water in it. The snow in the willows surrounding the slough, however, was still eight feet or more high. We decided to slide down the snow banks, otter-like, into the icy water, swimming a few strokes when we hit. We did this for perhaps two hours. All things considered, it was a fair trade: we didn't learn how to swim but we didn't catch cold. Father, of course, would never allow us to try to swim in the North Saskatchewan River; the undertow was too dangerous.

There were other light moments. Indeed, to the last days of his life in June 1971, my brother Elmer loved to tell the story of our venture into an experiment in air flight. The Mennonite people were understandably proud of the achievement of the Wright brothers, the first to fly a heavier-than-air craft. Elmer and I were enthused by their success. It was Elmer, I think, who conceived the idea that we should try to emulate their achievement. There were indeed many serious air-flight experiments in the West during this early period, but ours was not one of them. Neither of us had any mechanical skill. The only things we ever built were stilts and a small wagon, about three feet in length by one foot wide, with wheels six inches in diameter, sawn directly from a tree. We thought that we might fly our wagon by attaching to it an improvised parachute. We planned to launch it from the haymow over the barn. On the day we inaugurated this new form of air travel, our parents were visiting neighbours. Our only problem was where to get a parachute. Mother had a highly prized parasol with a gold head and a mother-of-pearl handle, a wedding present. We took the wagon into the hay-mow, sat our dog Tip in the box (we had nominated him as pilot), tied the open parasol to the end of the wagon's tongue, and shoved off. Down it went. Mother's parasol turned inside out and ripped. Tip we did not see again for three days. Mother was angry with us; Father a little more resigned. We finally saw an aircraft actually flying in 1910 when Lucky St. Henry put on an exhibition at the Saskatoon Fair Grounds.

On Sundays on the homestead we usually went to church services at Halcyonia School, even in the blizzard months of January and February. We would return home around one unless we went to one of our church friends for dinner. At other times one or another family would come home with us for a visit and a meal. Often, if it was too stormy, church services would be held at our home. Once or twice a month there would be a community singsong at our place, and from time to time, itinerant ministers of all faiths would spend a day or two with us. They had a hard life, these servants of the Lord. I remember one, the Reverend Mr. Marty, who made several visits to the homestead. Totally unused to pioneer life, he came to the Borden district after some years as a missionary in China. He had been in a beleaguered garrison during the Boxer Rebellion and his recital of the terrors of the siege are as vivid in my mind as they were when he described them. Also, Elmer and I at one time did some colporteur work for Mr. W. C. McCheane, the leading Quaker in Halcyonia, where several families belonged to the Society of Friends. He had us distribute well-bound morocco-covered Bibles in English and German to the Mennonite neighbours. I still have one of these volumes.

Elmer, unlike me, was fond of music, and from the time he could stand in front of the organ and reach the keys he played by ear. When he was old enough, Father taught him to play by note. He would stay at home and play the organ for hours on end. He wanted to be a musician or a medical doctor, but things did not work out that way, a source of great regret to me. When the opportunity came to him in Saskatoon, years later, he learned to play the pipe organ. I think he could have been a superior musician. It is interesting for me to recall that as boys I was the more bashful, Elmer the more outgoing. He was always very warm in his relations with others and very trusting. Everyone, no matter what his past may have been or what the suspicion of his friends might be, was regarded by Elmer as a decent, good person. He was generous to a fault; he had some of Father's traits in helping others. He could also be very outspoken and unusually stubborn when he thought something was not right. Throughout his life, he gave his all for me; whatever befell me, he was always my stand-by and unselfish helper and confidant. If I could sum up his life in a few words, I would say of him the words I placed on his tombstone, "He found happiness for himself in bringing happiness to others." I do not think I ever really showed him how much I owed him. But to no one do I owe more than to him.

Father, as I have mentioned, loved to hunt chicken, even though all he could afford was a rather decrepit one-barrel shotgun. With Elmer driving him, frequently he would hunt on his way home from school. Elmer seldom, if ever, fired a shot at birds, although he would go along on a shoot for company. And Father, ardent outdoorsman that he was, never hunted larger game. I remember a neighbour lent Father a .32-calibre rifle and suggested that he should bag a jumper deer or two, as they were then quite plentiful. Father simply would not shoot a deer and this aversion was inherited by me. On occasion, I have been along on a deer or moose hunt, but when the prospective victim came within shooting distance, I dropped my gun, much to the amazement and derision of the rest of the group.

The winters during our first few years in the West were frightening in their severity. On Christmas eve, 1906, such a continuing blizzard set in that Uncle Ed's school was closed for five weeks after New Year's. We stayed at home cutting extra firewood to keep us warm in temperatures that reached fifty degrees and more below zero and for a month were never warmer than fifteen to twenty degrees below zero. But the winter of 1907-08 stands out as the coldest of all. We were still travelling by sleigh in mid-May. In those days blizzards often took the lives of people who lost their way. Whenever a blizzard blew up or threatened, Father, as nightfall approached, would light a lantern and hang it outside as a guide to wayfarers. During the 1965 election campaign, a number of press and radio newsmen went out to the old homestead with Elmer and me. Elmer told those in his car about Father and the lantern. They found the lantern hook still there. As a result of this trip and of the interest it aroused, the late Premier Ross Thatcher of Saskatchewan had both homestead shacks removed to Regina and restored; I shall always be deeply indebted to him for doing this.

Father, Uncle Ed, Elmer, and I became lost on two or three trips, but, except for one occasion, only for an hour or so. Bronchos would not face a blizzard and would turn to left or right to avoid the flying snow; the driver would have no way of knowing that the pathway had been lost until it was too late. The eleventh of March is a date that I remember every year, for it was on that day in 1908 when

I nearly froze to death. At Halcyonia School, concerts were held occasionally by some of the talented English immigrants who lived in the district. The first concert of the year was advertised for 11 March and Uncle Ed and I decided to stay after school to attend. That morning, as the temperature was relatively warm—around zero, I decided to discard the Elmira felt boots which we all wore and put on a new pair of leather shoes given to me at Christmas-time. To complete my "Sunday" dress, I wore my cloth coat and Persian lamb cap. The concert began in the early evening. Within an hour a blizzard began. Uncle Ed became alarmed by the increasing intensity of the storm and decided that we should start for home, fearing that my parents would be concerned if we were delayed. We started out. As always, we were in an open sled. The storm became more violent. The temperature fell rapidly. I became very cold. There was an elevation about two and a half miles from home and as we passed this height of land, we saw the light of Father's lantern. Then it was blacked out as the northeast wind assumed gale proportions. The drifts wiped out the pathway. The horse, seeking relief from the pounding snow, turned off to the west, as we found out the next morning. Suddenly, the sled came to an abrupt stop and the horse almost disappeared from view in snow piled deep over a small willow bluff. We were stuck. Any attempt to find our way on foot would have been suicidal. We had lost all sense of direction. Uncle Ed, who had not discarded his winter wear and had on his felt boots, dog-skin coat, and Balaclava cap, gave me the only covers we had, two horse blankets. As the snow drifted high around the sled, affording some protection from the wind which screamed and moaned with an almost human sound, I fell asleep in the hay on the floor of the sled. Many times I was awakened by Ed during the night. Asleep, I dreamed of being in a warm room, then again of picking apples in my

Grandfather Diefenbacker's orchard as I had done in 1902. Awake, I would shiver, my teeth chattering, my uncle's words of encouragement lost on my numbed senses. My feet and legs lost all feeling. At daybreak, the blizzard was still raging. Then, almost without warning, it subsided. Uncle Ed got the horse free from the shafts, and the three of us started through the drifts. My legs were like blocks of wood. After a long hour or more, we arrived at the homestead. We learned to our surprise that Father and Mother had not been concerned for our safety, since they had assumed that we were storm-bound at the school. Both my legs were frozen to the knees. Medical attention was fifteen miles away, and Father and Mother became physician and nurse. She wrapped my legs in blankets which Father hour after hour filled with snow. Gangrene set in, but by the end of three weeks I was able to get about. Although there were no lasting physical after-effects, I developed a blizzard phobia; for years thereafter I was afraid to go outside our house, even to the woodpile, when blizzards were blowing.

In the summer of 1908, Father's brother Henry (a mechanic by trade and engaged in making carriages), who lived in Waukegan, Illinois, came to visit us. After hearing of our experience, he decided to build a canvas-covered shelter on each of our cutters to shut out the winds and the cold. He then equipped each of them with a small eight-inch heater, the stovepipe sticking some eight inches above the canvas roof. Thereafter, however cold or stormy the weather, we travelled in comfort. In the succeeding years, there were many who followed our example, some even calling the cutters "Diefenbaker schooners".

Year after year, a few more acres were brought under cultivation. We came to understand the vicissitudes of pioneer life. Rainfall was always uncertain. During one year there was frost in every month. In another, we were partially hailed out. One year we experienced a prairie fire; there is nothing to compare with the helplessness of those in its path. If Father had not acted when the danger became evident, we would have lost our buildings and some forty loads of hay. He got out the team, hitched them to the plough, and turned two furrows around the hay stack and buildings; then he ploughed two concentric furrows fifty or so yards away and burnt the intervening area before the prairie fire reached us. The income from the farm for wheat, oats, and barley amounted to one hundred and fifty dollars a year, if averaged over the four years that we were on the homestead. There were many worse off than we were, but at that economic level, even with Father's salary as a teacher, we were unaware of, and suffered no effects from, the financial panic in 1907.

Without doubt, the best time of year on a farm came with the harvest. When the threshers arrived, this was an occasion for hard work and the best of meals prepared by Mother. These were so appreciated by the threshing crew that it seemed to me that they slowed up the work near the end to have one more meal with us. I worked cutting the twine on the sheaves as they were pitched on to the separator platform and was paid one dollar and fifty cents for a day that began at six in the morning and ended at dark. My parents were opposed to my doing this work, since it was not uncommon for workers to lose the ends of fingers when they allowed the monotony of the job to make them momentarily forgetful of danger. I suffered no injury and on the threshing gangs in each of two seasons made twelve or fifteen dollars.

Our wheat was marketed mainly in Radisson. At six a.m. on Saturdays, after the wagon was loaded with thirty to thirty-five bushels of wheat, we hitched up the two bronchos and off to the elevator Father would go, accompanied during the long hours of the journey by Ed and either Elmer or me. The wheat was from virgin soil, or nearly so, and except for a few weed seeds it was clean. It was dry, for rain was unusual, particularly in the autumn. On our arrival at the elevator, before dumping the load, the elevator operator (there were few exceptions) would plunge his hand into the load and claim that it was damp. Then, taking a sample in his hand, he would claim dockage for weeds of anything from eight to ten per cent. When the grain buyer's "diagnosis" was questioned, he would suggest going to a rival elevator in the town, where those who followed his advice would have a repeat performance. There were competing elevators but there was no competition. The treatment of the farmer was cruel, but the agents were not to blame. They were acting under instructions.

I have never forgotten this exploitation of the Western farmer, the pioneer, by the great grain interests. For the thirty bushels of wheat we would get nine dollars. We had hauled it all that distance and we were deprived of the petty amount of about three dollars to which we were entitled. Senator the Honourable Tom Crerar has described these swindles in his book on the subject of grain-handling practices. Of course, there was provision in the regulations that the farmer had the right to have a grain sample sent to Winnipeg for government inspection, but this meant delay and, worse, hauling the wheat back home, and it was seldom carried out. While the lords of the grain trade lived in opulence in Winnipeg, the farmers were subjected to practices that soured their thinking and seared their souls.

Farmers' associations were launched on the prairies to secure justice for the wheat farmer. The first were the grain growers' organizations in the south of the province, along the main line of the CPR. The first of these in Saskatchewan was in Abernethy or Indian Head, just after the turn of the century. In our area in the north, a Farmers' Institute was established in Halcyonia School by the

Canadian farmers in the district—the Orchards, the Tallises, the Clarks, the MacDermids, the Saloways, the Wrights, the Piprells, the McCheanes, and so on. Meetings were held regularly to discuss current problems—difficulties in selling wheat on a fair market, getting the railway to provide loading platforms so that we might load our own wheat, the malpractices of certain farm machinery companies, and the inability of the individual without means to stand up squarely against these powerful interests in the courts. There were problems with livestock, and often the means to counter diseases afflicting horses and cattle by our own action were considered, as veterinaries were not available. I recall being perplexed over the discussions at Institute meetings on the subject of contagious abortion among cattle. When I got home I sought enlightenment in the dictionary but it gave me no clue. Since it was the kind of subject that a young boy could not ask detailed questions about, it was ten years before I understood what was meant. I used to stay after school to listen to the homesteaders voicing their complaints. At one meeting I became so angered over the dubious, if not unscrupulous, practices to which homesteaders were subjected that my shyness momentarily disappeared. After all, I was one of them. I would be about thirteen, old enough to be expected to do a man's work. I got up and said, "This thing is wrong. Some day I'm going to do my part to put an end to this." I was so frightened that I could hardly get out the words. The twenty-five or thirty present applauded my brief and to-the-point remarks.

CHAPTER FOUR

THE POLITICS of the prairie frontier, the people involved, and the anecdotes about them, have always fascinated me. As I have mentioned, when we lived in Carlton, in Hague, and on the homestead, the schoolhouse was the centre of community activity. There, when political meetings were held, everyone attended. And audience participation was expected, especially by the Englishmen present, who had mastered the fine art of heckling, of taunting politicians as formidable as Joseph Chamberlain. Elections gave rise to bitter controversy, even between normally friendly neighbours; but those meetings provided unrivalled public entertainment. I never missed one. The fact that I was too young to understand all the issues in no way diminished my enthusiasm as I viewed the proceedings from my front-row seat.

The dominant political figure in northern Saskatchewan was Thomas Osborne Davis, known as "T.O.". An opponent once described him, in an election pamphlet depicting his corruption of the voters, as Thomas "Odious" Davis. He created a political machine that dominated Prince Albert politics for years. T. O. Davis had an attractive personality; but in politics he was thoroughly unreliable. In 1896, when Wilfrid Laurier won in the constituencies of both Prince Albert and Quebec East, Davis was his Prince Albert lieutenant. When Laurier became Prime Minister, he automatically vacated his memberships-elect. It was the practice, indeed it was the law, at that time and for many years thereafter, that an M.P. vacate his seat and seek re-election when he accepted an emolument from the Crown. Laurier chose to seek election in Quebec East, leaving Prince Albert open. Several Prince Albert citizens wanted the nomination. The constituency, which until 1907 was called Saskatchewan, embraced the entire northern part of the province. There were four strong prospective Liberal candidates. Mr. Davis approached each of them in private and in the strictest confidence; he said in effect, "If you support me and I'm elected I'll put you in the Senate." He thus silenced his opposition and was nominated and subsequently elected to the House. When the long-expected Senate seat was provided for under statute, he took it for himself. In so doing, he explained that, in fact, he had pleased them all; had he chosen any one of them to be Senator, they would have been mad at each other and there would have been only one fewer annoyed and angered with him.

I saw him only once, in the federal election of 1904. By this time he was Senator. There was a meeting at the school where he spoke on behalf of John H. Lamont of Prince Albert, who later became a judge of the Supreme Court of Canada. After his speech, the old Senator put his arm around me and predicted, in typical politician style, that I would have a great future. He had no doubt, he said, that some day I would be "Member for Prince Albert and even more". In later years, I rather disturbed the equanimity of the Davis descendants by trying to make the Senator's prophesy come true.

A politician whom I greatly admired was Frederick W. G. Haultain. He was father of responsible government in the Northwest Territories and its one and only Premier before the Autonomy Acts of 1905 which created Saskatchewan and Alberta. Haultain opposed Laurier's policy of dividing the Northwest. Consequently, he was passed over when the premiers of the two new provinces were selected. The Conservatives were driven out of office in both the new provinces. A. C. Rutherford was asked to form the government in Alberta and Walter Scott, the Liberal federal Member for Regina (Assiniboia West), was brought back from Ottawa to form the government in Saskatchewan. Haultain became Opposition leader in the Saskatchewan Legislature. In the early provincial elections, the Conservatives, under Haultain's leadership, were known as "Provincial Righters", which perhaps tells the story.

When we were on the homestead there were often joint (two-party) political meetings at the Halcyonia School. This was not an unusual practice, and opposing candidates often travelled together. Thus, in the provincial election campaign of 1908, Frederick Haultain and the Honourable W. F. A. Turgeon of Prince Albert, Attorney General in the Scott Liberal government, on occasion travelled the political circuit together, sharing the same buckboard. Intimate friends, they were bitter political controversialists. It is said that when on one occasion Haultain was ill and unable to be present at a meeting, Turgeon first delivered the speech Haultain would have delivered had he been present, then delivered his own. Finally, he answered the arguments advanced by himself on behalf of the Conservative leader. I suppose they made the same speech night after night; but since there was no modern means of communication, they were held responsible neither for changing their views nor for repeating what they had already said. They remained friends and, in my time at the bar, both became in turn Chief Justice of Saskatchewan. Incidentally, Sir Frederick received his knighthood in 1916, probably the only person ever knighted wearing sneakers.

Of the local stalwarts who appeared on the hustings, I can clearly recall George E. McCraney, Gerhard Ens, George Langley, and Archie McNab. McNab, in 1936, became Lieutenant-Governor of the province, one of the most popular ever in Saskatchewan. The finest stump performer in the early years, however, was R. B. Bennett, then a distinguished lawyer in Calgary. They called him Richard "Bonfire" Bennett, an appropriate appellation if ever there was one. He spoke at the rate of two hundred plus words a minute, each perfectly articulated and delivered with power. Even when the audience only numbered twenty or thirty, they got the full two-hour speech every time.

There were some strong Conservative families resident in our area. Among the more outstanding were the Bakers. Fred and George Baker had a large department store in Prince Albert. The Bakers and the Davises were sworn enemies. Sam J. Donaldson, one of the original North West Mounted Policemen, was another. He ran the best livery stable in Prince Albert. He advertised his political faith in a sign painted on the front of the stable:

Sam J. Donaldson Prop.
TORY IN POLITICS

The Bakers and the Donaldsons, however, were not exactly friends. They might join forces to oppose the Davis group, but apart from that they had little but enmity for each other. Irrespective of their reasons for dissociation throughout the 1885-1914 period (and each was convinced of the certain rightness of his own), the two families came together for a brief moment in 1914, never to speak again.

James McKay, K.C., of the famous Prince Albert family mentioned in Chapter Two, had been elected to the federal Parliament as the Member for Prince Albert in the

1911 general election, the only Conservative from Saskatchewan. In 1914, he was appointed to the Court of King's Bench for Saskatchewan. It used to be said of him that while most judges took three days in court and two more in Appeal, he always took four days in court and there was no time wasted on appeals. Following his resignation from the House of Commons, a by-election was called for 1 February 1915. The Great War was in progress and the Liberal executive decided that they were not going to contest the seat. Naturally, a number of Tories wanted the nomination. Sam Donaldson, the provincial Member for Shellbrook, had gained a reputation for his prowess as a political magician. George Baker approached Sam one day in early November 1914: "There's no reason why we should forever be enemies. I don't want that." Sam said: "I don't either." From there the conversation, certainly as I heard it reported, led to the fact that George Baker, from his earliest days in Belleville, Ontario, had in mind being a Member of Parliament. Sam said: "It's a fine idea." George then asked whether Sam would take over his organization. Donaldson agreed that he might. "So, how much money? What do you need?" asked George. "Well," Sam looked thoughtful, "it'll take about six weeks to cover the area. Ten thousand would carry me through. I have the fastest horses in my livery stable, the best equipment, and I'll need money to hand out here and there." It was so agreed and Sam went off to work the constituency.

Prince Albert was the hub of northern Saskatchewan. Founded in 1866 as a religious settlement by a Presbyterian minister, the Reverend James Nisbet, it was by the 1880s one of the largest centres in the Territories. It was then, and it has not changed with the years, a political centre as well. During the days of the boom, Prince Albert enjoyed great prosperity. It had a magnificent opera house, where the finest of theatrical entertainment was available. Cost was no object. Between 1909 and 1911, the Prince Albert Club was the most elegant in all Saskatchewan. It is said that during the Christmas season of 1910, the secretary of the club wired a wholesale liquor dealer in Montreal a twelve-thousand-dollar order for champagne and wines. The wholesaler wired back, "There must be a mistake." To which the reply, "There's no mistake, double it." That's how the newly rich lived. When the boom collapsed, most of them went bankrupt.

The Conservative nominating convention was held in Prince Albert's Empress Theatre. Sam Donaldson returned two days before the event. He immediately met with George Baker. By this time there were several very strong candidates in the running. I've heard that Sam's assessment of the situation, when asked by Mr. Baker, went like this: "It looks all right to me, George, but it's going to be a long convention. Fortunately for us, the others are not wise in the ways of politics. But it's going to be touch and go. Nobody will get a majority on the first three ballots, but I think it would be a good idea if I let my name stand to take off some of the votes that would go to Dawson or Braden." "Whatever you say, Sam." There were sixteen hundred delegates. On the first vote, George Baker got thirty-five votes and Sam Donaldson about six hundred. That fine new friendship ended right there. Sam was chosen after several ballots as the Conservative candidate. Sam stepped down in the election of 1917 in favour of Andrew Knox, who ran and won as the government-endorsed Unionist candidate. Sam was promised elevation to the Senate, but it went to someone from Regina instead.

Sam was a great fellow. In 1916, he was Lieutenant-Colonel, Officer Commanding the 243rd Overseas Battalion, which he took to England. Only his age prevented his seeing active service at the Front. When I moved into Prince Albert in 1924, I stayed at his home. Indeed, it was he who got me to stand for election in 1925. In business, he was Prince Albert's equivalent of Robin Hood. The rich never forgave him but the poor loved him. He became very wealthy during the days of the boom. When he died in 1927, his land title certificates had a valuation that would have amounted to one million one hundred thousand dollars during the boom days. The actual value of his properties, however, was closer to five thousand dollars. He was not a good speaker, although he expressed himself very clearly in what he had to say. In the 1925 provincial election, Sam spoke for the Conservative candidate at a joint meeting some twenty-five or thirty miles from Prince Albert. Two Liberals were on the platform, with Sam the second speaker. After some argument, it was agreed Sam was to have five minutes for rebuttal at the end of the meeting. The first speaker told of Sam's alleged corruption over the years. Then came Sam. He did not reply to the charges. The second Liberal spoke and described more of Sam's alleged wrongdoings, and there were many. Every time he dealt with one of Sam's sins, he said, "What do you think of yourself now, Sam Donaldson?" The audience, mainly Liberal, reacted with partisan gusto. Sam's concluding speech was a masterpiece of effective political oratory, but does not appear in any collected works. "Here I am. You, your parents and grandparents have known me through the years. Imagine these two fellows saying to me, 'What do you think of yourself now, Sam Donaldson?' Me—in between them—what do you think of yourself now? I asked myself that question and I answered it to my own satisfaction. 'Sam, you're a number one kernel of hard wheat in a whole barrel full of rat manure.' " That ended the debate.

In the early days, electoral corruption was practised quite openly. Liquor flowed freely on election day and bribery was not uncommon. Where a candidate was without a dependable scrutineer in every poll, the consequences could be dire. Father served at least twice in this capacity and was loud-spoken in opposing electoral wrongs. To steal an election by fraudulent means was regarded by some as evidence of political acumen and electoral smart practice. This was, of course, a frontier, and politics tended to reflect that fact. But there were limits to what might be stolen, as demonstrated by, if I may use yet another Sam Donaldson story, the "Rabbitskin Election".

This stemmed from a Liberal attempt to deny victory to Sam Donaldson in the 1905 provincial election. As the campaign in Prince Albert progressed, it was apparent to all that the outcome would be close. On election day, the returns for the largest polls made it clear that Donaldson would be elected. The unreported polls, most of them far distant and insignificant numerically, had to send in their returns by wagon over many miles, a journey of several days. It did not appear possible that Donaldson's lead could be overcome. Among those polls not yet reporting was Red Deer Lake, now Waskesiu Lake, some seventy miles north of Prince Albert. In a last-ditch effort to thwart Donaldson's victory, several Liberals hied themselves to the Red Deer Lake poll the day after the election and went into action.

In those days polling places could be changed without difficulty. Their polling place was the outdoors. Since there was no table on which to place the ballot box, they used a muskrat house. These co-workers in crime had a happy time. They knew the Election Act well and scrupulously followed its provisions. Each ballot was marked with an X after the Liberal candidate's name. Before it was dropped into the ballot box, the counterfoil was removed by the Deputy Returning Officer and the name of the voter recorded in the poll book. To speed up the process they had whole families vote. And among those entered in the poll book were the Rabbitt family: Johnny

Rabbitt, Peter Rabbitt, Henry Rabbitt and so on. Then came the Ratt family, in the same order as the Rabbitt family: Johnny Ratt, Peter Ratt, Henry Ratt. Then came the Rabbitskins, all voting in the same order as the Rabbitts and the Ratts. My memory is not clear on the exact number who voted, but the voting did not end until the conspirators had agreed that, come what might, enough votes were in the ballot box to ensure defeat for Donaldson. They then returned to Prince Albert and delivered to the Returning Officer the records of the ballots cast, together with the pertinent election-day documents. The count complete, their candidate was declared elected. (I do not believe he knew what his supporters were up to.) Unfortunately for those responsible, the shenanigans at Red Deer Lake poll could not be kept secret; the numbers voting far exceeded the normal population. An action was launched to set aside the election. As the plot unravelled, criminal prosecutions were taken against the alleged wrongdoers, who were charged with conspiracy to defraud Donaldson of his seat in the legislature, and jointly and severally with having obtained the election of their candidate by false pretences. Warrants were issued by a Justice of the Peace in Prince Albert and the conspirators were lodged in the common jail to await preliminary hearings.

The story should have ended there but it did not. The men charged were loyal Liberals whose only crime, in the eyes of Prince Albert's Liberal establishment, was that their enthusiasm had run to excess. The machine rolled into action. The authorities in the Attorney General's office in Regina cancelled the appointment of the Justice of the Peace by an order purporting to have been dated some days before he had issued the warrants. Habeas corpus proceedings were secretly held and the Judge before whom the application was heard ruled that the Justice of the Peace had not had the authority to issue the warrants. He thus ordered the accused released. This, of course, was no more than a stopgap. It was realized that further proceedings could be taken, and plans were made to get the culprits out of the jurisdiction of the courts. Since no province or territory in Canada afforded sanctuary, it was decided they should go to Chicago until it was safe for them to return. To ensure they would not be on the unemployment rolls, each of them was to receive seventy-five dollars a month. With their first monthly allowance, their railway fares, and money for incidental expenses, they slipped away that same night.

Once they were safely out of the way, their mentors in Prince Albert forgot about them; only one or two of the monthly instalments ever reached them. Unable to find steady employment and on the verge of virtual starvation in Chicago, they finally decided to return to Prince Albert and face jail. They were immediately charged, arrested, and found guilty of having obtained the return of the Liberal candidate by false pretences. An appeal was launched. The Court, sitting "en banc" in Regina, quashed the conviction. Thus ended the Rabbitskin Election Case. If the wrongdoers finally escaped jail, at least Sam Donaldson got his election. So flagrant was the abuse that the legislature, even with a large Liberal majority, voted to seat him. Of course, as a boy on the homestead, I was unaware of many of the specific details outlined above. As I have often remarked, the only protection Conservatives in Saskatchewan enjoyed in those early days was afforded by the Game Laws. Yet they had pluck and courage and character. And they stood fast against a Liberal establishment that by the 1920s was to develop, under the Honourable James G. Gardiner, one of the most vicious political machines this country has ever seen.

I mentioned that we had in our home a large single-volume encyclopedia of about a thousand pages which

Father had bought second-hand from Britnell's in Toronto. I read it from end to end, from front to back and from back to front. Possibly because of my father's interest in them, I was attracted by the biographical sketches of those who fought the great battles for political freedom during the reign of Charles I, particularly the great Leveller leader, "freeborn John" Lilburne, who gave new meaning to the "liberties of England". Beloved by the people, he defied the infamous Star Chamber's suppression of the press and was flogged in the streets for his trouble. Exiled in turn by the Rump Parliament that tried Charles I, he was forbidden to return to England on pain of death. Return he did, and was arrested. But no jury in all London could be found that would convict him. He deserves a far greater place in history than has ever been given him. Later, when I was in collegiate and had to make short speeches at the Literary Society meetings, I spoke of Lilburne, Pym, and Hampden. We also had two volumes on Lincoln in our library, one, that uncertain biography by his law partner, Herndon, the other, a book on his wit and humour. Lincoln, a small-town lawyer, was to become the symbol of American democracy, tribune of his people, a man whose origins were those of a pioneer on the United States frontier. One story particularly impressed me with Lincoln's humility. Having been elected President, he returned to Springfield, Illinois, his home town, where there was a celebration in his honour. The mayor asked him how it felt to be President-elect of the United States of America. Lincoln replied that he was reminded of a coloured man, Josh, who about twenty-five years before had become engaged in some extramural and even extramoral activities resulting in his being tarred and feathered and ridden out of town on a rail. Lincoln continued, "I said to him when he came back three weeks later, 'Well, what did you think of the whole thing, Josh?' And Josh answered, 'Mr. Lincoln, if it hadn't been for the honour I would have sooner walked.' "

Every little boy or girl has some ultimate ambition, to be a farmer or a train engineer, a nurse, a schoolteacher, or a doctor, and no doubt in every case the best possible. Some pursue their ambition with a single-minded devotion and attain it. Others, caught in the byways of life, find more attractive or more realistic goals. As one looks back over life from the vantage of many years, it is difficult not to be fascinated by the "ifs" of his experience. Perhaps it would be simpler if one's theology embraced the concept of predestination. Mine does not. It would seem to me that we are given opportunities, not guarantees, and that all we can do is to strive forward, contributing as we can to the common good, trying to make certain that our decisions and actions are not inconsistent with our highest ambitions. Our ultimate future depends so much on character and circumstance. I was eight or nine years old when I said to my mother, "Some day I am going to be Prime Minister." She did not laugh. Always a practical woman, she pointed out the near-impossibility of anyone's realizing that ambition, and in particular one living far out on the Prairies. I was deeply concerned. Uncle Ed provided me a more sympathetic audience. As we walked or rode to and from school each day, I told him of my thoughts and ambitions, and discussed the things that I had read. He was a wonderful person, with a lively, inquiring mind and all the time in the world to listen to the dreams and plans which Elmer and I might unfold. From my earliest boyhood I was given to a romanticization of the future in which I would be able to do something for my country.

In the year 1909, the question came up frequently as to whether we should remain on the land and, if so, whether we should buy an adjacent quarter section, since Father was about to receive the patent (title) to our homestead. Mother thought that we should move to Saskatoon where educational facilities (both collegiate and university) would permit Elmer and me to get the best education within our parents' means. No final decision, however, was to be made until August when the Department of Education results were published for what are now grades nine and ten, then described as Forms I and II. Under the regulations then in effect, a rural student could write his grade eight entrance examination at the school he attended, but for high school subjects, departmental examinations had to be taken at designated central locations. I had studied under my Uncle Ed for Forms I and II and was now required to take my examinations in Saskatoon. I might mention that until then the only subject with which I had any real difficulty was art; I could not draw to save my soul.

My father took me to the city and lodged me in Madills' boarding house on Avenue C, where I was to stay during the examinations. He returned to the homestead. A block and a half away there was an ice cream parlour, the Maple Leaf. Mother had made ice cream occasionally on the homestead as a special treat. There was ice at the bottom of our well year round; we may not have had potable water but we certainly had refrigeration. I had a little money given me for the week, ice cream was not expensive, and here was the opportunity to have as much as I could swallow—heaven indeed. This was the end of June, and very hot. The departmental regulations required that if a student failed on one examination he lost all of them, no matter how well or poorly he did on the rest. On Friday, the last day of the examinations, I had about a quart of ice cream for breakfast. I felt squeamish during the morning examination, but everything seemed to go well enough. At lunch I walked over to the Maple Leaf for more ice cream. I felt still less well. To make a long story short, back in the examination room, I took sick and had to leave at the end of half an hour. I lost my year. That was the determining factor in my parents' decision to move to Saskatoon. There is indeed "a tide in the affairs of men". We moved on a flood of ice cream.

We left the homestead early in February 1910. Father had gone ahead to look for employment; he did not wish to continue teaching. Saskatoon was booming, afire with activity. Its population was nearly twelve thousand. Fortunes were being made overnight. There were reportedly more real estate offices in Saskatoon than there were houses. Everyone said that Saskatoon was going to become a metropolis. Warman, thirteen miles to the north, had the same ambition, and the optimism of Biggar, some fifty miles west along the CPR mainline, knew no bounds. When you reached the town limits, there was a sign: "New York may have a larger population but this is Biggar". In 1916, when I was overseas, I saw a sign in Birmingham advertising lots in both Saskatoon's River Heights and miles beyond. The leader read, "GET RICH".

Father took a position with the provincial government as desk clerk in the Land Titles Office. The salary was seven hundred and twenty dollars a year. He did not inform Mother before he accepted this and she was not very happy when she found out. He had had one or two better opportunities. In 1911, he moved to the employ of the federal government and, until his retirement in 1938, was a gauger at the Saskatoon Excise Port, testing liquor, gasoline, and the like. Father rented a house for us at 823 Avenue I South, "just a short step along the river", he told us as we got off the train. It seemed a short step to him because he had been taken out in a Brush automobile by the real estate man at the breathtaking speed of fifteen miles an hour. It was a fairly long step when we had to walk. We soon moved, buying a house at 411 - 9th Street.

The year 1910 was that in which the world last saw Halley's Comet. Many people were deeply aroused by its appearance, taking it to be a harbinger of calamity, or of good fortune. (I suspect that when it appears again in 1986, reaction will be similar.) Although Mother was inclined to entertain a remote Highland belief in the supernatural, Father normally dismissed superstitions as nonsense. Yet, when we saw Halley's Comet, all bright and beautiful in the southwest sky, it was Father who said, "It's propitious."

Elmer was in grade five at Queen Alexandra School. I attended the Saskatoon Collegiate Institute. This was only about one block from the Maple Leaf Café, but I stayed away from it as from a pest-house. I rewrote my grades nine and ten examinations in the summer of 1910 and passed without difficulty. Although I was less than enthusiastic about chemistry and physics, the only subjects I ever found difficult in high school were bookkeeping and penmanship, and there was little that James W. Neilson, my teacher, afterwards Bursar of the University of Saskatchewan, could do to help me. Fortunately I did not have to take art.

I was in grade eleven when Father came home one day greatly pleased because the Northern Crown Bank was prepared to offer me a job at a salary of twenty-five dollars a month. Father had two cousins who had become general managers of their respective banks, and he was most enthusiastic about my prospects. Mother, despite the fact that Father's salary was small, took a strong stand, and Father, on reflection, agreed with her that I should be given an opportunity to complete my education. Ironically, one of the reasons why the bank wanted me was that I had taken bookkeeping.

I cannot recall any particular change of attitude resulting from our move from the homestead. I was no less amused than the other students, and my parents no less shocked than theirs, when one Hallowe'en night some of the school's "bad boys" changed the "T" on the sign over the door of Saskatoon's Teapot Inn Restaurant to a "P".

Like the school at Halcyonia, this one was ninety-nine per cent English-speaking. Indeed, the only student of French origin whom I remember was a chap called Robillard, and he refused to speak French. I took little part in high school athletics (in university, I ran the three-mile race). Certainly, I was delighted to be at a school that did not have grades one to twelve in a single room, and was intrigued by the proceedings on the upper floor of the collegiate where, during 1911 and 1912, the fledgling University of Saskatchewan held its classes. I was sorely tempted to move on to university after my Junior Matriculation (grade eleven) and often wondered if it was not a mistake to stay on at collegiate to finish my senior year. In those days Latin was a prerequisite for university entrance. I began it only halfway through my last year and passed with good marks. Latin has been a favourite study with me ever since, and, I might add, a study of considerable benefit. In the early 1930s, when I was a member of the Senate of the University, a motion came before us to eliminate the Latin prerequisite. There were only two of us who voted to keep it and both were lawyers.

One of the teachers at the collegiate, C. Roscoe Brown, arranged a public-speaking course after school hours. I always had an ambition to be able to speak in public, but my diffidence and nervousness were hard to overcome. Father had tried to help me on the homestead. We spent some time studying the short story (Father was an ardent admirer of O. Henry), but whatever I learned did not seem to result in a solution to my problems. In Mr. Brown's class, we were assigned a series of five-minute speeches. I made mine on those historical figures to whom I attached particular importance: Coke and Selden, Pym, Hampden, and Lilburne, Pitt and Burke and Fox, Disraeli, Gladstone, and Sir John A. Macdonald. I became engrossed in following the development of the parliamentary system, the various landmarks of freedom

beginning with Magna Carta, the famous Parliament of 28
January 1265, the Habeas Corpus Act and the Bill of
Rights, the Long Parliament of 1641, and the debates taking place at that very moment in the British House of
Commons, where Lloyd George under the Asquith administration forced legislation through the House of
Lords by threatening to have sufficient peers appointed to
assure the passage of bills approved by the Lower House.
I did learn some of the principles of articulation, and a
fair amount of constitutional history. Also, I observed
that a large proportion of those who achieved a position
of leadership had followed the legal profession. This, no
doubt, was one of the reasons, subtle but significant, that
caused me to decide on law as a career. Father had high
hopes I might win the Gerald Willoughby Gold Medal in
the collegiate oratorical contest. I had placed first in the
preliminary round. There were five finalists. I carefully
prepared and memorized my speech. All went well until
my concluding remarks. My mind went blank. I had the
speech in my pocket, but nothing ever proved more elu-
sive than that final page. When the results were announced, I did not place. Father was greatly concerned.
Three years later, Elmer won the prize and we all were so
very proud of him.

In our family, we had little money. Everyone had to
pitch in to make ends meet. We kept a cow which we
tethered in the very centre of present-day Saskatoon
south, around First Street, about half a mile from home.
My brother and I sold milk for a year and a half or two.
In addition, Father bought two twenty-five-foot lots, one
hundred feet long, and these he had ploughed up for vegetables. Elmer and I sold papers. That was an experience,
since by this time I was almost fifteen years old, and in
grade eleven. I soon learned that one has to choose his
friends in public because those students who were my
friends in school often chose to pass on the other side of

the street when the noisy newsboys came along. "*Saskatoon Phoenix*, half a dime, keeps you reading all the time. The more you buy the better for me." It was not long before a sign went up in the window of Saskatoon's best café, the B.C. Restaurant, owned by Chinese partners, the Marks Brothers, "Dogs and newsboys not admitted." In the fall of 1910, I began to sell papers on a larger scale, finally coming to the point where I had four or five boys working for me. I was an entrepreneur, a distributor and active agent on the streets for the *Winnipeg Telegram* (the first paper in the West with a funny-paper insert). The papers were delivered to me in Saskatoon for half a cent, and the boys paid me two cents on every paper sold. This averaged out to about $3.50 on weekdays and $5.00 on Saturdays. The *Calgary Eye-Opener*, that marvellous production of Bob Edwards, was a good seller (it was considered "dangerous" literature) when it on occasion arrived; we paid five cents a copy but were able to sell it for twenty-five. I have a statuette in my office of which I am proud, commemorating my honorary membership in the Newsboys' Association of America, an association that has included United States presidents Hoover, Truman, and Eisenhower among its members.

We took every sort of odd job. Elmer worked after school delivering parcels for a men's wear store. In the summers of 1910 and 1911, I worked as janitor in Warner's Book and Stationery Store on Second Avenue, cleaning the floors and windows before store hours and dusting the merchandise. Any acquaintance with the winds of Saskatoon will give an idea of the dust that came off the unpaved streets, settling on everything in sight. I was paid twenty dollars a month. During a convention in Saskatoon, I worked four twelve-hour days and earned six dollars in total. We did very well selling memorial ribbons in May 1910 during the period of official mourning following the death of King Edward VII. By July 1912 Elmer and I had got together a few hundred dollars and decided to get into the real estate swim. We bought lots in River Heights. In October, the bottom fell out of the boom and a year and a half's work simply disappeared. Father had earlier bought two lots on Victoria Avenue. If I recall correctly, the normal terms were ten per cent down; the lots cost about twelve hundred dollars each. Within a short period, he was offered the opportunity to realize a thousand-dollar profit, but he held on. A year later these lots too were valueless.

On the social side of my life, I had no particular "girl friend". As I remember it, the girls at school were all very pleasant to me. A couple of the daughters of families to whom we sold milk would come over to our house in the evenings and we would sit on the porch and talk by the hour. But they went home alone each time.

Elmer and I became members of the First Baptist Church in Saskatoon in 1910 during the ministry of the Reverend Idell Hartson Wood, a preacher of unusual ability, who in some ways reminded one of the evangelist Billy Sunday. He was always opposing some instrument of the devil. I recall that he took strong objection to the Saskatoon Brewing Company, which described its Saskatoon beer as "liquid bread". The brewing company brought out arguments to prove the beneficial and nutritive values of its products. They were violently disputed by Mr. Wood. After some months of harsh exchanges, the debate wore itself out, neither side having made any advance in convincing the other. A schism arose in our church when a leading Baptist theologian, the Reverend A. Eustace Haydon (later to become Professor of Religion at Chicago University), preached against the Virgin birth and various revelations in the Old Testament, including Creation. We were among those who formed a new congregation on the west side of Saskatoon, known as the Riverdale and Nutana Baptist Church. The Reverend E. J. Bridgeman, my uncle by marriage on my mother's side, was our minister.

Mother was completely convinced that only the Baptist faith professed the true religion. Father, a Methodist, did not have strong convictions on the subject of denomination. He joined the Baptist Church in 1912. Thereafter, he was immersed in all areas of church work. He was on the finance board and was a Deacon for at least thirty years. There were few occasions, indeed, between our arrival in Saskatoon and his death in February 1944 when he missed a Sunday morning service.

In politics, I remember well the election night of 1911. It was a cold September night. I arrived home about midnight. The returns came in slowly. Although Saskatchewan had voted strongly Liberal, Laurier was out. Reciprocity and the Naval Service Act had combined to ensure his political undoing in Ontario and Quebec, with a little help from Manitoba and British Columbia. There was a belief in Saskatchewan that night that we were in for a period when the good accomplished under the Laurier administration, such as Sir Clifford Sifton's work in bringing in immigrants, would be swept aside. I know that Father was concerned that the Prime Minister, whom he regarded as one of Canada's greatest builders, had been defeated. And yet, I remember him saying on one occasion during the campaign, "There must be something to Borden's claim because Sir Clifford Sifton is against Reciprocity." By the same token, he was suspicious of the opposition to Reciprocity of Thomas White (the anti-Reciprocity Liberal who became Borden's Minister of Finance, 1911-19). He argued that White and the powerful Eastern financial interests that he represented were more concerned with selfish ends than with national welfare.

The election had a profound influence on me, and perhaps more than anything else made me a Conservative. I attended all the meetings in Saskatoon. There was widespread feeling that if Reciprocity with the United States was accepted, economic union would result, ultimately leading to political absorption. This belief was strengthened in the last few weeks of the campaign when one of the outstanding leaders in the United States Congress, J. G. ("Champ") Clark, Democratic Speaker-designate of the House of Representatives, stated that he had supported Reciprocity because he hoped "to see the day when the American flag will float over every square foot of the British North American Colonies clear to the North Pole." His statement had an effect far beyond any other. The Conservatives stood for "one Canada", free from United States domination. The bands at Conservative meetings played, and the faithful sang, "We're soldiers of the King". "Rule Britannia" had its place in those programmes as we cleaved to our British heritage in defiance of American manifest destiny and Grit continentalism. The result was a tremendous revelation of Canadian determination to be Canadian. This impressed me greatly.

As a matter of fact, I had met Sir Wilfrid Laurier the year before when he was in Saskatoon to lay the cornerstone of the University of Saskatchewan. His private railway car was at the station one morning when I went over to pick up our newspapers. There he was, standing on the platform, taking the morning air. This memory of him will stay with me always, his dignity, his plume of snow-white hair. I sold him a newspaper. He gave me a quarter—no better way to establish an instant rapport with a newsboy. We chatted about Canada. I had the awed feeling that I was in the presence of greatness. That afternoon, when he laid the cornerstone, he included in his remarks a reference to his conversation with a Saskatoon newsboy which, he observed, had ended with my saying, "Sorry, Prime Minister, I can't waste any more time on you, I've got work to do." I took some pride in July 1957, after I became Prime Minister, in the fact that my railway car was stationed in exactly the spot where Sir Wilfrid's had stood.

CHAPTER FIVE

MOTHER HOPED that I would become a minister of the
Gospel. To Father, banking and teaching might be
added to the ministry as the preferred professions. These
things I knew. Yet my ambition was to study law. Fortunately, I experienced no direct pressure from either par-
ent in making up my mind, nor did Elmer. Once I had decided on the career I wanted to pursue, Father helped me
select the courses that would be of maximum benefit.
Concentrating on English and Latin, I took a general
Bachelor of Arts course. Beginning in the academic year
of 1913-14, and while still an undergraduate, I had my
first introduction to the law, taking courses in contracts
and in criminal and constitutional law. I took readily to
the study of law; I was absorbed by it, and wanted to
read all the law I could find. I suppose my appetite had
first been whetted by a law book for laymen called *Law
at a Glance* which Uncle Ed had on the homestead, and
in which almost every conceivable legal problem was
considered.

I will never forget my first day at university in the fall
of 1912. I was unceremoniously heaved into the decorative pool in front of the present administration building,
at that time the University of Saskatchewan's only building. I had arrived in short pants and was saved from be-

ing the victim of further horseplay only by the fact that I
was a "fresh-soph"; though it was my first year at the university I was actually beginning my second year of studies. For the freshman, hazing was particularly cruel. I
suppose that in surviving it some acquired a sense of belonging to the university but it was a practice that often
became other than amusing, and universities today are no
poorer for its disappearance. During my first year, I took
little part in student activities; I was too shy and I had little spare time. I still had newspapers to sell, morning and
afternoon. In my second year, however, I became a little
more outgoing. I joined the Debating Union. Later, I was
elected to the Students' Representative Council. As well, I
was president of my law year.

Except when I took my Master's and in my law
courses, my marks as a student were average. For one
thing, I spent more time than necessary seeking
clarification of theories enunciated in class. I was reluctant to accept unchallenged what I was told, and always
wanted to follow propositions through to their logical
conclusion. Although probably I did not realize this at
the time, much of lasting value that I acquired at university was not to be measured in marks but in work done
on my own. I simply accepted the fact that I would never
be a top scholar, and I enjoyed my university years immensely. As I recall, twenty-four credits were required
for a baccalaureate degree; I took half again as many.

I was extremely fortunate in that, although the University of Saskatchewan was small and new, I had a roster
of outstanding professors. Students came to know them
personally and to benefit directly from their scholarship.
Dr. Walter C. Murray, the university's first president, was
an able organizer. Without him, I doubt that the university would have got off the ground. While his was not the
age of student rebellion, his actions often resulted in
strong opposition. Indeed, he and I were to come into

each other's firing lines on a number of occasions, both when I was a student and over the years, one equalling the other in the expression of unreticent opinion. For example, in 1919, four outstanding professors whom he without cause suspected of trying to undermine his authority were fired arbitrarily. By this time, I was in practice as a lawyer. But I was the only graduate, up to that time, who had received three degrees from the university (B.A., M.A., and LL.B.). I was ashamed that my Alma Mater would allow this action to pass unchallenged and took part in calling for a special Convocation to revoke the dismissal of these men. When it met, I was one of the lead speakers. My remarks were not designed to placate the President, the other professors, or the majority of the Convocation, who at that time were ninety per cent *ad eundem* (those who had become members of our Convocation in 1908 by reason of their graduation from other universities). It was a fiery fight. Ninety-five per cent of the actual graduates of the University of Saskatchewan stood together, but we were overwhelmed. I spoke of burning my diplomas in public to show my contempt for an institution capable of dismissing its leading scholars. The general public, however, believed that President Murray was right, reinforced as he was by the strong support of the Convocation. Nevertheless, the dismissals were a heavy blow to the integrity of the University and had an unfortunate effect for many years.

Among the professors whom President Murray discharged was Dr. Ira Allen MacKay. No one had a greater influence on me in university than he. He was my professor in political science and law, and he had that quality essential to a great teacher, the power to inspire. He was a man of much wisdom and I remember many of his lessons. He judged that a people can never be made good by legislation, a point that many of us never learn. His words come back to me when I think of the Morgentaler case:

"The law is not what should be; the law is what the consensus in the community ordain that it shall be." An acceptance of that principle would have vitiated the Volstead Act in the United States and the attempts to enforce prohibition in Canada. But Ira Allen MacKay was also a man often remote from the ordinary things of life. On one occasion, he came goose-hunting with three or four of us. We dug the pits, a surprise to him, and put out the decoys. Before long, a flock of geese began their approach. When they were about a hundred yards away, he stood up to proclaim: "Never, in all my life, have I ever before realized the meaning of the poetry of motion." That was the end of his goose-hunting with us! When my friends Hugh Aird and Allan Macmillan and I were ready to go overseas, he arranged a tea for us. Typically, he presented me with a volume which he hoped I would carry throughout the war, William James's *The Principles of Psychology*. To Hugh he gave a volume of Sophocles; to Allan an equally unmartial book. He was a dreamer, an idealist.

Among the others whose names I will never forget were Donald Maclean and Arthur Moxon. Maclean was a fine lawyer; appointed to the King's Court Bench, he was a tower of justice. Like MacKay and Maclean, Moxon was also a Nova Scotian. A Rhodes Scholar, he could have touched the heights in law. He had a great heart, and his knowledge and appreciation of jurisprudence brought that subject to life for us. No student I know who was privileged to have had him as professor but would agree with me that no one was his equal as a teacher. Certainly, he inspired in his students a determination to emulate his erudition, however small our success in the attempt.

By the summer of 1913, I was becoming too old to sell papers. It was impossible to find work in Saskatoon. My Uncle Ed got me a job as a farm labourer at twenty dol-

1. John and Elmer Diefenbaker, about 1902

2. William Thomas Diefenbaker and Mary Florence Bannerman on
their wedding day, May 1894. Their attendants are the bride's sister,
Mrs. Sadie Bridgeman, and the groom's brother Ulysses.

3 & 4. *(Above)* William Diefenbaker with the pupils from Greenwood School north of Whitby in 1899. Four-year-old John Diefenbaker would frequently sit in with the other pupils. He is the blond curly-headed boy in the middle of the second row (eighth from the left). *(Left)* Grandfather George Diefenbacker (the spelling he used) in 1905

5 & 6. *(Above)* the homestead house near Borden, Saskatchewan, where the Diefenbaker family lived from 1906 to 1910. *(Below)* William Diefenbaker and the pupils at Hoffnungsfeld School near the homestead. Elmer is sitting at his father's left. John attended the nearby Halcyonia School where his Uncle Ed was the teacher.

7. Uncle Ed Diefenbaker and his Cleveland bicycle

8 & 9. *(Right)* John G. Diefenbaker in 1915 when he received his B.A. degree from the University of Saskatchewan. *(Below)* Lieutenant Diefenbaker in England, 5 November 1916, with two friends from Saskatoon, Lieutenant Hugh Aird, who was later wounded, and Lieutenant Allan Macmillan, who was later killed in action.

10 & 11. *(Above)* The young lawyer at Wakaw in 1919 with the old Herd railway handcar he sometimes used to travel to neighbouring villages. *(Below)* The little house in Wakaw where John Diefenbaker batched during the early years of his law practice.

12. Mrs. Florence Diefenbaker in 1920

lars a month, with forty dollars during the harvest
months of August and September. Duncan Jamieson, my
employer, lived some twenty miles south of Blaine Lake.
Duncan was a bachelor and prepared our meals, invariably salt ham and potatoes. The work was hard but man-
ageable, and I did every possible type of farm job. What
with Jamieson's jumpy team of horses, near catastrophe
became an every-second-day occurrence; they would
bolt on the least provocation. I didn't even enjoy an easy
day when it rained; rainy days were set aside for hauling
manure. The only respite I had was on Sundays when occasionally his sister-in-law invited me to the adjoining
farm to have a meal. One of those Sundays remains in my
mind. The bank manager from a neighbouring town and
his wife were there for lunch. He gave dissertations on all
current problems and, as I thought I knew something
about economics, I volunteered an opinion. His response
was that I should mind my own business, that it was bad
enough to have a farm labourer sitting at the family table,
but to have him trying to express his views was totally
inexcusable. Near the end of my employment in late September, I developed a carbuncle at the base of my neck,
no doubt as a consequence of our diet. Treatment for it
cost me more than my total summer wages, intended to
carry me through the coming university year.

In the following summer, that of 1914, I taught grades
one to five at Wheat Heart Public School, some seven
miles west of our homestead. It was a thrilling experience
to be surrounded by boys and girls eager for education.
They would come to school however early I was prepared to come, and stay as late as I could stay with them.
Sometimes we were there from seven in the morning until six in the evening. I had taken the complete course in
pedagogy (two three-hour lectures!) before starting out,
but in order to get my teaching licence approved for the
following year, I had to have a satisfactory report from

the inspector. As fate would have it, School Inspector Magee arrived one afternoon about two-thirty. The children were busy with their work but I was nowhere in sight. He found me at the back of the yard with a .22, shooting gophers, which were so numerous as to be almost a plague. I did not get my certificate. I could only conclude that gopher-shooting was not on the curriculum that year.

We live in a world still suffering from the consequences of that summer of 1914, when the Western World marched to war. I was at home in Saskatoon on Saturday and Sunday, the first and second days of August. There was great excitement. Europe was in turmoil. Germany had issued its ultimatum to Belgium. Everyone was tense, waiting to see what Britain would do. We were still waiting when I caught the train to Borden that Sunday afternoon. Tuesday war was declared. Old-countrymen rushed to the colours in a surge of patriotism, encouraged in many instances, I am sure, by the thought that if they did not hurry they would miss a free trip "home". Gone too was that character whose presence lent a special colour to the prairie scene, the English remittance-man. All heard the call to King and Country. Many were positive that it would be a short and glorious affair, over by Christmas. It is hard now to believe that we entered the holocaust that was the First World War, if not exactly in the spirit of light opera, at least as if it were no more than the natural course of events. The West would never be quite the same again.

For me, it was back to university to finish my final undergraduate year. My classes went reasonably well. In the university's Mock Parliament, I had become leader of the student Conservative Party and Leader of the Opposition in 1913. There was no chance of my becoming premier since the ratio of Conservative supporters never exceeded about a third of the Liberal supporters. At that time, there was no third party to create uncertainty. I have always believed that there should be a clear choice in politics and not a fading out of political colour such as developed in subsequent years, first with the Progressive Party in 1920, and later with the CCF (now NDP) and Social Credit. At the university, we met regularly in Mock Parliament. We debated what had been debated in the House of Commons two weeks earlier, since it took two weeks for Hansard to arrive. Our Speaker knew parliamentary rules and procedures, and we learned them, not by rote, not by being able to point out a, b, c, d in Bourinot, but by a detailed examination of each confrontation as it arose. I remember those debates with pleasure. They were exhilarating and we learned a great deal. In my first year in university, I attended the first Boys' Parliament in Regina. In 1913, when it met in Saskatoon, I was defeated by one vote for the premiership. And it is of some interest, possibly, that in the graduation number of the University of Saskatchewan magazine, *The Sheaf*, in May 1915, which prophesied the destiny of students forty years hence, I was marked as the Leader of the Opposition in the House of Commons by 1955. It was in error by one year.

I was to graduate in May 1915. Imagine my consternation when I went to look over the list of those receiving degrees and found that my name was not included. I was devastated. Mother, always calm, said, "There must be a mistake." Father and I felt there could be no mistake; I was out. Those moments of panic disappeared when I found the Dean. A line had been missed by the printer. My nervousness, however, remained. When my name was called, I proceeded up the steps to the Chancellor's throne, received my sheepskin, turned about, and fell straight down the stairs.

I had decided that I would go on to take my Master of Arts degree in economics and political science (Father very much wanted me to) in the fall of 1915. The John A. Hertel Company of Toronto was to provide me with a whole series of memorable experiences in that last free summer of my life. A classmate of mine, Stanley Mighton, and I were given a short course on sales pitches. Equipped with sample books and order forms we set off on our bicycles to bring "new opportunities for self-betterment" to the populations of small towns in central Saskatchewan. In fact, our books were worth buying: the Bible in symbols, a magnificent book; a book of Bible lessons; a layman's law book; an excellent book on the first six months of the war, replete with pictures and readily saleable. The costs ranged from $7.95 for the Bible bound in morocco to $2.50 for the war book. We were to collect a deposit, the balance when we later delivered the volumes. Our commission was forty per cent. We tried our luck in Watrous, Nokomis, Outlook, Hawarden, and Hanley, and in every town in between. I was amazed that with the same selling technique, one week we would outsell all the students in North America, and the next week we would sell nothing. Dependent as we were on the deposits to keep us alive, we were either opulent or broke. When we were unlucky, we didn't eat and had no place to sleep. We became acquainted with a great many straw and hay stacks. There is nothing to compare with a hot summer night on an old straw stack with every species of the bug world concentrating its undivided attention on you.

Our first experience with the police was in Outlook, where we were aroused from our slumbers in the grandstand of the fair grounds. We had no money and were sent packing as vagrants. In Hanley, where we had money, we were arrested for selling without a licence and taken to the police office. We were out in an hour or so; the local policeman, after much argument, agreed that we might leave our bicycles as security until our appearance in court the next week. The charges were dropped when it was discovered that our employer had the necessary licence and our bicycles were returned to us. I never pass through Hanley without thinking of that burly constable jumping from behind the organ in Mrs. Brown's living room, as Stanley was writing up her order, saying, "You're under arrest!"

During the academic year 1915-16 I completed my Master's degree requirements, including a thesis on the operation of inland grain elevators. I also continued my law classes. My graduate marks were much better than those of my undergraduate years. I was now twenty years old. In March of 1916, I volunteered for overseas service in the war and went to Winnipeg to take the officer-training course. I was to receive my M.A. in absentia that May. The officers' training was well organized and compressed into a strenuous six weeks. The pay was $1.10 per day. I still have the notes I made during those lectures. As army stores were depleted at the time, we were the first class through the school not dressed in khaki uniform. We wore the red jackets and blue trousers of the peacetime militia. But more serious was the boot shortage; we had to take whatever was available, no matter how approximate the fit. The blisters induced by a combination of Portage Avenue pavement and those ill-fitting shoes were beyond belief. Apart from this, I enjoyed the training, and I passed near the head of my class. There was, I fear, no lack of evidence to show that commissions were excessively handed out on the basis of political and personal friendship. I had to wait for mine.

Thus, after finishing my training course, I returned to Saskatoon and began my Law Articles under Mr. Russell Hartney. Since I wanted to keep in training while awaiting allocation to a unit, I trained every night with the Home Guard. The company sergeant-major was an old British regular. I doubt that there was a better-drilled

outfit in the land. When I read in the newspaper that, because of heavy casualties on the Somme, a draft of junior
officers was to be sent overseas at once, I got in touch
with Colonel Norman Edgar, District Officer Commanding, Regina. The next day I received the message: "Accepted". Hugh Aird and Allan Macmillan, my close
friends from collegiate and university, had gone with me
to take the officers' course in Winnipeg. Like me, they
were also articling law students. I found them that day at
the Land Titles Office and told them my news. Since they
had no intention of remaining behind, we three went off
to war.

We went to Regina to be sworn in and, after a two-day
leave, proceeded to Camp Hughes, Manitoba, near
today's Camp Shilo. After some confusion, we received
our orders. We were to go overseas immediately. I recall
that while we were celebrating, Major Bateman, formerly
my professor of English, said (paraphrasing Walpole) that
it would not be long before we were wringing our hands
rather than bells. We paid him no heed. We were on our
way. At Halifax, we were held up for a week; there was a
submarine close at hand. Then we joined the convoy. As
it turned out, our destroyers missed us northwest of the
Giant's Causeway. We were in a potentially desperate
position; but we saw nothing to indicate the danger.

I had never been on a ship before. Fortunately, I wasn't
seasick, and never have been, either back and forth
across the Atlantic or across the Channel. I had a very interesting time on board. Among other people, I met Sir
George and Lady Perley. Lady Perley enjoyed
shuffleboard and I was one of her partners. As we arrived
in Liverpool, she said to me, "If there is ever anything you
want done, you go to my husband and it will be done."
Sir George was High Commissioner, representing the
Borden government in London. Later, when I became a
Member of Parliament, Lady Perley took some pleasure

in telling the consequences of her promise. I was on leave
in London in December 1916, at the time when the Asquith government was in its last days. The king-maker,
Sir Max Aitken (later my friend Lord Beaverbrook), had
decided that Prime Minister H. H. Asquith must go and
that the Right Honourable David Lloyd George was to replace him. The day before Lloyd George was to make his
initial appearance as Prime Minister in the House of
Commons, I went down the Victoria Embankment to the
High Commissioner's office: "I want to see Sir George
Perley." I made no progress with the officials, but I stayed
around and argued. Finally, one of them asked, "Have
you a card?" Of course I hadn't, but I wrote my name on
a piece of paper and it was taken in. Out came Sir
George. He welcomed me and ushered me into his office
and asked what he could do for me. I told him that I
wanted a ticket for the gallery at Westminster the next
day. He replied: "If you came to me and wanted a promo-
tion to the rank of Major, it would be so easy, but this
can't be done." I said to him, "Now, you heard Lady Perley's promise." I got my ticket and was one of a half-
dozen Canadians to hear Lloyd George on that memorable day. He raised the horizons of the British people from
the frightful slaughter on the Somme to the hope of ultimate victory. I recently read that speech, and in cold
print it is not particularly inspiring. Churchill's speeches
read well; Lloyd George's ability to move his audience
depended on the contagion of his emotions, his gestures,
his eyes.

When on leave in London I spent my time either in the
Gallery of the House of Commons at Westminster or in
the Law Courts. I saw and heard some of the giants of
what were to be my two loves, law and politics. London
became forever a place dear to my heart. I could not have
imagined then that the honour of the Freedom of the City
of London would some day be given to me, the 250th to

be conferred in 500 years. Nor will I forget one evening in Crowborough when I, along with several other officers, had dinner with Sir Conan Doyle (I did not cry "Excellent!", nor he "Elementary").

To get back to our arrival in Liverpool, there were about one hundred and fifty junior officers in the draft. We proceeded by train to Shorncliffe, near Dover. The arrangements for our travel were somewhat primitive. We had, for example, to catch our food on the fly at station stops. I remember the stop at Crewe. One of the young officers, that is, younger than the rest of us (he had lied about his age), slapped down a handful of half-crowns and ordered, "Pie." None of us knew the value of the money. However, we arrived without incident at Shorncliffe, where Napier Barracks was to be our temporary home away from home.

I should add that home—Saskatoon, that is—never seemed far away. I remember being in Edinburgh on leave. Darkness came, there was a blackout, and I was soon lost. I have a chronic disposition never to ask directions. I do not like to admit that I don't know my way. I started to walk this night in Edinburgh, and I walked and I walked until finally I heard music. At least, it was music to my ears. A group of soldiers were singing: "We don't give a damn for all the rest of Canada, we're from Saskatoon". The leader of that band of good cheer was Allan Bill, afterwards editor of the *Calgary Herald*.

A few years ago when I was in London for a special dinner, the first in history given by Her Majesty's Imperial Privy Councillors in honour of Her Majesty the Queen, it occurred to me to visit Shorncliffe. My British driver, who was also somewhat vague about directions, headed the car towards Folkestone and we finally found Shorncliffe. It was after hours when we arrived, unannounced. The colonel commanding the base (it is now occupied by British regulars) kindly took me around, and I relived that first night in October 1916. There had been no accommodation. We bunked on the concrete floor. There was one officer with us who had come over on the first draft for 4th Division some months earlier. He had already been to the front, had been wounded, and was now recovered enough to have another try. Every time we tried to get to sleep, he decided to calculate how many of us would be alive by the end of the year. With the occasional echo of artillery booming across the Channel as background, he went on and on with reassurances: "Do you realize that sixty-five per cent of you will be pushing up daisies within three months?"

The carnage at the front was incredible. Young officers would leave today to appear in the casualty lists the day after tomorrow. Generals seemed to measure their success by the number killed in action; there were no territorial gains worth mentioning. The outpouring of blood on the Somme, when the Newfoundland Regiment went into action, was in my opinion one of the most disgraceful episodes in history. However, we had come to fight for King and Country, and the devil take the hindmost! There were some who had a premonition of death. Allan Macmillan was one. When we were sworn in at Regina, he said, "Well, that's the end of my life." He was killed on 9 April 1917. Another was the most brilliant poet I have ever met, J. Douglas Cumming. I had known him from my earliest days. He had no fear, only a realization that he would not survive. Nor did he. My wife's cousin, Bernard Freeman Trotter, was yet another. His poems reveal him to have been the Canadian Rupert Brooke. The genius of almost an entire generation perished. No wonder world conditions have become what they have.

I enjoyed army life. We worked hard. The drill was heavy, the hours long. Trench work was our forte. From Shorncliffe, I was transferred to Crowborough in Sussex for further training. At the conclusion of one day's work we were cleaning up. I was at the bottom of a seven-foot trench when someone, unaware of my presence, threw in a heavy entrenching tool, a combination shovel and pick-axe. It hit me squarely on the spine and down I went. I haemorrhaged most severely. Blood always seems more than in fact it is, but I would think that I must have lost a couple of quarts. My concern at the time was that if I reported to the medical authorities I would miss my chance to go to the front with my friends. My brother officers, and in particular Hugh Aird and Allan Macmillan, wanted me to report but I demurred, my contention being that if I did, I would be put in hospital and everything would be over. I booked off duty for a few days. The haemorrhage eased on the second day, but on the fourth day it started again. The single line in my diary for that day reads: "Bleeding today from the mouth." Perhaps, had I immediately reported my injury, nothing would have been different, but I shall always wonder.

After being hospitalized, I was medical boarded again and again. Finally, what I had tried to avoid became a reality: I was invalided home. I did manage to get them to agree and recommend that, if I became fit again, I could return to active service. However, this was not to be, for after being boarded a number of times in Saskatoon I was put in Category E; in other words, totally unfit for further service. When it was suggested I was now eligible for a pension I refused to consider the idea, although on three occasions thereafter, over a period of twenty-five years, I haemorrhaged as a direct result of my injury. The impact on my back caused my heart to be moved out of alignment. In the early 1920s I underwent surgery. In 1925 I was still unable to get life insurance except subject to a lien of 50 per cent, reducible by 5 per cent each year for ten years, at which time the full amount of the policy would be payable.

During the summer of 1917 I decided that I might be

able to serve in the R.C.A.F. and made arrangements to be seconded with my rank, but a medical examination ended that hope. The Defence Department transferred me from the Active list to the Reserve of Officers being subject to recall to active service. I joined the Great War Veterans' Association in the autumn of 1917. The Canadian Legion, a combination of various veterans' associations, was formed in 1925; I became a member of the Prince Albert Branch and hold the fifty-year pin. Many years later, when Prime Minister, I recommended to the Queen, and obtained, permission for the Canadian Legion to use the designation "Royal", the first of all the soldiers' organizations in the Commonwealth to be so designated.

The conscription election of December 1917 was the occasion of my first active participation in politics. I campaigned for the Union candidate in Saskatoon, Mr. James R. Wilson. My speeches in those days were short; I was still experiencing difficulty. I tried to memorize what I was to say. Not having anything approaching a photographic memory, I failed.

In the autumn of 1917, I had started in the law office of Ferguson and MacDermid to complete my Law Articles. Under the regulations in effect during the First World War, a law student's time—three years for university graduates and five for non-graduates—continued to be credited while he was in the armed forces. If in the service long enough, he was not required to write his first- or second-year law examinations before admission to the bar. However, he had to take the final examination. In the Law School a similar rule applied. I decided not to take any of the classes, because of my army service, but to write all the examinations. I worked very hard between 1918 and May of 1919. In June of 1919, I was called to the bar of Saskatchewan.

My first experience in making a presentation to the Court was on some very simple "ex-parte" application. I approached the Judge's chambers in fear and trepidation. Seated behind his desk was the District Court Judge His Honour Judge E. A. C. McLorg. He greeted me abruptly and asked what papers I had. As I endeavoured to produce them, I stepped forward and into a wire wastepaper basket with which I became so entrapped that for the next several minutes my time was taken up not in explaining to the Judge the nature of my business, but in extricating myself from a mortifying position.

In the law office of Lynd and Yule where I was next articled, the work of routine mortgages and simple estates was boring. In consequence, I was not a good student in the performance of my office duties. Neither was my fellow law student, Emmett Hall. I was paid fifty dollars a month, which was then regarded as tops, and was promised that on graduation I would be elevated to the splendour of seventy-five dollars a month.

The passing years have not dimmed my memory of signing the Roll of the Law Society in Regina. The Secretary of the Society was Mr. J. Kelso Hunter, an Englishman, who showed me where to sign and said, "Do it fast, I want to play golf." On returning to Saskatoon after signing the Roll, I went to see one of the leaders of the bar of Saskatchewan. It was late at night and he was in his private office. I said: "I was called to the bar today," to which he replied, "You don't know any more law than you did yesterday." "That's true; but I came to ask you, as a leading counsel, for your advice." I must say that had some whom I recall followed his advice, the world would be much better: "Do right and fear no man. Don't write and fear no woman. Now get the hell out of here."

CHAPTER SIX

AS A YOUNG BOY, I had set my mind on becoming a lawyer. My ambition was now realized. What my boyish
determination had not included was an understanding
that a call to the bar was a beginning, not an end, and that
indeed there was no end to the law. Canadian law, like
English law, is a living thing, subject to constant change.
That combination of tradition, statute, and judicial decision constituting the law provides at any one time the
most exact and complete expression of what we are as a
society. Thus, the full majesty of the law is the reflection
of a free people in the civil conduct of its business. Of
course, I have lived a long time and my view has been
formed by all I have experienced; but I do believe that
from my earliest days I regarded the system of law
evolved under the British Crown as the greatest single
guarantee of individual liberty for Canadians. I have not
changed my mind. Nevertheless, I have always been conscious that law as a human institution is not unaffected
by human frailties. When we were on the homestead, I
remember attending courts presided over by a Justice of
the Peace. These courts were not always models of justice, since often the Justice of the Peace knew little about
the law. In England the office of Justice of the Peace was
a mark of class distinction; in Saskatchewan, it meant little other than that the office-holder was politically

qualified. But it was an office hotly pursued, since it created the right impression in letters home to the old country: the holder of this honour had clearly moved into the
ranks of the gentry.

There are many amusing stories about the J.P. courts.
One concerns a Justice of the Peace who had brought before him information that Mr. X had removed from a
slough a small boat—a punt—that did not belong to him.
The J.P. had his copy of the criminal code. He went
through it and concluded that the offence committed by
the alleged wrongdoer was not theft. Theft was defined
among other things as taking from the possession of him
who has. He decided that since the punt was on the
slough it could not have been in possession of its owner.
He finally came on to what he regarded as an appropriate
charge: piracy on the high seas. It was only after Mr. X
was convicted that the Justice of the Peace discovered
that the penalty for piracy was death! I remember ap-
pearing before a J.P. of Central European origin. The
charge, as read, against my client was that he did "in-
sault" the complainant. I said, "What is this?" The J.P.re-
plied, "You, a young lawyer, don't know enough English
to understand that? You know what hits is, that's assault.
You know what bad words is, that's insult. This is both."
Fortunately, little of great consequence came before Justices of the Peace; they had their part to play in the administration of justice at the local level in the absence of
properly qualified Magistrates, dealing with offences
summarily punishable and requiring no jury.

After we went to Saskatoon in February 1910, whenever the High Court was in session, I would make my
way after school to the back of the courtroom. There I
heard the greats of Western Canada. Of the defence
counsel, at least half a dozen would have taken a place of
eminence anywhere in our country: P. J. (Paddy) Nolan,
immortalized in the pages of the *Calgary Eye-Opener*; A.

G. MacKay, one-time Liberal leader in Ontario, subsequently a Minister in the Alberta Cabinet; R. A. Bonnar from Winnipeg, a fabulous counsel for the defence, and many others. For the prosecution: R. B. Bennett and P. E. Mackenzie, afterwards a judge of the Court of Appeal in Saskatchewan, both masterful in their knowledge of the law and in the presentation of their cases. In watching and listening to these various counsel addressing judge and jury, questioning witnesses, protesting the unfair or prejudicial, I began to develop my own approach in court cases. It may be that unintentionally one becomes a composite of all those to whom one has listened. At law school, I, of course, participated in moot trials where I had a chance to test my theories and knowledge of the law. In addition, in my final year in law, we established a student court where our peers were tried for various disciplinary offences. But, as I have indicated, a call to the bar assures only that one has read and learned enough law to begin in earnest the process of learning the law.

I have already recounted my fascination as a boy with the lives of the great tribunes of freedom. No doubt unconsciously impressed by the fact that almost all had been lawyers I decided at twelve years of age to become a lawyer. My parents from time to time had attempted, if not in fact to discourage me, at least to temper my eagerness for the law as a career by pointing out that in many cases known to them the relative wealth or poverty of the litigant or the defendant seemed to affect the outcome; that law and justice were not necessarily synonymous. There was, of course, no system of legal aid in those days to ensure that the poor were always represented by competent counsel. Instead of discouraging me, these observations aroused in me a determination that when I became a lawyer, no man who sought my services, if I were free to act on his behalf, would through his poverty suffer prison or other grave injustice.

My profound respect for human life is based on religious conviction. I do not believe in capital punishment. However, as Prime Minister, when a capital case came before Cabinet for review, as it must under the law, and where there was no recommendation of mercy from the jury and no new evidence to cast doubt upon the prisoner's guilt, I never allowed my personal beliefs to stand in the way of the law. Nevertheless, to take a life for a life has always been in my judgment wrong and antiquated. Not only do I consider the arguments in favour of capital punishment as a deterrent to be specious, but the fact that innocent men have been hanged (I have had a client hanged whose innocence was made clear after his execution) casts a pall over any jury of twelve honest men and women assigned to this grave and final responsibility. Thus, believing as I do, I made it a rule to follow the British tradition of the bar, where, however difficult the case, I would make myself available to act for the accused in a capital case if my services were requested.

My immediate problem in 1919, however, was not how I might practise law but where. Should I remain in Saskatoon in someone else's law office or should I open my own? My ambition was to spend as much time in the courts as I could; the work of the barrister rather than the solicitor appealed to me. This hardly seemed possible for a junior in an established law firm; the senior partners would naturally get all the challenging work and I would be relegated to duties not much more interesting than those of an articled student. Further, a starting salary of seventy-five dollars a month was not exactly princely, and I was considerably in debt. Then, if in my own office, the next question was, where? The city of Saskatoon was out, as was any other centre abounding in law firms; it would take years to establish any reputation or clientele. A young lawyer could die of boredom or starvation, or both, in such centres.

I talked the problem over with a friend, a very good lawyer in Saskatoon, David Kyle. Together we surveyed the province, taking account of criminal and civil court cases in each area. Two places, above others, seemed to commend themselves: Theodore, a village near Yorkton, and Wakaw. I decided on the village of Wakaw. It was in that part of Saskatchewan which I knew best and was about equidistant from Prince Albert, Saskatoon, and Humboldt, where the High Courts were held. As a matter of historical interest, in Wakaw today there is a replica of my original law office, reconstructed in 1971 by the local Lions Club. In June of 1919, however, it seemed that I might not have an office there of any kind.

I encountered an unexpected problem on my arrival in Wakaw. I knew, of course, that I was breaking in on a lawyer who had set up practice the year before. I had, however, known him in law school and I knew that he was not particularly interested in litigation. What I did not know was that many of Wakaw's leading business-men, out of friendship for him, were determined to shut me out if they could. I found, for example, that I was not too welcome at the local hotel, which provided the town's only decent public accommodation. I was forced to spend my first two months in a rented room about seven feet by eight, a near approach to an enlarged piano box. My meals were taken in a small restaurant run by the near-blind son of a famous Budapest surgeon. Not only were they gastronomic abominations, they were followed by coffee into which he always dipped his never-too-clean thumb to measure the degree to which the cup was full. An office I could not find at all. Finally, Mr. J. H. Flynn offered to let me build, at my own expense, on a lot he owned on the front street. That was fine, but I had no money. I had arranged to buy the law books and office supplies I needed on credit. Now I had to seek credit for building supplies and find someone to build my office on faith. In this, I was saved by the North American Lumber Company (the other lumber company in town had refused me credit) and a French-Canadian carpenter by the name of Joe St. Pierre, who, when I asked him, said: "Sure, I'll help you out, boy." My office was built, and I opened for business on 1 July 1919. My first client was my brother Elmer, who had come from Saskatoon to spend his vacation with me. He sought my advice on a particular matter and, expressing the belief that those who practise law should be paid in cash, he gave me one dollar, which in his words was worth more than any advice I could give.

I was not in practice many days before a farming family from around Cudworth, a few miles to the southwest of Wakaw, appeared at my door. The husband and father of the family had been arrested and charged with attempted murder in the shooting of a neighbour. His quarrels with the victim were common knowledge and he freely admitted that he had several times threatened to shoot him, although he strongly denied that he ever intended to make good his threat. His story was that he had heard a noise near his corral. He had been bothered by coyotes, which had already that year carried off two of his calves. It was dusk. He saw what he took to be a coyote near the corral and fired. The shotgun blast hit his neighbour in the side of the face and shoulder, generally disfiguring him, removing part of an ear, and blinding one eye.

Trial was set for the fall assizes in Humboldt. I agreed to act for the accused, and got my client out on bail. I worked for weeks on the defence. The Crown was well represented by Mr. Ernest Gardiner. A man of advancing years, he was a good prosecutor, fair and responsible, with a full conviction that no matter what the outcome of the trial, the Crown never loses. Chief Justice J. T. Brown of the Court of King's Bench was the trial judge. The role

of a defence counsel in court is essentially to take the part
that his client would have taken if he were acting for
himself. I argued the case as best I could. My belief in my
client's case was strengthened by the fact that he stood
up well under cross-examination by an experienced prosecutor who obviously believed him guilty. My aim was to
have him acquitted but, failing that, to get a verdict for a
lesser charge of malicious wounding or assault occasion-
ing actual bodily harm, rather than one for attempted
murder. The trial went on for four days. The Chief Justice, when charging the jury, stated that if they determined that the facts amounted to negligence revealing a
shocking disregard for the rights of others, but not an intent to murder, they might convict on a lesser offence.
The jury retired. They came back for instruction. After
three hours they returned. The Clerk of the Court asked
the familiar questions: "Gentlemen of the Jury, have you
reached your verdict?" Their answer was, "We have."
"How say you. Is the prisoner guilty or not guilty?" "Not
guilty."

I had expected this verdict. The Crown counsel and the
Chief Justice had not, and obviously were surprised. That
evening, Chief Justice Brown inquired of some of the jurors who were staying at his hotel how they had come to
the conclusion that the accused was not guilty. In fact, no
juror should be asked, nor should he have the right to di-
vulge, what took place in the jury room. The Chief Justice's curiosity, however, got the better of him. It would
appear, if their version can be believed, that they had
been swayed more by the sincerity of my arguments than
by their quality. The story went something like this: "As
soon as we went out, we agreed that because it was the
young lawyer's first case we would find on a lesser
charge. Having so decided, we were just about to come in
when one of the jurors said, 'But this is the kid's birthday.' We reconsidered the verdict and decided that under

the circumstances we had to find, 'Not guilty'." That once-in-a-lifetime verdict launched my legal career. That there is nothing that succeeds like success is more than a trite epigram. I began to get cases on every hand. It has been estimated that I had more High Court cases in my first year of practice than any lawyer in Western Canada.

As a footnote to all this, my client was never again in trouble with the law, so far as I am aware. I cannot say how the victim took the verdict at the time, but when I met him again fifty years after the trial, he told me that he had always held me in deep affection because I had not attempted during the trial to be anything but sympathetic. I might add that in the full course of my practice at the bar I never questioned the character of any man or woman I believed was giving honest testimony.

In mentioning my first case and the manner in which the jury supposedly came to its verdict, this does not mean that I question the extent to which the jury system preserves and maintains justice in freedom. They may be wrong on occasion, for human beings are not infallible. But often I have seen jurors ignore the implied direction of the judge and bring in a verdict of not guilty, to find beyond any doubt months later or years later that they, not the judge, were right. I stood against the reduction of a jury from twelve to six members. I considered that a six-member jury would not work. It is of interest that the Saskatchewan Legislature, after experimenting with the smaller jury, decided to restore the original number. Further, I do not believe that any Court of Appeal should usurp the historic right of the citizen in our society to be judged by his peers where his life or liberty is at stake. No doubt it can be argued, as it is, that those trained in the law are the best qualified to judge in matters relating to the law. It is also true, however, that those involved in the day-to-day administration of the law, whether judge,

Crown counsel, defence counsel, or policeman, may become so enured to the processes for securing justice that all becomes routine; the man in the dock today is not seen to be any different from the man in the dock yesterday. Assembly-line justice is a contradiction in terms. Those who would place a premium on efficiency in the courts unwittingly open the doors to dictatorship. Juries prevent this by injecting a fresh perspective into every trial. Theirs is the common sense or social sense of the community. Jurors are not required to possess any knowledge of the law. History has proved that twelve honest men and true are competent to judge the facts related to guilt or innocence in any criminal case, and that generally they are right in the verdicts they render. Due process ensures justice so far as justice may ever be ensured. Those who administer the law must, like the Crown counsel in my first jury trial, have ever before them the concept that the Crown never loses.

My own short experience as a prosecutor in the 1930s is sufficient to prove to me that there are lawyers temperamentally unsuited to the role of Crown counsel. It was only after two or three jury cases in which I was successful in securing convictions that I began to realize that something was wrong. No matter how hard I tried to refrain, I became an active participant in the trial. My proper function was to aid in securing justice, not to be an advocate. I quickly concluded, and I think rightly, that, possessing a competitive temperament, I must thereafter limit my role to counsel for the defence.

To return to my early days in Wakaw. With clients coming in on every side, I was soon out of debt. The tensions arising from my arrival in town eased, and within a few months I rented a larger office across the street, and turned my original office into living accommodation. To handle the solicitor side of my practice, I had arranged, while still in Saskatoon, to have a law student in my office. That student, Michael Stechishin, many years later became District Court Judge in Wynyard, Saskatchewan. He was of great help to me in those initial months of my practice. I might mention that Michael had a knowledge of English classics unequalled in my acquaintance, no mean achievement for someone who, on emigration from the Ukraine in 1913, knew no English at all. He used to tell the story of his first instruction in the language, one unfortunately not uncommon for immigrants to Canada. The first expression he learned was, "Thank you very much," or that is what his friend told him it meant. Mike was riding aboard a freight train one day when the brakeman came along. The brakeman spoke to him. Mike didn't understand, but thanked him for the free ride. To his amazement the brakeman turned on him and threw him from the train. His leg was broken in the fall, a rather painful way to learn that his version of "Thank you very much" cast grave doubts on the brakeman's paternity.

In 1919, the population of Wakaw was about six hundred. The inhabitants of the village and its immediate surroundings were mainly Ukrainian, although there were also Germans, Scandinavians, a few old-country French and English, and settlers from Ontario and the United States. The people were particularly litigious, in court at a moment's notice, and for a while arson seemed the favourite local sport. Indeed, in relation to the latter, my office was burned out on at least two occasions by the spread of fires set in buildings farther up the street. When the insurance companies finally stopped making cash settlements in fire claims and began to replace burnt-out buildings, arson somehow ceased to be an important item on the calendar of local crime. If the Wakaw of today would not recognize the Wakaw of yesteryear, I can only suggest that it is because it took a generation for many of the non-British immigrants to Western Canada to settle into their new-found freedoms under the British Crown. It is true that in civil cases they revelled in having their day in court. However, in those areas of human interrelationships likely to result in criminal charges, some took longer to adjust to the fact that we had in Canada a civil order backed by a system of criminal law built over the centuries to assure the safety and freedom of the citizen.

There is a special joy that accrues to the lawyer, a joy not necessarily shared by his client if he does not win the case, when the judgment on a hard-fought appeal establishes a precedent. When some great principle is at stake, the pathways of new law often become the highways of justice. Here, the counsel may participate in a step forward or backward in man's march towards justice. Take the case of *Sikorski v. Lozinski.* My client, Sikorski, was a man of many parts. He loved to go to public meetings. He would get himself a front seat and spend the evening interrupting the proceedings. One evening, he exceeded even his usual performance. He climbed right up on the stage. The chairman of the meeting, Lozinski, objected. Sikorski insisted on his rights: "I came to this country for freedom of speech," and began a rather abusive address. Lozinski said, "You shut up." My client remonstrated. Lozinski gave him a shove and he fell from the stage. The local band had been playing for the audience earlier in the meeting. Sikorski fell on the bass drum and the sound was like a cannon shot. Pandemonium ensued. Sikorski hurt his leg in the fall and sued Lozinski for damages. I lost both the case and the appeal. However, that case did establish in law for the first time in Canada that the chairman of a public meeting had the right to keep order, and that he could use such force as was necessary to maintain order so long as he did not exceed what was necessary. In the years since that judgment I have probably participated in as many political meetings as anyone in Canada. Sometimes these meetings have been noisy, raucous, and threatening, but I have always paid every attention to any directions that came from the chairman!

Most of the court cases attracting the public's attention are sensational. The details of a murder, wounding, or robbery trial commend themselves to the press and to the popular mind. The accused and his alleged victims share stage centre, and any advance in the law normally passes unnoticed by those to whom it ultimately matters most. Further, and just as naturally (although I was never particularly conscious of this), the defence counsel is often identified in the popular mind with the actions of his client.

A case involving human drama of blood-and-thunder proportions was *Rex v. Harms* in the 1930s. It became ideal material for any western or detective pulp magazine. But its significance was not its sensation.

Harms was a trapper in Saskatchewan's Lake Athabaska region. A man of about sixty, he had come north from the United States, where his record with the law was questionable. "A little fast with a gun," they said. A young man by the name of Anthony was his victim. Anthony, a Canadian in his early twenties, had gone north for the sheer adventure of it and was down on his luck when Harms took him in. Their normal relationship was harmonious.

Fifteen miles away from Harms's shack lived another trapper, Clark. Clark had a beautiful common-law wife who had recently borne him a child. Harms had taken to paying calls on this woman when Clark was away on his trapline. So had Anthony, and of course neither man's activities were known to Clark or to each other.

On the morning of the day in question, Harms and Anthony set off in opposite directions with sled and dog team. Each was certain that the other would be busy checking traps and collecting furs. Harms circled wide and headed for Clark's. He had just arrived when Anthony appeared. It was a stand-off as far as potential romance was concerned. Harms was indignant. He ordered Anthony home and followed him to make certain that he was obeyed. Fifteen miles across the snow with only the cry of the wind, the crack of the whip, and the bark of the dogs to temper the seething anger of the two partners. As they got in the door of Harms's shack, Anthony turned and criticized Harms for being a dirty old reprobate. Harms lifted his rifle and shot Anthony between the eyes.

Anthony dead, Harms returned to the Clark woman. When he arrived at Clark's the woman refused to let him in for the night, so he camped on her doorstep, drinking home brew and eating raw moose meat, a presence more menacing with each passing hour. Finally, the woman in fear and desperation agreed to return to Harms's shack with him, her baby bundled in her arms.

It was dark when they arrived. As the woman entered the cabin, she slipped. "What's this?" she asked, putting her hand to what had caused her fall. "It's Anthony's blood," Harms replied. With that, she screamed and, clutching her child, fled into the cover of the storm. Harms searched the night for her. The woman, hiding when necessary and pushing on at every opportunity through the blowing snow and sub-zero temperature, covered the fifteen miles home on foot to safety.

Harms was subsequently charged with Anthony's murder, tried, convicted, and sentenced to hang. I was retained for the appeal. The year was 1936. There was no question of guilt or innocence; rather, the question was whether the circumstances of the crime warranted conviction for murder or for manslaughter. The law provides that if insulting words are used that would unseat the mind of the person to whom they are directed, the conviction should be for manslaughter, not murder. As there had been no one else present, the only account of what had in fact taken place was that provided by Harms himself. It was for the jury, however, to decide, on instruction from the judge, whether Anthony's words, as recounted by Harms, had constituted sufficient provocation in this case. Harms was convicted of murder and I appealed his case to the Court of Appeal. I argued that the jury had not been charged to consider the extent to which provocation, if established as sufficient to dethrone reason, might be increased by intoxication. The evidence showed that Harms had been drinking his own home-made brew both before and after the killing. A new trial was ordered and Harms was convicted of manslaughter. *Rex* v. *Harms* has become a leading case in establishing the principle that if words of provocation uttered by the victim actually deprived his assailant of the power of self-control, then the jury could consider the degree of his intoxication in deciding how much greater his mind would have been unsettled because of the liquor consumed.

The defence of a man accused of murder that has caused me intense concern and worry through the years was undertaken because I believed in the innocence of the accused. Being virtually penniless, he had not been able to secure a defence counsel and I agreed to act for him. The man was a White Russian who had served with General Wrangel's army before his emigration to Canada. He worked as a section hand for the railroad. He was a womanizer, an adulterer, and anathema to most of the people in the town where he lived. He was charged with the murder of his paramour. The Crown's star witness was the dead woman's husband. I advised my client to stay off the witness stand and accept a probable sentence of manslaughter. He said, "I'm innocent, why should I?" I pointed out that if he took the stand, all his various adulteries would be brought into evidence and that he would be hanged, not for murder but for adultery. For obvious reasons, I could not convince an innocent man that he should willingly accept the possibility of ten years in prison. And I could not prevent him from taking the witness stand. The consequence was as expected.

Subsequently, I took the case to the Court of Appeal, where it was dismissed. I then made representations to the Department of the Solicitor General in Ottawa, but without success. When the hangman arrived at his cell for the final tragic end, I am told that the condemned man spoke most defiantly to him, "God won't let you hang an innocent man." A few months after the execution it was established that he was innocent.

CHAPTER SEVEN

AN UNSWORN ENEMY OF INJUSTICE, particularly against the weak, I have spent my years on the side of the individual against the powerful establishments of our nation, whether public or private. One never had to worry about who was looking after the interests of the powerful; they had minions without number. The individual, uncertain of his rights, with limited means, too often frightened by the pomp and panoply of the courtroom, required not only every advantage that counsel could obtain for him but, most of all, the belief that justice would be done him.

One of the great offenders in its lack of regard for individual rights has been government bureaucracy. The Hicks case is one that I remember with pleasure in that it provided a major challenge to the unfair practices of bureaucratic tribunals. Hicks was a man possessed not only of a considerable physical presence but blessed with two Christian names of distinction and theological greatness, Calvin Knox. It was in the month of May that he travelled to Canora, Saskatchewan, and there purchased a large supply of high-grade antifreeze. In those days, antifreeze was still made from grain alcohol. The police could not have been reassured by the fact that he shipped his purchase by rail to a point where there were not only no mo-

torcars but no roads within forty miles. His insatiable desire for antifreeze may have led them to the obvious conclusion, but the purchase of antifreeze even in large
quantities and in May was not evidence of anything ille-
gal in itself. However, when the police cannot get you for
one thing, they often get you for another. They moved in,
seized Hicks's shipment, and charged him with failing to
pay the necessary excise duty. He was brought up under
a section of the Excise Act that provided for his examination under oath by any inspector of police or high official
of the Excise Branch of the federal government. His hearing was to take place in the village of Hudson Bay, Saskatchewan. This is where I came in. Hicks retained me as
his counsel and I accompanied him to the hearing.

When we entered the RCMP office, the inspector informed me that I could not be present for the hearing,
that under the Act, Hicks was not entitled to be represented by counsel. I said, "I realize that, but the purpose
of my being here is simply to ask that my client be
granted protection under the Canada Evidence Act; that,
under Section 5 thereof, anything he says cannot be used
against him excepting in a prosecution for perjury." The
police inspector replied that Hicks was not entitled to this
protection and invited me to leave. I did.

It was a hot day, so I sat on the steps of the police station. Only a screen door separated me from Hicks and his
interrogator. The dialogue went something like this: "You
are Calvin Hicks." "Calvin Knox Hicks." "I now swear
you," and he was sworn. "You reside at——[whatever the
place was]." "I don't intend to answer that until you allow me to have my counsel present and until I have protection granted under the Canada Evidence Act." "You're
not entitled to counsel and there's no right to protection."
Next question: "Were you at Canora on such and such a
day?" "I refuse to answer on the ground that my counsel
isn't here, and he's a good one, I'll tell you that—that's

why you don't want him; and until I get protection." The police inspector asked him a number of questions and received the same answer. The police officer said: "I have to read you the law. For every question you don't answer you're liable to a penalty of twenty-five dollars costs or one month in jail or both [or whatever it was]." "Well, look a little further down and see how much I'll get if I do start to talk."

Hicks was convicted and I appealed. On appeal it was found that he was entitled to have counsel. Mr. Justice Taylor ruled that whatever the statute said, the individual cannot be placed in a secondary position by being brought before an institution analogous to a court without having those fundamental rights which are our heritage and have been for generations. I must admit that that principle was not followed in Nova Scotia within a year thereafter. The courts there decided that the statute in question was above natural justice. However, the Hicks case was one in keeping with my own philosophy throughout the years: that the state is not our master. Today, under the Bill of Rights, the right to counsel is guaranteed.

When I first began as a lawyer, approximately fifty per cent of my practice was in criminal law. It was not long, however, before the balance of my cases began to shift, and by the time I moved to Prince Albert in 1924, ninety-five per cent of my work was with civil law. Yet, throughout my thirty-six years at the bar (I retired from active practice when I became Leader of the Progressive Conservative Party in 1956), I remained identified in the public mind as a counsel for the defence. Of course, one has little choice in these matters. Juries were very good to me. When I appeared, they concluded that there must be something of injustice in the case. I represented to them what a defence counsel should be. In all the years, no one ever suggested that any witness I called had a manufactured story. I took what I was given in every case, although I seldom called on the accused to give evidence. I was searching in cross-examination, but only if there was untruth. "Lord help you if you lie to him" was the common assessment. As a consequence, because I did not treat them as though they were flies to be pinned to the wall, police officers were always anxious to give all sides of the evidence in their testimony, not only what would be helpful to the prosecution.

Of all my jury trials, probably the one best remembered was the Canoe River case in 1951. Certainly, this is one not forgotten by railway men. On 21 November 1950, two Canadian National Railways passenger trains met in head-on collision near Canoe River in the mountains of British Columbia. The wreck took the lives of twenty-one people, most of them Canadian soldiers en route to Korea; some sixty others were injured. The cause of the tragedy was immediately labelled as human error by the railway officials and by the then Minister of Transport, Lionel Chevrier. Responsibility for the crash was finally laid at the door of Alfred John Atherton, a twenty-two-year-old CNR telegraph operator. It was alleged that the collision had occurred because Atherton had improperly relayed an order originating with the CNR's dispatcher in Kamloops, and he was consequently charged with manslaughter.

I was in Australia attending a Commonwealth parliamentary meeting when I read the press reports of these events. An outstanding lawyer in Australia remarked to me, "Now there's a likely case for you." "Well," I replied, "it might be very interesting but I don't belong to the B.C. bar." Little did I know that already in motion was a course of events that would greatly influence my future. I thought no more about the Canoe River tragedy, as the business of the conference provided interest and problems enough. On my way home, I planned to spend three or four days in Hawaii, where my first wife, Edna, was to meet me. Instead, there was a cable waiting saying that she would meet me in Vancouver. At Vancouver, there was yet another cable, this time from our doctor, stating that my wife was in hospital in Saskatoon, dangerously ill. After some difficulty in arranging a flight, I arrived in Saskatoon to find her near death.

Ill as she was, her thoughts were not for herself. She said, "Jack Atherton has been to see me. Everyone in the CNR is running away from responsibility for what appears to have been a grievous disregard for human lives." She went on to give me the details of the Canoe River collision. The soldiers who had been killed and injured had been travelling in wooden cars preceded and followed by steel cars. When the crash came, these wooden cars had simply folded, accordion fashion. I agreed with my wife's assessment but explained to her that the fee for joining the British Columbia bar was fifteen hundred dollars. She said, "I told him you'd take it." Finally I agreed that I would. She did not live to see the event, for she passed away 7 February 1951.

I interviewed Atherton. Everyone's hand seemed to be against him. His seniors, who should have been held responsible, if anyone, were able in turn to exculpate themselves by passing the blame down the line. Finally it came to the telegraph operator. I considered it unjust. Atherton had only one passport and that was marked "prison".

I contacted the British Columbia Law Society to make the necessary arrangements. I sent my fee. However, one could not belong to the B.C. bar without a very intensive examination on the statutes. I travelled to Vancouver. The benchers met in solemn conclave. The Treasurer of the Law Society conducted the examination: "Are you ready for your examination?" He cautioned me against any premature attempt at the examination and made certain that I was aware that in the event of failure there was a set period before I might have another opportunity. I said, "I appreciate all that, but I'm ready." Then the oral examination began: "Are there contracts required by statute to be in writing?" I took a moment for judicial consideration before I made my reply (a first-year law student, or even one who wasn't, would be able to answer). I said, "Yes." The second question: "Name one of them." Again, a moment of contemplation. "A land contract." The Treasurer, who is in effect the president of the Law Society, said, "You have passed your examination and it will interest you to know that you are the first in the history of the bar of this province to have passed with a mark of one hundred per cent!" I then appeared before Mr. Justice Manson of the Supreme Court of British Columbia to take the barrister's oath. I was admitted to the bar that day along with Mr. Gilbert Kennedy of the University of British Columbia Law School, whose father was the renowned Professor W. P. M. Kennedy, Dean of the Law School at the University of Toronto.

From Vancouver, I went on to Prince George for Atherton's preliminary hearing. Widespread interest was shown by the numbers who turned up for the preliminary. The Crown was brilliantly represented by the Deputy Attorney General of British Columbia, Colonel Pepler, who had achieved his rank in the First World War. At the conclusion of the preliminary, Atherton was committed for trial on the manslaughter charge. I arranged a continuation of his bail and went ahead with the preparations for the trial in early May.

In law, you win cases if you know more than the other side, everything else being equal. You learn so much, you have to know so much, about the particulars of the case. But this has no lasting value; when the case is over, it has all gone with the wind. In the famous Tichborne Peerage case in the United Kingdom in the 1870s, the solicitor against the claimant for the baronetcy spent four years of solid work. He won. But this is all labour lost. I spent weeks on Atherton's defence. I studied the inside and the outside of the transmission of messages, and got to a point where I knew the rules better than anyone else. The rules had been in effect since the year 1908. They were loosely drawn. During the trial, the Rule Book was plugged so full of holes that two teams of horses could have walked through them. Their revision was one result of that case.

Atherton's trial began on 9 May 1951 in Prince George. The Crown claimed that the accused, in his position as a CNR telegrapher, in relaying an order to the conductor of the westbound troop train, had failed to include the last two vital words of the message, "at Cedarside", which would have sent the train on to a siding to await the passing of the eastbound passenger train. The Crown contended that Atherton had thereby brought about the fatal crash.

It was true that the message received by the conductor did not include the two words in question. It was also true that the omission of these words brought the two trains into direct collision, head on. My client, however, was certain that he had included the entire message given him by the dispatcher in his transmission. The only record of a message broken in transmission had occurred in rather extraordinary circumstances. A seagull flying overhead dropped a fish on wires covered with fresh snow, breaking the transmission. This example was not well authenticated but it was all I had. And it was basic to my case because it demonstrated the possibility of something other than human error as the cause of the accident. The night before the Canoe River tragedy there had been a heavy snowfall in the mountains and the wires were covered with snow.

I never revealed this during my period at the bar, but always when I had a jury trial, I had someone in the courtroom to keep me informed about the reaction of the audience; there was a fair probability that what was overheard as members of the public talked among themselves would indicate the trend of the jury's thinking. For the trial in Prince George, I had with me General Pearkes's son, John, a young man, then going into law, and now a barrister in Vancouver. On the first day of the trial, the Crown called several witnesses during the morning. I just sat and listened. The Crown counsel had the appearance of having been a colonel; there was something about his manner and appearance that could be associated with some senior officers. I asked no questions. Witnesses came and went. At noon, I met with young Pearkes, who told me, "Everybody's thoroughly fed up. They thought you were a good counsel and you haven't said a word."

During the afternoon, the Crown called a high Canadian National Railways official. It was simply a matter of identification, but it was under his jurisdiction that the composition of the train was determined, not that he personally had anything to do with it. So I asked him the question that everyone seemed to be running away from: "I suppose the reason you put these soldiers in wooden cars with steel cars on either end was so that no matter what they might subsequently find in Korea, they'd always be able to say, 'Well, we had worse than that in Canada.'" Well, everything broke loose. The Crown counsel said that he was shocked, that this was the British Columbia bar, and that they did not have that kind of thing out there. The judge said he thought it was improper, in that it was a statement rather than a question. I said, "My Lord, it was made clear by the elevation of my voice at the end of the sentence that there was a great big question mark on it. This man is an intelligent man. Right up at the top of the hierarchy. It's a long question, but it won't be difficult for him. He'll be able to break it down."

We argued back and forth, and finally he said, "Well, I'm very doubtful but—" Just then the Colonel interjected: "I want to make it clear that in this case we're not concerned about the death of a few privates going to Korea." What he no doubt meant was that the charge did not include them as at the trial the charge was restricted to the four members of the train crew who had been killed. "Oh," I said, "you're not concerned about the killing of a few privates? Oh, Colonel!" There were two old soldiers from the First World War on the jury, and in a voice you could hear all over the courtroom, one turned to the other and said, "Do you hear what that blankety-blank said?" From then on, things went along in an agreeable way. I concentrated on cross-examination; I did not call any evidence. I hammered home my one example of the bird and the fish. I did not call the accused to give evidence. Thus, I had the last speech to the jury before the judge summarized. However, during the last three days of the trial, my hearing was not quite acute. It did not matter what question the Colonel asked, whether favourable to me or to him, I would say, "I didn't quite hear you, Colonel." Every time I said "Colonel", the reaction of the jury was not such as would have been judged entirely warm towards the Crown or its case. The jury acquitted after a very short consideration of the case.

I suppose, had I wanted to, I could have earned a large income. The offers were there. An amusing story about two of the greats at the English bar might perhaps illustrate what counsel could aspire to in fees. Sir Rufus Isaacs and F. E. Smith (later Lord Birkenhead, Lord Chancellor of England) were opposing counsel on the famous Lever Brothers–*Daily Mail* action. Smith lost. It was a great day for Sir Rufus. Smith had perhaps the best legal mind this century has seen. Further, in the past, Smith had gloated over the degree to which he exercised dominion over Rufus Isaacs. Now the tables were turned. Afterward, they met for a few drinks. The question came up:

"What fee did you get?" After a few more drinks they decided to write the amount of their respective fees on separate chits which they then exchanged. Now these are not the exact figures, but they are very close. Smith's fee was, in Canadian money, $115,000. Isaacs's was about $65,000. Sir Rufus looked at him and said, "F.E., and you lost. Almost thou persuadest me to be a Christian."

For myself, when I accepted a case where I thought someone's rights were being violated, often the person couldn't pay me, or did so only after many years. From the beginning of my practice, I never charged a Métis or an Indian who came to me for advice. I was distressed by their conditions, the unbelievable poverty and the injustice done them. I was touched when Maria Campbell, in her book *Halfbreed*, wrote of me:

He would represent anyone rich or poor, red or white. If they had a case and no money he would help. . . .He helped us, and the important thing was that he did so when no one else would.

It was because of my concern for the Indians that in 1939 I carried to the Court of Appeal the case of *Rex v. Smith*. Smith was an Indian who had been charged and convicted of hunting on a game preserve. Under the treaty applicable to him, Indians had the right to hunt for all time on "unoccupied land". My contention was that these treaties had been shamelessly broken, which was true. I saw them broken every day. But there was no recourse. The wronged individual had no appeal to the courts except with the consent of the Government of Canada. Fortunately that situation no longer exists. In the case of Smith, I argued that when the treaty was made, "occupied land" meant land on which there was settlement. There was no such thing as a game preserve at that time. Therefore, it could never have been contemplated that forest reserves would be anything other than unoccupied Crown land. The Appeal Court held otherwise, however. I insisted when I was Prime Minister that the treaties be upheld. They were.

Of course, it is impossible for me to recall my cases as a lawyer without mentioning Grey Owl. Grey Owl was one of the most remarkable men Canada has ever produced. He was a genius; no doubt a charlatan, a poseur, and a faker, but no one in North American history ever left behind him such a treasure of concern for what he described as his furred brethren of the soil and his feathered brethren of the air. He pretended to have been the son of George Belaney, an Englishman, and a Navaho princess. I was never taken in by his claim to Indian blood. I remember an elderly Indian woman, wise in the ways of the world, saying, "That Owl isn't telling the truth. He has white man's eyes." But all of this being so, his writings may well become immortal. I once went over to his camp with Superintendent Wood of the Prince Albert National Park, who was a great admirer of his. He came down to the dock when we pulled in and handed the Superintendent thirty or forty pages of manuscript to forward to his publisher. I read them on the way back to Waskesiu; they were clothed in masterly English and filled with an imagery that only a lover of nature could possibly possess. I saw his beavers, Jelly Roll and Rawhide. He spoke of them as individuals, his friends. He developed what he called the first beaver dictionary in all history, forty-six or forty-eight words and expressions; this I never saw.

Never has any Canadian since the days of Laurier so captivated the British people. He filled the halls. He became the embodiment of the movement against cruelty to animals. He spoke in Albert Hall, eloquent, direct. On his return he described that event at a meeting at the Legion in Prince Albert, of which he was a member: "Before I got up to speak I wondered whether it would be possible for me to articulate my aspirations and my achievements, my message to them. I had never spoken to such an audience before. Comrades, you'll excuse me for my lack of knowledge of the English language, my vocabulary is so limited, my choice of words so restricted. There I was, the cynosure of all eyes, six thousand pairs of eyes on Grey Owl. I wondered to myself, 'Will I be able to speak.' My throat dried. What was my inspiration? What impelled me? What gave me the ability to express myself in a way that they understood? Just before I got up, I saw you, my comrades of the Prince Albert Branch of the Canadian Legion, and I said to myself, 'I'll not let my comrades down.' And then I saw in my mind's eye my beautiful Anahareo; it was inspiring. [He had gone through a native marriage ceremony with her. She was his devoted helper, a very able woman.] But that wasn't enough, even then I was in a state of deep dubiety. What finally gave me the compelling impetus to speak, to convey to these people a message never before heard by them, was that I saw to my right and to my left, as clearly as if they were there in person, Rawhide and Jelly Roll, seated on their haunches; and in unison they spoke to me, simultaneously raising their right paws in doing so, 'Grey Owl, do your stuff.' "

On his way back from his final trip to the United Kingdom, Grey Owl met a girl in Montreal, Yvonne Perrier. He immediately fell in love with her and married her. She did not know that he was in no position to take another wife. He died soon after. He left a will which provided that half his estate be given to her. The other half was to go to his daughter, Shirley Dawn, daughter of Anahareo. Grey Owl's books and lectures had earned him a small fortune. The true wife was in Ontario's Temagami region, Angele Eguana by name, the Indian woman whom he met when he first came over from the old country. She taught him Indian lore. She bore him a family. He went overseas during the First World War, became a sniper, and was wounded in action. Following his return to Canada he lived intermittently with Angele, finally deserting her in 1925. He then went to northern Quebec, where he married Anahareo. Anahareo could make no claim against Grey Owl's estate but Angele could. She saw his picture in the papers announcing his death (it was taken from a portrait painted by the renowned Sir John Lavery), and identified him. She sought the advice of local lawyers, who started proceedings to gain her a share of the estate. I acted for Miss Perrier.

Under the law of Saskatchewan no one can disown his wife if she is living apart from him as a result not of her own misconduct but of his desertion. However, a wife is not entitled to share her husband's estate if she is living apart under circumstances that would disentitle her to alimony. In other words, adultery would deny her any share of the estate. It came out in the evidence that two years after Grey Owl had left her, Angele Eguana had a son. She quite frankly admitted this in the examinations for discovery, but she said that she had been raped. The alleged wrongdoer and father of her child denied the charge. Her story was that one day while returning from the lake with two full pails of water, she was suddenly set upon and criminally assaulted. Her story seemed obviously false for she further testified that none of the water was spilled in the act. I felt sorry for her. She started the Owl on his path to greatness. Now she was old and destitute. During the trial I spoke to my client about it and she agreed that in fairness and equity Angele should share in the estate. I so advised the judge. Read his judgment. It is a masterpiece. Mr. Justice P. M. Anderson found that while the story of Angele's alleged ravishment was one that might not be acceptable among those of us who live in a different atmosphere and milieu, it could nevertheless be true; therefore, he accepted her evidence at face value. Angele received one-third of the estate.

In general, from the very beginning of my legal career,

cases in which principles were at issue were always attractive to me. My first reported case, *Mackie* v. *Boutin and Ethier*, in 1922 had to do with two school trustees near Domremy, a French-speaking area south of Prince Albert, who were jointly charged with permitting French to be used as a language of instruction beyond the first grade. When Wakaw Justice of the Peace E. H. Firneisz found them guilty, Rémi N. Ethier and Léger Boutin came to me. I undertook their appeal. I considered that a grave injustice was being done the people of French origin in Saskatchewan through the failure of the provincial government to assure them their constitutional rights and their language. Mine was an unpopular view. At that time, there was a strong, even bitter, anti-French-Canadian attitude in Saskatchewan and Alberta. My friends, knowing that I wanted to go into politics, warned me not to defend Ethier and Boutin. It would be a roadblock to any future in politics, they cautioned. I answered that it might be unpopular but that it was right. I won their appeal. My fee, interestingly, was paid from a subscription organized by L'Association Catholique Franco-Canadienne de la Saskatchewan.

There are, of course, many of my reported cases that are leading cases. They helped to advance the law in relation to all manner of things, from well-digging to trespass, to lotteries, to the rights of the individual—the workman, the employee, the independent contractor—to private international law, to the statute of limitations, to agency and fraud, and to many more legal questions. In this chapter and the one preceding I have treated only those few of my cases that I consider to be of general interest. I intend at some future time to deal with those other important cases in full detail.

While on the subject of my career in the courts, I must add that, to my knowledge, I have never had a client who, after serving his sentence, ever committed a second offence. I used to talk to these offenders. I am afraid that too many people fail to be aroused over the sufferings of others in matters of punishment for crime. Too often people whose lives are free from wrongdoing to the extent that they are never charged with crime develop a sense of superiority over those unfortunates who run afoul of the law. This is natural enough, I suppose, but I have always felt that, "There but for the grace of God go I." All of us, at some time or another, apart from the most perfect—and few belong in that category—might have been in serious trouble with the law, if more often by neglect and inadvertence than by intent.

I find it shocking that some seventy per cent of those who go to penitentiary become recidivists. The fault for this must lie with the rest of us. We seem to be not nearly so much interested in rehabilitation as in punishment. In most cases, when a person is arrested on a first offence, I believe that he feels a deep sense of regret for what he has done and a determination to do better. To send such a person to prison destroys any possibility of redemption. A man emerging from prison is immediately faced with a barrier of public fear: we refuse to take him into our businesses because, after all, he may commit another crime. If he is on probation, being obliged to report regularly not only has a demeaning effect on him but advertises the fact of his criminal conviction. Many a man going straight finds himself suddenly dismissed, his services no longer required, when his employer finds out about his prison record. There is no way in which that person can carry on in the face of a punishment that he does not deserve except to turn in deep resentment to activities likely to return him to penitentiary. No commission of inquiry will solve this most difficult problem until the public is prepared and determined to resolve these questions: where does punishment end and when does rehabilitation begin?

Of course, crime that results in the taking of human life is in a category by itself. I will never have the experience of defending a person for murder when conviction does not bring the death penalty. However, I consider that in recent years society has been worse off in some respects than during my time at the bar. It may have been that in the past juries acquitted more often than they would have if there had been a mandatory sentence of twenty years for murder. It may have been that hanging was not an effective deterrent (and I've already expressed my views on that). But I have had men say to me: "I'm charged with murder. Well, I'd sooner be executed than spend my life in prison." And that tells the story. One of the reasons that the crime rate in our country has been increasing over the last decade is that the Pearson and Trudeau governments have ignored their oath of office to carry out the law. In consequence, the worst of murderers have gone free after ten years in penitentiary. As long as there is no certainty of punishment, there is no fear of punishment. This may be considered a harsh view for one with some degree of humanitarian feeling; but I consider that if the conviction for what is now called capital murder carried a sentence of twenty years, without possibility of parole, it would be an effective deterrent. I am not here referring to homicides of passion. I am talking about those who set out deliberately to kill. Society must be protected from those who murder for profit, or who regard murder as an occupational hazard in the commission of robberies or kidnappings. It must be protected from gang murders and from the most shocking of killers, in my view—the poisoner. I have seen a great deal of life and am not easily shaken; but the insidiousness of destroying another person through slow and deliberate administration of poison over a long period of time (to avoid medical detection in post-mortem examination) is a crime that my compassion can never embrace.

Murderers whose crime is one of passion, however, are not likely, on release from prison, ever to kill again. From what I have observed, if they have no previous criminal record, this is about ninety-eight per cent certain. I remember a lad whom I defended for murder; I just barely saved him from the gallows. His sentence was commuted. I will not go into the particulars, but he had murdered his own father, an act more of desperation than of retribution for the treatment, the beatings, and the misuse he had endured over many long years. One night I was sitting in the House of Commons thinking about him. He had been in prison then for thirteen years. I had kept in touch with him. His conduct had been exemplary. He had promised me, when his life was spared, that it would be. The Second World War was in progress. I went over to Mr. Louis St. Laurent, the Minister of Justice, and told him about the case. I said, "He shouldn't be there. He should be out on ticket of leave. He wants to join the army." Mr. St. Laurent undertook to review the matter, and the young man was released for military service. He became a sergeant. I recall one afternoon in July 1945; my wife and I had been out for a drive and had returned home. My wife came into my study and said, "There's a soldier out here who wants to see you," and there he was. A striking-looking fellow, he was now about thirty-five. We talked for a while; then guests arrived and he stayed to help serve the refreshments. As he was leaving, he turned and said, "John, I can never thank you. You've been like a father to me." I replied, "Don't carry that too far." He went on to a new name and a new life. We still keep in touch, and I have had reason to be proud of his success as a father, as a husband, and as a businessman.

CHAPTER EIGHT

I WON MY FIRST ELECTION in 1920, my second in 1940. In the years between those two victories, I was defeated five times. Let me state at the outset that I ran for public office because I wanted to. Although there were those who urged me to run on each occasion, and those who faithfully supported me when once I entered the electoral fray (and to each of those who worked for me I shall always remain grateful), I was never able to stand before an audience and say: "I am in this contest as a candidate because of overwhelming and irresistible popular pressure. The phone calls, the letters, the delegations of influential people from the community finally convinced me that it was my duty to run for office." At a bar dinner in my honour in Regina after my election to the House of Commons in 1940, it was said that I had been pressed into being a candidate over the years. I responded by reminding those present of the story about the elderly maiden lady who never touched a drop of liquor. She became ill. The rural doctor to whom she went for treatment was one who drank to excess. He made a short examination and said, "I'm sorry to tell you, madam, but you've got to cut out your drinking. Your pulse shows it." She not unnaturally was indignant. She was a charter member of the Women's Christian Temperance Union. She told him off and swept from his office. Only then did the doctor realize that he had been feeling his own pulse. I must say that those people who relate how they have been dragooned, hijacked, and forced into being political candidates sometimes remind me of that doctor.

Saskatchewan was solidly Liberal. In the federal elections of 1908 and 1911, the province returned only one Conservative to Ottawa. In the provincial field, Liberal success was unbroken from 1905 until 1929. In the 1921 provincial election, only two Conservatives were elected. The federal election of 1917 saw sixteen Unionist candidates victorious, as opposed to one Laurier Liberal, but that was in fact a vote for a wartime coalition government and conscription. The 1921 election, which defeated the first Meighen government, resulted in a temporary upset of the federal political system. In Saskatchewan only one Liberal was victorious, but no Conservatives were elected. The other fifteen seats went to the Progressive Party. In 1925, however, the results were fifteen Liberals against six Progressives, and again, no Conservatives. It is clearly an understatement to say that Saskatchewan was not the most promising ground on which to stake a Conservative future.

The reasons for Saskatchewan's adherence to the Liberal Party throughout virtually the first quarter-century of Saskatchewan's existence were essentially threefold. First, the immigrants from continental Europe who came to Canada under Clifford Sifton's immigration program were brainwashed into the Liberal Party. They constantly had drummed into their heads the idea that "Liberal" was synonymous with "liberty" and "Conservative" was synonymous with "the tyranny of land-owning autocrats". And, of course, the Conservatives added substance to this destructive myth with the passage of the Wartime Elections Act of 1917, a scandalous piece of legislation which deprived naturalized Canadians of the right to vote because of their enemy racial origin. Without too much exaggeration, George v, if allowed to vote, would have found himself under condemnation by this Act, except that he had a son in the armed forces. While I supported the Unionists in December 1917, I nevertheless strongly condemned that legislation.

The second reason for Liberal success was one to which I have already alluded. When Saskatchewan was created in 1905, the Laurier government in Ottawa intervened to make certain Walter Scott rather than F. W. G. Haultain formed the provincial government. Thus, a government that by all right and reason should have been Conservative was instead Liberal. The principal sequel was that the Liberal Party was placed in a favourable position to court and win the political hand of the Saskatchewan Grain Growers' Association. The S.G.G.A. was the most powerful farmer organization in Saskatchewan until the early 1920s, and Saskatchewan was a province entirely dependent upon agriculture. Thus, the Liberal Party, which was in time to style itself the Government Party, was also able to style itself the Farmers' Party by adopting the programs of the S.G.G.A., thus bringing the leading grain growers into the provincial Cabinet. In 1921, of a total of eight provincial Cabinet members, four were former S.G.G.A. officers. Charles A. Dunning, who became Liberal Premier in 1922, was a former S.G.G.A. vice-president, and former general manager of the Saskatchewan Co-operative Elevator Company. In consequence, the Liberals were able to get away with labelling the Conservatives as antipathetic to agricultural interests, and irredeemably protectionist. In fact, the record shows that the Conservatives were no more protectionist than the Liberals, and might have been considerably less so, had the government of Saskatchewan been formed, as it ought to have been, by Haultain in 1905.

Last, but far from least, the Saskatchewan Liberals created a political machine unequalled in Canadian history. It was certainly comparable to anything to be found during the worst days of machine politics in Boston, New York, or Chicago. Party supporters were given civil service jobs, especially in public works. We witnessed a classic example near Prince Albert: a highways inspector who could neither read nor write. His job was to line up the Ukrainian vote. Much to the amusement of the Ukrainians whose votes this character was supposed to deliver, my brother Elmer designated him "Inspector of the northern lights". "He turns them on and off," said Elmer; it was a description that stuck. Highways inspectors served as district organizers for the party. Officials from other government departments or liquor store managers were placed in charge of individual ridings. In the rural constituencies, practically every government employee was a Liberal Party heeler. Provincial policemen or lesser government employees would serve as poll captains, and collected information on each person within their areas. Liberal Party headquarters in Regina had a dossier, compiled at public expense, on practically everyone in the province. Nothing was neglected to bring pressure to bear on anyone who might conceivably be swayed to the Liberal cause. It was said of the 1925 provincial election that had every government employee engaged in Liberal Party work been obliged to wear a uniform, a visitor to Saskatchewan would have thought that the province was under the heel of an army of occupation.

Once James Garfield Gardiner took over the machine, it became a vicious instrument for the personal destruction of political opponents. "Fighting Bob" Gould from Estevan was one of its early victims. Gould had been elected as a United Farmers candidate in a by-election for Assiniboia in 1919. He retained that seat for the Progressive Party in 1921. Prohibition was then in effect in Saskatchewan. Gould was a non-drinker. He was visiting

his constituency during the summer recess when the provincial police called on him one afternoon at his hotel
charging him with having illicit liquor in his possession.
Today, the effect of this charge would be more or less
equivalent to an M.P.'s arrest for possession of narcotics. A
bottle was discovered under Gould's bed. The penalty, on
conviction, was two hundred dollars, *and* one month in
jail. He was found guilty. On appeal, the conviction was
quashed, but Bob Gould had been destroyed. I came per-
ilously close to sharing Gould's fate during the 1926 election. Prohibition was ended in 1924, so this time the plant
was a jar of bootleg moonshine. Fortunately, I found it
before the police, who seemed once more to know exactly where to look for the incriminating evidence. I have
heard stories about the Hon. William Pugsley, Laurier's
Minister of Public Works and master of pork-barrel politics; but Slippery Bill was a child compared with Gardiner. Able, brilliant, an excellent parliamentarian, and a
good administrator, Gardiner was entirely lacking in political scruples. He never forgot a friend or an enemy. He
was an implacable foe. He carried his politics into everything he did. In time, I became the object of his destruction. No candidate running against me ever found himself
lacking any necessary assistance.

For ninety days in 1930 I served as government counsel
for the Bryant Charges Commission in Saskatchewan.
The Gardiner Liberals had been defeated in the election
of 1929. The slogan of the combined opposition parties
had been "Break up the machine". Once elected, Dr. Anderson's Conservatives and the Independents and Progressives who supported Anderson were united on the
question of civil service reform. The Bryant Commission
was charged with the task of investigating some of the
more blatant irregularities and scandalous practices of
the 1926-29 Gardiner government, particularly as they related to the provincial police, the Weyburn Mental Hospi-

tal, and the provincial jails. The Commission's report, the work of three High Court Judges (two of them outstanding Liberals before their appointment to the Bench; one a Conservative before his appointment), documents the whole sordid story of the early Gardiner machine. On 3 March 1931, I received the following letter from J. G. Bryant, Anderson's Minister of Public Works, whose charges had resulted in the appointment of the Royal Commission:

I have been so busy since the report of the Royal Commission has been filed, reading the report and making notes on the evidence, that I have not had the opportunity of writing you and thanking you for the very splendid manner in which you conducted the case. I appreciate very much the fact that you have given such careful and close study to the details of the evidence, and feel that great credit is due you for bringing out the evidence as you did, particularly in view of the fact that you received a good deal of discouragement at times.

I felt when I made the affidavits and looked into the question in the first instance that the facts could be proven, and I am very pleased, indeed, that it has turned out the way it did.

Unfortunately, when the next provincial election came in 1934, the electorate, desperate to find some escape from the worst of the depression and drought, forgot about the Bryant Report and returned the Gardiner Liberals to power. The machine again was back in business, and the civil service reforms brought about by the Anderson government were undone. Within months, over ten per cent of the Saskatchewan civil service either had been fired or had resigned.

I, of course, had not required a Royal Commission to inform me on Liberal political practices. I had known the stories of Liberal pork-barrel politics from my boyhood. I was to watch it at first hand when I began to practise law. I remember a court case in 1921 when I defended a cor-

poral in the Saskatchewan Provincial Police charged
with a variety of offences, from bribery to perjury to ob-
taining gain under false pretences. T. C. Davis of Prince
Albert and I were his counsel. The corporal was a political activist for the Liberal Party; there was nothing he
would not do, whether within or without the law, to bring
about the election of Liberal candidates. The preliminary
hearing was held before a magistrate of unusual ability,
the late Tom Murray, a strong Liberal but a man of integrity. As the preliminary progressed, the accused asked me
how we were progressing. I replied, "You haven't a hope.
There is no possibility of an acquittal. Even by chance,
this could not happen." The next morning, Mr. Davis, after consultation with me but with no reference to my conversation with the accused, asked for an adjournment for
four or five days, and this was granted. Four days later,
an official in the Bureau of Public Health was dismissed
by Premier Martin for having attempted to influence
Magistrate Murray to dismiss the charges against the police officer. The corporal was dismissed from the police
force. Because the Minister of Municipal Affairs, the
Honourable George Langley, was implicated in the action
of the official (Municipal Affairs encompassed Public
Health), the charges were never resumed.

During my Wakaw days, however, the machine had yet
to sink to the depths achieved under Gardiner. Premier
W. M. Martin was a man whom I greatly admired. He had
been a Member of Parliament for Regina in 1916, when a
colossal highways fraud shook Premier Scott's administration to its foundations. Martin returned to become Premier. Indeed, he could have become Prime Minister of
Canada if this had been his ambition. He attended the
Liberal Convention of 1919 where the great clash was between Mackenzie King, Laurier's former Minister of Labour, and the Honourable W. S. Fielding, former Minister
of Finance in the Laurier Cabinet and one-time Premier

132 / Diefenbaker: One Canada

of Nova Scotia. Martin was urged again and again from all parts of the country to stand. He would have been a perfect compromise candidate, but he refused. King defeated Fielding by a small margin. In later years, I chatted with Martin on many occasions; I can only say that he knew he would have won the Liberal leadership had he so chosen.

Among the greatest of Saskatchewan's premiers was Martin's successor, Charles Dunning, who held office from 1922 to 1926. Dunning subsequently became a member of Mackenzie King's Cabinet. He was a man of courage and vision when neither of these attributes seemed to be cherished by the national leader of the Liberal Party. King did not like Dunning, who stood out as a potential successor to the Prime Minister. But Charles Dunning, an English immigrant, was a great Canadian who rapidly rose through the Grain Growers' movement to become a Member of the Legislature, Provincial Treasurer, Premier at thirty-seven, federal Minister of Railways and, finally, federal Minister of Finance. He resigned from the King Cabinet in September of 1939.

Immediately after my establishment in Wakaw, the leading Liberal organizers tried to enlist me for party work and as a possible candidate. During the elections of 1921, both provincial and federal, they came to me on two or three occasions. I declined. They continued to press, however, and one weekend when I was out of town, the Wakaw Liberal Association elected me Secretary. They appear simply to have taken for granted that anyone interested in political life would want to be a Liberal. I returned on the Tuesday from Saskatoon and was amazed to find the Liberal Association minute books and paraphernalia in my office. I immediately delivered them back to the local Liberal president, Mr. J. H. Flynn. It all seems somewhat curious in retrospect; but these people were apparently not convinced of the sincerity of my political convictions until I stood as a Conservative candidate in the election of 1925. Indeed, just before my move to Prince Albert in 1924, I was approached to be the provincial Liberal candidate in Kinistino.

Nineteen twenty-one was the year of the Progressive Party in Canada. An agrarian party, it swept across the West and rural Ontario like a raging prairie fire. I was never approached to join the Progressive Party, since, I imagine, I had expressed myself strongly against political parties based on occupation or established for specific economic purposes. My father had held similarly strong views on the Patrons of Industry in Ontario. I could not disagree, however, with the objective of securing for Western and Eastern farmers better returns for their labours. The Progressive candidate in Prince Albert, Andrew Knox, was a farmer and a fine citizen in every sense. He had been the Unionist candidate in 1917, and a worthy Member of Parliament, a devoted supporter of the Hudson Bay Railway. In 1921, the population in the Prince Albert constituency was relatively small, but he won a majority of over 3,500. In 1925, despite his excellent representation, he was defeated by over 2,600. Nothing did greater harm to the Progressive Party than T. A. Crerar's decision not to become Leader of the Opposition in 1921 when the party standings were: Liberals, 117; Progressives, 64; Conservatives, 59; others, 4. When Robert Forke, M.P., the sage of Pipestone, became House Leader of the Progressive Party (ultimately he became its national leader, succeeding Crerar), the philosophy of the party collapsed. Mr. King promised to implement many of the principles for which the Progressive Party stood, and thus its rationale disappeared. By 1930, it had ceased to be a factor in Canadian politics. The Progressive movement, it is interesting to recall, never won much support from those Canadians of Central European origin. The outstanding example to the contrary was Mike Luchkovich, who was elected in Vegreville as a United Farmers of Alberta candidate in 1926, the first Canadian of Ukrainian origin to become a Member of Parliament.

I ventured into politics in 1920 by contesting the office of Councillor in the village of Wakaw. I do not exactly remember why I decided to run. The incumbent, Alec Andrew, the hotel-keeper, was a good citizen. It turned out to be as hot an election campaign as ever I have contested. To everyone's surprise I won the election by some twelve or thirteen votes. I served on the Village Council for three years. Although we did noticeably improve the appearance of the town, particularly its streets and sidewalks, and built a new Town Hall, I was not overly impressed with the time required for Council work when measured against what was actually achieved.

My life in Wakaw was a pleasant one. I was busy in the law. Each day, after hours, I made it a point to spend two or three hours reading law. I was on the Village Council. The fishing and hunting were good. I had a summer cottage on Wakaw Lake. My back injury prevented my enjoying the new golf course, now roughed out. I wish I had been able to curl; there was a sport that Western Canada could call its own! And, although I could not play, I did become the very enthusiastic manager of the local baseball team. One year we even made the finals in our league, playing teams from Cudworth, Domremy, and two or three other small towns. When I could manage it, I would spend the weekends in Saskatoon. When I could not, the Village Hall was the important social centre for dances, suppers, meetings, and the like.

It was in Wakaw that I bought my first automobile. A new 1921 Maxwell, it was a thing of beauty, if not a joy forever. It was the worst fraud ever perpetrated on anyone. The only good thing about it was its name. If you drove a thousand miles without something major going wrong, you were in clover. I lost all count of the flat tires.

But I loved to tour. There is still nothing I would enjoy more than to take a camping outfit, climb in the car, and push off into unknown territory. In the summer of 1921, I drove to Vancouver, a trip never to be forgotten. The road from Lillooet to Hope, down the Cariboo Trail, was as it had been for generations: makeshift, narrow, with incredible gradients, sheer drop-offs, and hairpin curves totally beyond belief; and the Maxwell didn't have a horn. I must have been enchanted by it, for in the summer of 1923 I got as far south as Los Angeles.

One motoring experience almost cost me my life, although not in a way normally associated with cars. One of the more prominent characters in the Prince Albert area was a Hungarian by the name of Lukacsffy. Fraud was his constant companion. Although he was quite a successful businessman, larceny was rooted in his soul. The stories about him are innumerable. His favourite expression was, "Damn, hell, what you believing in!" He owned a McLaughlin Buick, a magnificent car. It showed him to be a man of opulence and distinction.

On this particular morning, I was driving from my office. I had purchased a Ford coupé, no longer desiring to own a car that would attract people's comments. Along came Lukacsffy. "Where are you going?" I replied, "To Saskatoon." "So am I. I'll race you. I won't start until an hour after you leave, and I'll beat you."

I set off. En route, I had to take the Gabriel ferry across the South Saskatchewan. The river was high, and the gradient from the road to the river was unusually steep. To manoeuvre a car onto the ferry required care and attention. As mine was the only car on deck, the ferryman directed that I park it on the south side of the ferry against which the river was flooding.

Just as we were ready to move off, a Buick came over the top of the hill. It was Lukacsffy and he was gaining speed. What happened was that he mistook the accelerator for the brake. Down came the Buick at a furious rate. As it reached the ferry, I jumped over the railing and hung on to the outside, as did the ferryman. Narrowly missing my car, Lukacsffy hit the chain at the far end and disappeared into the river.

It was over in seconds; but so vividly does the mind record such an alarming experience that everything seems to be happening in slow motion. Thus, it seemed that we had been standing staring into the water for a long time when out of the foam, if not quite like Aphrodite, Lukacsffy's head appeared. Turning to me, he shouted, "Damn, hell, what you believing in! Don't worry J., I standing on the cushion." I laughed until the haemorrhaging that I had suffered overseas began again. Back in hospital for a major operation, I had a narrow escape. Had I died, no post-mortem examination would ever have traced the cause of death to the antics of an eccentric Hungarian.

Next to James G. Gardiner, who was in a class of his own, my principal antagonists over the years was the Davis machine in Prince Albert. The eldest son of the old Senator, T. C. (Tom) Davis, honest and aggressive in political contests, now ran northern Saskatchewan's Liberal establishment. Tom was a well established lawyer, and the mayor of Prince Albert from 1921 to 1924. It was in the professional area that we had our first differences. Under the rules of the Law Society of Saskatchewan, a law firm was not permitted to open a branch office run by an articled student. Tom's younger brother, while still articled, opened a Davis branch office in Wakaw. I called this young Davis to account on a man-to-man basis. The storm arose. I obviously had not realized that the rules were made only for us mere mortals. Tom Davis wrote me a letter (which I suspected from its tone had been drafted by his brother) in which he said that if I did not realize the power of the Davises, I would be in for grave trouble and more. I replied that it was they who were courting trouble with the Law Society. Their Wakaw office was shortly thereafterwards closed. This was an encounter that did not augur well for our future relations.

In 1924, I decided that it was now time to move my law practice to Prince Albert. A friend of mine, Ed D. Wright, manager of the Western Trust Company, had worked out the details of a partnership for me with Colin Baker, the City Solicitor. At the last moment, Baker, who was also a close friend, backed out. This was a setback, but I made the move to Prince Albert despite it. Wright offered me space in the Western Trust office suite, and I set up shop. Initially, business was extremely slow. It would be an excess of charity to say that the Davises were less than helpful to me. It is adequate to note that when I did have a case before the courts, the Prince Albert *Herald*, owned by the Davis family, refused to mention my name; always "a lawyer from Prince Albert" represented Mr. X. I persevered; clients began to come to me, and in 1925, I formed the firm of Diefenbaker, Cousins, and Godfrey.

F. C. Cousins, a First World War veteran, was from London, Ontario. A good lawyer, he had been very badly shell-shocked and had been invalided home. One evening, Cousins and I worked until about midnight preparing for a case. The next morning, he failed to turn up at the office. I went over to where he boarded and found him dead. At the age of twenty-seven, he was the victim of an attack of delayed shell-shock.

On moving to Prince Albert, I kept my Wakaw office open. It was run by a series of partners. R. B. Godfrey ran it for a time. Alec Ehman, whose son Gerry was to play in the National Hockey League from 1964 to 1971, was another. Its final occupant was Alexis Philion, a French Canadian, older, very experienced. In 1929, I closed the Wakaw office for good, since most of my clients were by this time coming to Prince Albert.

Among the various partners whom I had over the years, none was more outstanding than John Marcel (Jack) Cuelenaere. I met Jack first in 1926. I was speaking at a meeting in Leask, west of Prince Albert, during the election campaign. Cuelenaere's father was a hotel-keeper and an officer of the local Liberal Association. After the meeting, Jack came up to me. He was in grade twelve. He said that he was going through for law and wanted to article in my office after he received his degree. I said, "That'll be fine." Without seeing or hearing from him in the interval, I never expected that more than six years later he would appear in my office, degrees in hand, to remind me of my promise. The year 1933 was not one I remember for its financial affluence. I was in fact trying to reduce my office staff and expenses. It was by no means convenient, but I said to Jack, "There's your desk." This was one of the best things I have ever done. He was a hard worker. Called to the bar in 1935, he became an excellent counsel. We were together on many cases. He was elected a bencher of the Saskatchewan Law Society in 1955, and in 1962 became its president. Like his father, Jack was a Liberal, active in constituency work and in the Saskatchewan Young Liberal Association, of which he was president. After two years as an alderman, he was elected Mayor of Prince Albert in 1946, an office he held with distinction for six years. Provincial member for Shellbrook, he became a Minister in the Thatcher Liberal government.

So much of political life depends on a balanced perspective, especially in personal and professional relations. Partisanship has its place and is necessary in maintaining the political health of our society. But there is a line that is crossed at one's peril; if one allows the battles of the hustings and the House to carry over into the other aspects of his life, he will inevitably be the loser. It is natural enough, given what is read and heard, that political personalities and issues often are confused in the public mind. All I can say is that many of my best friends were those with whom I had the greatest political battles. The fact that Jack Cuelenaere was a hard-working Liberal in no way affected our partnership or our friendship. The fact that Tom Davis and I were opposing counsel on many cases, or that he was Mackenzie King's lieutenant in Prince Albert and Gardiner's Attorney General, or that I ran against him in 1929, did not stop me from liking him. In the House of Commons, I numbered Ian Mackenzie, C. D. Howe, and Paul Martin among my personal friends. An editorial in the Prince Albert *Herald*, following the 1925 federal election and my first campaign, commented, I think, wisely:

In so far as the candidates themselves and their prominent supporters are concerned, the fight has been a remarkably clean one from which bitterness has been entirely absent. This is as it should be, for men who are good neighbours one day do not suddenly become the most undesirable people in the community simply because they happen to be candidates for political office and hold political views which are wide apart, but which they conscientiously believe to be in the best interests of the country.

On 6 August 1925, in Prince Albert's Memorial Hall, I was unanimously chosen as the Conservative candidate to contest the Prince Albert federal seat. My name was placed in nomination by Mayor S. J. A. Branion of Prince Albert, seconded by Mr. A. Ostrovsky of Wakaw. The writs had not been issued but we expected an election in October. It was to be on the 29th of October. The sitting Member was Andrew Knox, Progressive. We had no idea who the Liberal candidate would be. As it turned out, neither did the Liberals; they were not able to hold their nominating convention until 21 September for want of a suitable candidate. Charles McDonald, druggist and ex-

Member of the Legislative Assembly, was their final choice.

For me, the election campaign was a test involving more than votes. I passed my thirtieth birthday during the contest. I had come of age politically, and my candidacy was a public declaration of my political faith. My conservatism was rooted in the traditions of Sir John A. Macdonald, of Disraeli, and of Burke. "A disposition to preserve and an ability to improve, taken together, would be my standard of a statesman." So said Edmund Burke, and so did I believe. Saint Paul, in his first epistle to the Thessalonians, wrote, "Prove all things; hold fast that which is good." But the acceptance of basic principles does not mean a philosophy of reaction. Too often have Conservatives in this country lost sight of the fact that change must take place to meet changing conditions, that the health of the tree is preserved by pruning the withered limbs.

I believed in a Canada free from the directing influence of the United States—a belief that served to emphasize my devotion to the Monarchy in Canada and to the Commonwealth relationship. Our institutional heritage and our Commonwealth citizenship gave Canada a uniqueness in North America vital to our preservation as a nation. I considered, as I said many times during the campaign, that our greatest asset was immigration and our greatest liability emigration. I could not understand why the King government forced Canada to be the only exception to the Commonwealth immigration scheme, nor could I understand why the tariff was not used to protect Canadian industry to ensure a level of industrial development adequate to stem the tide of Canadian emigration to the United States.

I began in 1925 my lifelong attack on hyphenated Canadianism. My whole purpose, from my university days, was to bring an end in this country to discrimination on a basis of race, creed, or colour. In the 1925 election, this emerged in a very practical way for me. I was labelled by some of the lower-level workers of my opponents as a "Hun". The younger reader will perhaps require the reminder that in 1925 Canada was but seven years removed from a war in which this little nation of eight million people had poured out its blood (over sixty thousand dead) and treasure on the battlefields of Europe to defeat the "Hun". There were no four-letter words to equal that three-letter appellation. Matters were made little better when I was simply called a German. I was not a German, not a German Canadian, but a Canadian. On the hustings, I tried to treat this issue lightly, humorously, and in a way that would be understood. On 8 October, to an overflow audience in Prince Albert's Orpheum Theatre, I said, "They call me a Hun! Probably the opposing candidates do not, but their minions most certainly do, and one of the leading Liberals has publicly apologized for this serious allegation. The only crimes they can pin upon me are those of youth and of German ancestry. Am I a German? My great-grandfather left Germany to seek liberty. My grandfather and my father were born in Canada. It is true, however, that my grandmother and my grandfather on my mother's side spoke no English; being Scottish, they spoke Gaelic. If there is no hope for me to be Canadian, then who is there hope for?" I suppose that those who have never experienced this sort of thing will never truly understand it. I have often wondered what the effect on my life would have been if my name had been my mother's, Campbell-Bannerman, rather than Dief-enbaker.

Arthur Meighen, who had been Prime Minister from 10 July 1920 to 29 December 1921, was the Conservative Leader. Born in humble circumstances at St. Mary's, Ontario, he came West in 1898, was first a teacher, became a lawyer, and moved to Portage la Prairie. There he received the nomination of the Conservative Party in 1908 and was elected to the House of Commons. He was an outstanding parliamentarian, but he never understood the people. If a problem came up for decision, no matter how the people might view the subject, his decision had to be based on logic. People are not logical; if they were we'd be nowhere today. Meighen, for example, considered it illogical that freight rates should be fixed by statute; all freight rates, in his view, should be fixed after full consideration by the members of the Railway Commission. This was one of the errors that defeated him in his bid to regain the Prime-Ministership. (When he did attain that office the next year it was not by the will of the people.) He would have won the 1925 election had he listened to reason, but reason is not always logical. The Crow's Nest Pass rates are the Magna Carta of the Western farmer, and I know what the effect would be if any section of them was removed. In 1925, Meighen's threat to abrogate the Crow's Nest Pass rates did more harm to the Conservative Party than any other issue, save one, that I can recall.

The other issue that lost him his chance for a majority was his opposition to the completion of the Hudson Bay Railway. To me his position was preposterous. The Laurier government had passed the necessary legislation for its construction; Laurier was the first Liberal Leader to grasp the importance of northern development. The Borden government proceeded and built some eighty miles before the war, when work was discontinued. There it remained. At that time, Fort Nelson, not Churchill, was to be the terminus. From 1921 to 1925, the demand grew in the West that the Hudson Bay Railway be completed so that the return per bushel to the farmer on grain exported to Europe would reflect the saving in freight rates. Nothing is stronger than an idea that comes of age; it is irresistible in politics. But Meighen would not be convinced.

I remember pleading with him before his campaign meeting in Saskatoon. As I recall his answer, it was to this effect: "Young man, you have all the ideas of the Western farmer, but you haven't got the national picture." I said, "If you don't go ahead with this we're going to lose all over Western Canada." "Well," he said, "we're going to win the election." At the meeting that evening, he made public his opposition to the Hudson Bay Railway.

In Prince Albert, I tried to counter Meighen as best I could. On 8 October, at a meeting in the Orpheum Theatre packed to overflowing, I declared that if I were successful I would resign my seat if rails were not being laid on the Hudson Bay Railway within two years of the date of my election. I carried my message to village and town throughout my constituency, to Domremy and Wakaw, to Rosthern, to Blaine Lake, Marcelin, Leask, and Shellbrook, to Briarlee, Wild Rose, and Honeymoon. My Liberal opponent and his principal supporter on the stump, Tom Davis, twitted me for campaigning on a platform different from that of my leader. My position was difficult; it need not have been. But I chose to speak for myself. Even today, my conviction on the use of the Hudson Bay Railway has changed very little.

I was becoming reasonably proficient as a platform performer. My first success in public speaking was not long after I moved to Prince Albert from Wakaw. I addressed a Kiwanis dinner on "Humour in the Courts". My remarks received a favourable reception and not long afterward Sam Donaldson approached me to determine my interest in becoming Conservative standard-bearer in Prince Albert for the 1925 provincial election. As a serious proposition, this left something to be desired. I was a relative unknown, and the Liberal against whom I would be pitted was Tom Davis. I was not so hesitant when the next opportunity arose.

On election day I lost, and Meighen lost what he could

have so easily won. He needed seven seats for a majority in the House. We elected no one from Saskatchewan. We lost in Saskatoon by a few votes, in Last Mountain by even fewer, and in Moose Jaw by a small number. There were constituencies in Manitoba and Alberta that could have been won. But these are the "ifs" of political life. Nationally, the Liberal Party suffered a rout, a debacle. Mackenzie King and seven of his Cabinet lost their seats. In Prince Albert, although I carried the city, I lost the constituency, and my deposit to boot. The victor was the Liberal candidate, Charles McDonald.

McDonald's career in federal politics belongs in Ripley's "Believe It or Not". He is the only person in our history ever elected to the House of Commons and appointed to the Senate who was never to sit in either. Mackenzie King, defeated in North York but determined to hang on to power at all costs, needed a seat. McDonald resigned immediately to make way for him. He was to be made a Senator. And indeed he was, but this was ten years in the coming. Finally appointed in 1935, McDonald died before he could take his seat in the Red Chamber.

13. The Conservative candidate for the Prince Albert constituency in
the federal election of 1925

14 & 15. *(Above)* A July 1 celebration at Macdowell, Saskatchewan, probably in 1925. Mr. Diefenbaker is seated in front of the speaker, near the centre of the photograph. *(Below)* Leaving the Prince Albert courthouse, the scene of many of his brilliant triumphs as defence counsel over the years.

16. With party colleagues following his nomination as a candidate in the 1929 Saskatchewan provincial election. (Standing) David L. Burgess, M.C., and Dr. J. T. M. Anderson, leader of the Saskatchewan Conservative Party; (seated) S. J. A. Branion, K.C., Mayor of Prince Albert, and Dr. Fred Maclean.

17, 18, & 19. *(Right)* The newly elected leader of the Saskatchewan Conservative Party, 1936. *(Far right)* Mr. Diefenbaker with his parents and his brother Elmer, about 1941. *(Below)* First session of Parliament as Member for Lake Centre. The House listens attentively to the budget speech of the Honourable J. L. Ralston, 24 June 1940.

20 & 21. *(Above)* Consulting with his law partners in Prince Albert, John Cuelenaere and Roy Hall, in 1948. *(Below)* A pointed comment for a Liberal Cabinet Minister across the aisle.

22 & 23. Mr. and Mrs. Diefenbaker in their home in Prince Albert in the summer of 1948. The first Mrs. Diefenbaker, the former Edna Brower of Saskatoon, died in 1951. *(Below)* Visiting with Sam Carle and Arnold Agnew, both long-time political supporters, at the Carle and Brownlee livery stable in Prince Albert.

24 & 25. Talking with friends
and admirers at a Memorial
Day gathering at Glenside in his
Lake Centre constituency, 1948.

CHAPTER NINE

MACKENZIE KING'S GOVERNMENT was in serious trouble from the day of the 1925 election. Badly defeated in the election, King nevertheless clung to power. The standings were: Conservatives 116, Liberals 101, Progressives 24, Labour 2, Independents 2. The Conservatives had emerged from the election not only with the largest number of seats, but with a national plurality of two hundred thousand votes. The Right Honourable Arthur Meighen summed up his view of this situation in a letter to Major P. W. Pennefather, President of the Prince Albert Conservative Association, on 19 February 1926:

What strikes me as utterly insufferable about the present situation is this: a Government defeated at the polls comes to Parliament and through the mouth of a Minister declares that it does not ask for confidence and continuation in office on the basis of its past record, but that it offers a new series of promises of future conduct fulfillable at the expense of the Public Treasury to a small group of Progressives, and asks these Progressives on the face of such promises to maintain it in power. The Progressives even more frankly state they are prepared to accept the offer and maintain the Government in office because of such offer. This is a shameless, brutal assault not only on the most sacred principles of British constitutional government but on common honesty.

Meighen's outrage, legitimate as it was, would change neither King's unscrupulous tactics nor the fundamental nature of the Progressives. As I pointed out earlier, political parties established for specific economic purposes have a future as limited as their objectives. The support of the Progressives was for sale, and King was buying with no thought of the cost. But Meighen had King on the ropes, and both of them knew it. Meighen hated King almost as deeply as King feared Meighen. Breaking around Mackenzie King's head was the Customs Scandal. The revelations were incredible. The Pacific Scandal that toppled Macdonald from office in 1873 was small by comparison, since millions of dollars in goods and in lost tariff revenues were at issue. The Progressives found that they could not maintain an alliance with this sort of dishonesty.

Within weeks of the 1925 election, the entire range of corruption began to emerge. Canadian customs officers were involved in a smuggling ring operating in Windsor-Detroit, in the Eastern Townships of Quebec, and throughout the New Brunswick-Maine boundary. Directing much of these operations was a senior Customs Inspector and implicated was the former Liberal Minister of Customs and Excise, the Honourable Jacques Bureau, who, instead of being sent to jail, had been appointed to the Senate by King prior to the 1925 election. As a result of Conservative pressure, a Committee of the House of Commons was appointed to investigate. Three Liberals, three Conservatives, and one Progressive heard the evidence, most of it brought forth by the RCMP, over a period of several months. Their report was damning; the King government was guilty not only of neglecting public business but also of knowing of the scandalous state of the Customs Department and doing nothing about it. When the Committee brought down its report, the Conservatives moved a vote of censure against the Liberal government.

Mackenzie King's plan was to have the House dissolved and an election called before the vote on censure could be taken. Never before in Canadian or in the whole of British parliamentary history had such a request been granted to a Prime Minister facing the censure of the House of Commons. Lord Byng, Canada's Governor General, rightly and properly refused King's request. Further, King had assured the Governor General following the 1925 election that in the event the Liberals were unable to maintain the support of the House, they would stand aside to allow Mr. Meighen his chance. But King now denied that "gentleman's agreement". He announced the resignation of his government and flatly refused to debate the issue.

Canada was without a government. Lord Byng invited Arthur Meighen to form one. All Meighen's lieu-tenants—Perley, Ryckman, Tolmie, Drayton, Manion, Stevens—said "No". It has since been generally agreed that, had their views been accepted and an election fought, a Conservative government would have been the result. Instead, Mr. Meighen accepted the advice of an Ottawa publicist, whose influence over him was greater than the combined experience and knowledge of the Conservative front-benchers of that day. Thus, Meighen accepted the seals of office and formed his famous "Shadow Cabinet" on 29 June 1926. Defeated almost immediately by a fluke vote in the House, he was forced to seek a dissolution, which was granted 2 July 1926.

Mackenzie King then produced one of the most transparent falsehoods of any man in any generation of our country. He claimed that Canada was in the midst of a constitutional crisis, that the Governor General, Lord Byng, had acted on instructions from Downing Street in inviting Meighen to form a government, and that he, Mackenzie King, would save the common people of our nation from colonial peril. King's "challenge of imperialism" was so phoney it made Barnum look like an amateur. There was no substance in it, either in law or in logic. But it attracted the public imagination, or at least King's performance did. Meighen treated King's synthetic arguments with contempt, refusing even to mention them. In the light of events, that was a grievous error.

Arthur Meighen was a man of integrity and principle, and of powerful intellect. He could have torn Mackenzie King to shreds on the constitutional issue had he been willing to recognize its existence. It is forgotten today that at the Prime Ministers' Conference in London in 1921 he took a stand that changed the course of history. Meighen stood alone in his opposition to the renewal of the Anglo-Japanese Treaty. Advocating its renewal were men as powerful as Lloyd George, Winston Churchill, and Billie Hughes of Australia. But before the Conference was over, Meighen had secured majority support for his point of view; and the abrogation of the Anglo-Japanese Treaty paved the way for closer relations with the United States in international affairs and, ultimately, for the entry of the United States into the Second World War.

In the elections of 1921 and 1925, Liberal politicians in Quebec had won by raising the standard of fanaticism. They pictured Meighen as the agent of British imperialism, his hands red with the blood of French Canadians who gave their all in the First World War. If the Liberal Party could win election after election in Quebec on the issue of conscription, then what success might be enjoyed in the West by trotting out the Wartime Elections Act to secure the votes of ethnic groups who had suffered from its provisions, as a complement to the constitutional-crisis scare. In Prince Albert, Mackenzie King deliberately stirred up racial strife. Advertisements were placed in the *Ukrainian Voice*, over the signature of Mr. King's official agent in Prince Albert, stating that the Conservative Party stood for the principle of depriving all naturalized Canadians of their right to vote. They went even further, as I stated publicly on 4 September 1926, at a meeting in Goschen, in the east end of Prince Albert: "Representatives of Mr. King are going through this constituency telling the non-English speaking people that, if the Conservative Government is returned, they will all be deported one by one without trial." I stood foursquare, as did the Conservative Party, behind the principle that anyone undertaking the responsibility of citizenship should be entitled to its privileges. But as proof of their racist charges, the Liberals used the unjust and callous statements of three Ontario Conservatives of minor importance deprecating Mackenzie King's choice of the riding of Prince Albert following his defeat in North York in 1925. During the last week of the campaign, Liberal advertisements appeared throughout the Prince Albert constituency, such as: "The Conservative candidate in North Grey, speaking on Mr. Meighen's platform at Owen Sound, hurled insult at the electors of Prince Albert. 'Mr. King' he said 'is running in a riding among the Doukhobors, up near the North Pole where they don't know how to mark their ballots.' Citizens of Prince Albert: Mark your ballot for Mackenzie King and reject this insult!" References to King's preference for the smell of garlic-stinking continentals in Prince Albert over the company of native-born Canadians in his old riding of North York had also been made, and were widely quoted. The fact that these statements were the very antithesis of my beliefs did not help to rectify the situation. What was said by these Ontario nonentities may have gone down well with their audiences but they did not speak for the Conservative Party. Indeed, they cost the Conservative Party several constituencies. Certainly, I knew in that last week before the election that they, more than anything else, had undone me in my campaign.

I might in this connection mention the provincial election of 1929, in which I contested the Prince Albert seat against Mackenzie King's chief local lieutenant, T. C. Davis, now Attorney General of Saskatchewan. I was accused of being hand-in-hand with the Ku Klux Klan, if not of being a member of it. A flash in the pan, the K.K.K. was first noticeable in Saskatchewan in 1926. It spread much in the same way as the Non-Partisan League or the Progressive Party before it. Based on a strong anti-Catholic, anti-Jewish, anti-non-English-immigrant, anti-coloured sentiment, it was fired by the oratorical powers of J. J. Maloney. Around it coalesced certain factions sharing a bitter hatred for the Gardiner machine. If left alone, it might have disappeared as quickly as it had emerged. Unfortunately for everyone, Gardiner began in 1928 to use it as a political straw man. He launched a series of political attacks on it in the Provincial Legislature, bringing the K.K.K. out of its obscurity, giving its leaders the appearance of political martyrs, and making it a recognizable centre of opposition to his government and its policies. Everyone who opposed Gardiner, his policies, and the viciousness of his machine was tarred with the dirty brush of Klan fanaticism. I met the Klan leader, J. J. Maloney, only once and then for a period of not more than five or ten minutes. He asked for legal advice on the financial difficulties of the K.K.K. arising when its American organizers absconded with a large part of the organization's dues.

I was fortunate, in the light of subsequent events, that Tom Davis defeated me in 1929. I was defeated by some four hundred votes. Had I been elected, I would have been the Attorney General, as promised by Dr. Anderson during the campaign, and responsible for bringing in legislation to end sectarianism in public schools. The Klan,

from its inception in Saskatchewan, had campaigned vig-
orously against a Roman Catholic presence in certain of
the province's public schools. The Conservatives were
pledged to end this sectarianism. When the legislation
providing for the removal of teaching nuns from the
schools was brought down, I was opposed to it. I wonder,
as I look back, whether I would have had the courage to
resign over the issue. I think my normal reaction would
have been, after my labours in three elections, "Why
should I resign?" That would have been my destruction. I
would have been irredeemably associated in the public
mind with the religious and racial bigotry of the period.
Indeed, in 1956, the Honourable Earl Rowe's group from
Toronto decided to prevent me becoming leader of the
Conservative Party by charging that I had been a Ku Klux
Klan member. This allegation was completely disproved
when a provincial Cabinet Minister, an outstanding Liberal and a man of recognized integrity, the Hon. Hubert
Staynes, who had a complete list of the Klan membership, denied categorically that my name was on that list.
He further stated that it was clear that I had never been a
member of that organization.

To return to the 1926 election, the issues in the campaign were much the same as in 1925: the Crow's Nest
Pass rates, the Hudson Bay Railway, the tariff. The major
change was the addition of the old age pensions question.
Mackenzie King, under pressure from J. S. Woodsworth
and A. A. Heaps, the two labour Members elected in 1925,
had brought forward a publicly financed pension scheme
that provided those over seventy and without means
twenty dollars a month. This was to be financed jointly
by the federal and provincial governments, and adminis-
tered by the provinces. I took the stand that no man or
woman could maintain a decent existence on two hundred and forty dollars a year. Throughout the campaign
Meighen opposed old age pensions. I vividly recall a con-

versation with him when I suggested that there was a strong feeling among older people concerning this opposition. "It's wrong," he said. "You must earn by the sweat of your brow, you cannot live off others. There can be no advancement for anyone with the promise of a pension held out." "Well," I replied, "don't you realize that this is the trend?" He could not understand that social legislation and socialism were not synonymous terms. He suggested that I had got my ideas from what he described as "socialist caricatures of fact." My views sprang from my personal experience. I have always been opposed to socialism. I believe that we cannot accept in a country such as Canada any system denying to the individual citizen the courage and initiative necessary to the development of a great country. When the private citizen takes a chance in business or enterprise and loses, he loses. When the state makes a mistake, the taxpayer picks up the loss. There is a vast difference, however, between the state that denies the citizen everything except the right to pay taxes, and the state that denies a decent measure of social security for the aged, the afflicted, and the disadvantaged. Mr. Meighen could not grasp the fact that old age pensions or mothers' allowances did not ultimately lead to socialism, or worse. In this, he was not much different from the Conservative reactionaries who condemned R. B. Bennett's "New Deal" legislation in 1935, and regarded R.B. as a traitor to his class. These were the same people who refused to support the Saskatchewan Conservative Party in the 1938 provincial election when, under my leadership, we proposed a progressive platform including social legislation. In 1945, when the Family Allowance legislation was introduced in the House of Commons, I was the only Member in our caucus, to begin with, not prepared to oppose it. It was demanded by some that I either oppose the measure or leave the Party.

Threats of that sort have never been effective with me. I knew what a difference it would have made to my boyhood. After long and stormy arguments over two or three days, all but one Conservative Member supported the bill. I was to be shocked and concerned again and again by the degree to which some in our Party seemed to regard the possession of wealth as a necessary preliminary to any sound conception of national interest.

To those who have labelled me as some kind of Party maverick, and have claimed that I have been untrue to the great principles of the Conservative Party, I can only reply that they have forgotten the traditions of Disraeli and Shaftesbury in Britain and Macdonald in Canada. The Conservative Party in Canada had literally to be dragged kicking and screaming into the Twentieth Century. I was a candidate twice under Mr. Meighen when I had to try publicly to explain matters that were unexplainable. During the 1926 campaign, Meighen had a tremendous meeting in the Third Avenue Methodist Church in Saskatoon. During the question period, an elderly gentleman by the name of Eby, something of a local institution and much beloved, who from 1885 had kept the daily records of rainfall and of temperature and atmospheric pressure, rose and asked, "Why are you opposed to old age pensions?" For ten minutes, Meighen took apart the old man as only he could. Support in that audience went down the drain. The only Conservative elected in the Prairies that year was the Honourable R. B. Bennett. And they tell me today that the Meighen name is magic in Canadian politics.

In Prince Albert, the results of the 1926 election were about what I had expected. This was a straight fight between Mackenzie King and me. The Progressives, well on their way to total absorption by the Liberal Party, had been pressured into not running a candidate. I had a fine organization. Mr. O. B. Manville, a highly respected businessman, was my official agent, replacing Mr. Richard Mulcaster, who had done an equally praiseworthy job in 1925. Because the Conservatives were the Government going into the election, I was able to have Major Percy W. Pennefather appointed as Returning Officer for Prince Albert. Penny was a wonderful man, one of the original North West Mounted Policemen. He had served in Prince Albert, Moosomin, Battleford, Macleod, the Yukon, and Lethbridge, before retiring as a Superintendent in 1922. I still think that I might have overcome the constitutional issue, the Hudson Bay Railway, the Crow's Nest rates controversy, and even the old age pension question, had it not been for the offensive racial comments of those Ontario Conservatives that I mentioned earlier. Despite this, I put on a good fight in the city; King's lead in the rural polls, however, was unassailable.

In October 1926, I went to Ottawa to attend the meeting of elected Conservative Members and the defeated candidates in the Railway Committee Room of the House of Commons. The word was that Meighen, personally defeated together with six of his Cabinet, had to go. Meighen himself seemed to recognize that his position was untenable, that his chance of leading the Conservative Party to victory had gone for good. It was interesting to observe that although he had little or no support from Quebec in the election (with the exception of four English-speaking ridings), the French Canadians were most eloquent in proclaiming that he was the greatest leader ever to lead the Conservative Party. Armand Lavergne demanded that Meighen must not be allowed to resign. All through the day the arguments went back and forth. Finally, Meighen's resignation was accepted. When he left that Committee Room, all but the elected Members left as well. As Arthur Meighen walked down the hall, I thought that I had never seen a more forlorn figure.

Before leaving Meighen, I should add that at the 1927 Conservative National Leadership Convention in Winnipeg he was anathema; he could not have been elected pound-keeper even in an area where there were no cattle. The Honourable Howard Ferguson, Premier of Ontario, whipped the Tory faithful into a paroxysm by condemning Meighen for his Hamilton speech during the Bagot by-election of 1925, in which he stated that never again should Canadian men be sent overseas except by the declaration of Parliament. That was the last straw for the hidebound Ontario Tories, the worst heresy ever uttered by a Conservative leader. Just as in the early 1880s, when Macdonald decided that Canada ought to have representation in London, some Tories said, "This is the end of the Empire, that's all." Meighen, as retired Leader, had the right to make his own speech, and he chose to reply. Never have I seen anyone take a hostile audience and turn it around so completely. That speech, "Unrevised and Unrepented", as it is now known, was the best political speech that I have ever heard, and in my time I have heard many of the great orators in the English tradition. He could have been re-elected overwhelmingly, had he chosen to stand.

I attended the Winnipeg Convention as a delegate and as whip of the Saskatchewan delegation. Saskatchewan's representative on the Party's national organization was Major H. E. Keown, who did a great deal for me over the years. Keown possessed a dry wit. Driving with him once some twenty-five miles north of Saskatoon, the car careened off the road near a sign which read, "Wild Grove Farm". Keown's only comment was to look at the sign and say, "Wrongly named." The 1927 Convention was the first at which a National Leader was chosen other than by caucus. My intention was to support the Honourable Hugh Guthrie. I felt that Mr. Bennett with his reputed millions could not hope to get the support of the average

Canadian. I was wrong. Guthrie had a commanding presence. He was a giant in parliamentary debate, as well as a giant of a man physically. He had entered the House of Commons for Wellington South constituency in 1900 as a Liberal. In 1917, he broke with Laurier on conscription and accepted a portfolio under Borden. When Union Government ended, he stayed on under Mr. Meighen and became a Conservative. He was re-elected by a very small majority in 1921. In 1925 his majority increased, and in 1926 increased again. When Mr. Meighen retired as Leader, Guthrie was chosen House Leader, and did very well in the succeeding session. When the convention came, it was decided, since he was Leader of the Opposition, that he should have the right to speak first. He stepped up to the podium: "Ladies and gentlemen, I welcome this, the greatest Liberal convention in all history." That ended his chances. It was one of those things which cannot be eradicated, cannot be erased. Mr. Bennett was chosen Leader. An exciting convention, there were quite a number of exceptional candidates: Bob Rogers, C. H. Cahan, Bob Manion, and Sir Henry Drayton.

I never ran federally during Mr. Bennett's tenure as Leader, although I came to develop a profound appreciation of his courage and political vision. Had I run in 1930 when offered the nomination in the constituency of Long Lake (Lake Centre in 1935), probably I would have been elected. Dr. W. D. Cowan, the Conservative candidate who took the nomination in my stead, won easily. But reasons of health prevented my considering the nomination. My haemorrhages had recurred, and the doctors ordered me to take a long rest. I was holidaying in Toronto when I received a wire from the Long Lake Conservative Association asking me whether I would accept the nomination. I replied that I could not. When the Convention was called, I received a second telegram to the effect that proceedings in the Convention were being held up pending my reply: "We hope that you will accept," their message ended. There was no possibility.

When I did stand again for Parliament in 1940, my constituency was Lake Centre. My association with this riding had a curious beginning in the provincial Arm River by-election of 1928. Arm River was contained within the federal constituency of Lake Centre. Our provincial leader, Dr. J. T. M. Anderson, wanted me to attend a meeting at Hawarden, a town on the Outlook–Moose Jaw branch of the CPR, where Premier Gardiner and his Minister of Agriculture, the Honourable C. M. Hamilton, were to speak. My job was to interrupt if either made any statements of questionable truth. This was a new role for me and I was reluctant to take it on, but over I went. I sat under the balcony at the rear of the hall. The lights were dim, if there were any at all. Mr. Hamilton spoke first. He was a fine gentleman in every way, but he made two or three statements which I did not consider correct, and I interrupted. After my third interruption, Mr. Gardiner, apparently annoyed that Hamilton had not squelched his heckler, stepped forward. The exchange that followed was along these lines: he demanded, "Who is this person? It takes us little time in Liberal meetings to put an end to characters like you. It's easy to sit down there and ask questions you've been sent to ask, and paid for. Well, I'm going to give you the opportunity to let this audience see and hear you. I'm going to give you the platform for twenty minutes." There were about three hundred at the meeting. The area was strongly Liberal. I arose and started down the aisle. When I came under the light in the main part of the hall, Gardiner said, "The offer doesn't apply to you. What are you doing here anyway? I wouldn't let you speak on my platform for anything." I said, "But you asked me," and I kept on until I was at the foot of the platform. He continued to object. I replied, "Fairness is essential in every walk of life. You challenged me, and I'm here." By this time the audience started to take sides and the pro me's outnumbered the con's. Finally, Gardiner yielded. "I want to be fair. I'll give you ten minutes." "No," some of the audience cried, "give him the twenty minutes you promised." Ten minutes was plenty. I asked a series of questions, all most embarrassing to the Premier. I still follow that course. I do not ask questions in the House of Commons just for the sake of amusing myself or to be reported in Hansard. That one never asks a question unless he knows the answer is basic to parliamentary questioning, although some Members seem to be under the impression that a reference in Hansard is reward enough. A question which can be answered without prejudice to the government is not a fit question to ask, unless there is some kind of political alliance between the questioner and the government. My questions were difficult for Mr. Gardiner to answer. He began his speech about 10:30 p.m., immediately after I had finished. His words volleyed and thundered out in a never-ending torrent. On and on he went, with no reference to me or to my questions. No one left the audience. After an hour or so, interruptions began, inquiring as to when he was going to answer my questions. Jimmy said, "You wait." More words. Finally, he looked at his watch. "It's midnight. I never discuss politics on Sunday. I believe we should keep Sunday as a holy day." "Jimmy and Johnny had met and Jimmy didn't answer the questions," was a reputation that stuck.

Out of that meeting at Hawarden stemmed my invitation to contest the federal seat of Long Lake in the 1930 election, my bid for a provincial seat in Arm River in 1938, and finally, my nomination and election to the House of Commons in Lake Centre in 1940. Before leaving Mr. Gardiner, I might add that my lasting memory of him is in the House of Commons answering Opposition questions without a note to guide him. He would stand with a glass of water, brimful, in his hand. I never saw him lift it to his lips, he just held it as he spoke. As you watched him you became fascinated by the glass: when would the water spill? With perfect self-control, he never spilled a drop.

I have known a number of men who have been exceptionally good on the stump. Gardiner was one. Another was my friend Major Keown. He had a magnificent voice, but sometimes he tended to view the facts as totally irrelevant. During the same Arm River by-election, we had a meeting at Bladworth. Keown arrived late: "What'll I speak about tonight?" "You'd better deal with finances." He said, "That's my niche," and started in. "Your debt is piling up. Your taxes are increasing. I'm not one of those who simply makes declarations on a platform without providing the fullest of information. Do you realize that the debt of this province is 12 million 543 thousand dollars? And if I went further I'd say, 'and 44 cents'." About ten minutes later a heckler yelled, "What is the debt of this province?" Keown said, "I'll not repeat it." "I want to know; you've told us you have the figures." "Well, I'll tell you what the debt is. Thirteen million 642 thousand dollars." The heckler thought he had him. "You said 12 million a while ago." Keown was not to be outdone: "That was a while ago. I'm giving you the figures right up to this very minute."

The peril to the political speaker is that when interrupted he may become annoyed and proceed to excoriate the heckler who has asked him an embarrassing question. Elections are lost that way. I have seen a rock-ribbed constituency for the party in power lost by the manner in which the leader of one of the political parties answered a question that was reasonable but embarrassing. Macdonald was a master of the art of handling such questions. An example was in the last days of the campaign of 1891. Sir John was very ill. He spoke near Ottawa. Those who preceded him on the platform were continuously interrupted. When Macdonald got up, frail, uncertain in gait, moving with difficulty to the table from which he was to speak, hecklers decided to howl him down. A big booming voice arose from the back of the hall. "Let us listen to what Sir John has to say. We have a reputation in this village for doing that. Let us have order." There was silence. Sir John said, "I want to thank you very much, sir." The voice replied, "Don't run away with the idea, Sir John, that I'd ever vote for you. I wouldn't vote for you if you were the Angel Gabriel." Sir John said, "My friend, you are so right. You would not be in my constituency." That is the way to deal with hecklers. Of course, when interruptions are from that small group whose purpose is to break up a meeting, to dislodge reason, and to destroy the right of others to listen, they have to be dealt with in an entirely different way.

My only active participation in the 1930 campaign was to persuade Robert Weir to run in Melfort. He had been a major overseas, a teacher, and a school inspector before his retirement, when he became a scientific farmer. I had attempted in both 1925 and 1926 to enlist him as a candidate in Melfort, but without success, although he would come in now and then to talk the matter over. He always explained that his election would interfere with his seed programs and his cattle-breeding. Finally in 1930 he agreed, provided that I would secure someone to run his campaign. I at once suggested David L. Burgess.

Burgess had run in the by-election that followed McDonald's resignation to make way for King in Prince Albert after the 1925 general election. The Conservative Party, as such, decided not to run a candidate in that by-election, but they did not want Mr. King to go unopposed. I received a telegram suggesting that an Independent candidate run. I was standing, this telegram in hand, looking out from my window at the traffic on Central Avenue below. It was a cold, blustery day in January 1926. Across the street I saw Dave Burgess. I sent one of my staff to ask him to come up. I knew Burgess well, and I respected his ability. His war record in the Royal Flying Corps was outstanding. When he came into my office, I said, "You have often told me that you'd like to be in Parliament. Well, how about running as an Independent?" Without hesitation, he agreed to do so. It was: "Dave Burgess, M.C., for M.P.". King, of course, was a shoo-in; to defeat the Prime Minister in a by-election is almost an impossibility.

In 1930, when Weir was elected and appointed Minister of Agriculture, Burgess became his Private Secretary. In the 1935 general election when the Bennett government went down to defeat, Weir lost his seat. Burgess continued in Ottawa as a civil servant under the provision in the law that anyone who had been a Private Secretary to a Cabinet Minister was entitled to appointment to an equivalent civil service position. Burgess was given an innocuous position in the Department of Agriculture under the King administration. It had title, but no substance. It gave him time, however, for his veterans' work. Later, Burgess became Dominion President of the Canadian Legion. It was at his suggestion that I secured the designation "Royal" for the Canadian Legion.

In the period between 1930 and his retirement in 1938, I came to know the Right Honourable R. B. Bennett well. He trusted me, and we had some frank discussions. A large man physically, he was inclined to be portly in appearance. Often brusque in speech, he tended to give many the impression that he was somewhat pompous. Always correct in manner, he was a man of considerable intellect. He was a dominant figure in the House of Commons.

From a humble beginning he rose to become a wealthy man and a director of large companies. In the courts, he often acted for the big interests; he was Chief Counsel for the Canadian Pacific Railway west of Winnipeg. On one occasion I said to him, "You were a great lawyer." He replied, "I was not. I was a successful lawyer." As noted earlier, I did not support him for the leadership in 1927 because of his close identification with the established economic interests. I had not reckoned in my assessment with either the independence of his character or the strong influence of his Methodist conscience. From the beginning, Mr. Bennett was his own man. In 1930, R.B. largely ignored the self-appointed Eastern bosses of the Party and, to their anger, directed and financed a large part of the national campaign. Canadians more and more are beginning to reassess his Prime-Ministership without being blinded by the appalling great depression in Canada, which was under way when he took office in July 1930. The demands placed on the Bennett government were greater than any ever placed upon a Canadian government. Yet, as you look about you today, at the Bank of Canada, at the Canadian Broadcasting Corporation, it is obvious that his was not a government that sat on its hands. To hold Bennett responsible for the great depression is about as logical as holding Mackenzie King responsible for the outbreak of the Second World War. The Farmers' Credit Arrangement in 1934 saved tens of thousands of farmers from bankruptcy and ruin; but this was not a measure to which the banking and mortgage institutions were particularly favourable. The number of people whom Mr. Bennett personally helped over the years will never be known because he refused to allow his many philanthropic acts to be made public. And, when every traditional method of government had been exhausted to meet the depression, and time had provided no respite, he shocked the great interests in Eastern Canada with legislation that could never have been expected from one of their own.

I was in Ottawa for a few days in that summer of 1934, and I remember him saying, "Something has to be done. These conditions cannot be permitted. I have tried, but no one seems to have an overall plan." And soon after, he decided to bring about in Canada something similar to Roosevelt's New Deal, subject, of course, to Canadian conditions. He had his brother-in-law, William Herridge, and his chief secretary, R. K. Finlayson, work out the details. He then enunciated his policies for Canada in a series of radio broadcasts in early 1935. The Bennett New Deal is as far-seeing when read today as it was statesmanlike when it was first introduced. Indeed, I think that had he gone to the country immediately, he might have been the victor. But events seemed to overwhelm him. Even in the election in October 1935, had Bennett been able to heal the rift in his Cabinet between the Honourable H. H. Stevens and the Honourable C. H. Cahan, or, more particularly, had he sided with Stevens and allowed Cahan to quit, the Conservative Party would have emerged from the 1935 election in a healthy state. I can recall arguing with him in Stevens' favour. R.B. would have none of it; for reasons I have never been able to understand, he was determined to keep Cahan.

In the 1930 general election, the Conservatives elected 137 members; in 1935, 39 members. The large difference stemmed from Harry Stevens' decision to break with the Conservative Party in 1935 and to found the Reconstruction Party. Harry was a great parliamentarian and an equally great orator. He was determined to do something about the lot of the common man, the factory labourer, the piecework slaves of the garment industry. Bennett's New Deal legislation, brought in after Stevens left the Cabinet, with its provisions for unemployment insurance, minimum wages, and maximum hours of work, its protection and advancement of consumer and producer interests, would have achieved all Stevens' objectives. In the event, the Reconstruction Party entered the fray and divided the Conservative Party to capture some four hundred thousand votes, but actually to elect only Stevens. I believe that we would have won at least forty more seats had Bennett been prepared to seek a reconciliation before Stevens moved irrevocably into his course of destruction. That would have given us seventy-nine seats, a number we were not to equal in the four succeeding elections, under three succeeding national leaders.

I had been elected Vice-President of the Saskatchewan Conservative Party in 1932. In 1935, when the President, J. M. Patrick from Yorkton, was appointed to the District Court Bench, I automatically succeeded him. It was in this capacity that I chaired a public meeting for Bennett shortly after the 1 July 1935 riots in Regina when the Communist-led Ottawa trek was broken up. It was as big a meeting as any hall in Regina could accommodate. To the left of the platform was a large group of those who had taken part in the riots: noisy, vociferous, offensive, and profane. There had been threats that the Prime Minister would be shot. The Regina Conservative Association took those threats seriously; the rostrum had been turned into a bullet-proof shield which came up to my shoulders. Mr. Bennett was sitting directly behind me in the cover of the rostrum. During my opening remarks I turned to him and he wasn't there; he had taken his big chair out in front. His courage calmed the audience. The speakers preceding him had a fairly rough time. Mr. Bennett just sat there. When he got up to speak, he was cheered. Courage, Barrie said, is the greatest attribute of all. This it is, next to integrity. Bennett had both.

On the day R. B. Bennett ceased to be Leader of the Party, Jack Anderson and I were with him. Anderson, an intimate friend of Mr. Bennett's from their early days, had become my most devoted political supporter, determined to make me Prime Minister of Canada. He was one of the most remarkable men I have ever known, self-effacing, dedicated to his country, and devoted to his Party. He was the only person I know who could get away with blowing smoke into Mr. Bennett's face during an interview. Jack would say, "R.B., you're all wrong. Now I want to tell you, R.B., you don't know what you're talking about." To which Mr. Bennett would reply, "Now Jack, I think you're going a little too far." Jack would rejoin, "I've just started." Mr. Bennett, of course, knew Jack to be a friend of unlimited common sense, and one who, regardless of whether his advice was acceptable or not, would give a frank, clear, and effective expression of his views. That evening, Anderson and I sat in Bennett's main office. Messages were coming in from all across Canada, deep regrets at his retirement. Rod Finlayson kept bringing them in. There was one from the Conservative Association in Kingston. In effect, it said: "Greatly regret your retirement. History will give you large place. Conservative party will now have to choose new leader. Suggest you get behind George Drew. He is going places." Mr. Bennett was indignant. He called in a secretary and, as I recall it, dictated the following: "Thank you. Will not be getting behind George Drew as suggested. He and Conservative Party not going same places."

In June of 1929 I had married Edna Mae Brower, who had taught in Saskatoon at Mayfair School. She was a most attractive and vivacious person, and a political helpmeet who made many friends and supporters for me in Lake Centre constituency in the elections of 1945 and 1949. It was our tragedy that through the last nine years of our married life she was seriously ill. She passed away in February 1951, widely mourned in Ottawa and in Saskatchewan.

During our chat in his office, Mr. Bennett had asked me if I was married. When I told him that I had been for eight years, he replied that a wife could mean a great deal to a public man, but unfortunately he had never married. He then inquired as to whether he had sent me a wedding present, and when I told him there was no reason why he should, that was the end of the incident as far as I was concerned. Three weeks later, on returning to Prince Albert, I found to my great surprise that he had sent me $2,-500 as a wedding gift.

On 29 October 1936, I became Party Leader in Saskatchewan, succeeding Dr. J. T. M. Anderson. I did not have it in mind to become Party Leader, nor did I campaign in any way for the office. But as President, it was difficult to resist the demands of E. E. Perley, M.P. from Qu'Appelle, and of R. L. "Dinny" Hanbidge from Kerrobert, and of other leading Conservatives that I allow my name to go forward. I told the Convention: "I'm not here to put my qualifications before you; but if you think I can lead this party to victory, I'll lead the party. If you think I'm not the man, then I'll get behind any man you choose and give him my wholehearted support." I was elected unanimously.

Mine was a formidable task. Dr. Anderson's government had been devastated in the 1934 election; not a single Conservative seat had been retained in the Saskatchewan Legislative Assembly. Ernest Perley was the only Conservative M.P. to retain his seat in Saskatchewan in the federal election of 1935. But we had enjoyed good leadership both provincially and federally. No scandals had occurred at either level of government under Conservative administration and, unlike the Liberals, we had never had to walk through the valley of humiliation. With re-dedication, a united party, and a policy based on Conservative traditions, yet brought up to date—"Radical," as

I told the Convention, "in the sense that the reform pro-
gramme of the Right Honourable R. B. Bennett was
radical"—I thought we had a chance.

CHAPTER TEN

MY LAST ELECTION CAMPAIGN in Prince Albert, until 1953, was in 1933 when I allowed my name to stand in the race for mayor. Mr. Fraser was my opponent. I was concerned over the extent to which the city's annual revenue was being eaten up by interest on old debts. In 1932, according to my figures, out of municipal taxes amounting to $267,000, $128,000 had been paid in interest charges. At the base of this problem lay a foolish, publicly backed venture from which Prince Albert had not had the chance to recover. Just prior to the First World War, during the boom, there had been a local power shortage. The city guaranteed the interest on the bonds for a hydro development on the rapids at La Colle Falls, just east of the city on the North Saskatchewan River. Today, there stands a monument to all this in crumbling cement. The project was never completed but the city-guaranteed bonds were issued. In 1933, one-hundred-dollar bonds were selling for twenty-five dollars or less. Members of the Davis clique were buying them up. I wanted the city to buy them. My opponent was not prepared to move on the bond issue. Even with the support of the Davis Family Compact, he beat me by only fifty votes. (Fraser challenged me federally in 1963 and lost by over fourteen thousand.) Of course, had I won in 1933, I would not have been in a position to accept the leadership of the provincial Conservative Party in 1936. The fascination with those "might have beens" in my experience does not lessen, though they constitute a world devoid of obvious reality. In retrospect, there seems almost a logic which was not apparent at the time.

In 1935 I was in line for appointment to the Court of King's Bench in Saskatchewan. When the expected vacancy on the bench did not occur, Mr. Bennett, in the midst of the election campaign, got in touch with me to ask whether I would accept appointment as a District Court Judge. That did not interest me. I am reminded of the story of a well-known American lawyer speaking before a Law Society meeting in Canada. He was introduced by one of the deans of the Canadian bar, who praised the greatness of the American system of jurisprudence, made much of the association of the Common Law of the United Kingdom with that of the United States, spoke of our shrines of freedom. But he found that in one particular the American system did not appeal to him: the election of judges. The American lawyer rose and, in acknowledging the fulsome introduction, said that, although he had not been in Canada very long, he didn't see very much difference between the way judges were chosen in Canada and in the United States. In the United States, with the exception of the two highest courts, judges had to be elected. In Canada, the major qualification was to have been defeated once or twice.

As the winter of 1936-37 began, I was the Conservative Leader in Saskatchewan. Like no other, our province was still locked in the grip of the world's most appalling depression. Drought, grasshoppers, and the lowest wheat prices in history transformed a land of optimism into a land of grim survival. The total Saskatchewan wheat income for the years 1922-29 inclusive was $1,559,000,000; for the years 1930-37 it totalled $449,000,000. In vast areas, one year of drought was followed by another, and by yet another. In the Prince Albert region, the conditions were very similar to those general throughout depression-ridden Canada. However poor the returns, the farmers could not complain about production. But travelling south from the park land into the northern rim of the Palliser Triangle was like moving from the Garden of Eden to the Dead Sea. The sandstorms were like unto the desert. The land simply dried up and blew away. Telephone poles stood three-quarters buried, and, in the fall, Russian thistle rolled the land.

In 1933, myriads of grasshoppers descended, leaving behind not a vestige of green. In 1935, there was rust. For poultry, there was no market whatsoever. Hog and cattle prices were not much better. It is no exaggeration to say that farmers who tried to get top prices for their cattle by shipping them to market wound up with a net loss. They would receive their bill: six cattle, at such a price; freight costs, at so much. The amount owed the railway was more than the value of the cattle!

Rural relief and agricultural rehabilitation were the major issues throughout the 1930s. The Saskatchewan Relief Commission, established by the government of Dr. Anderson in 1931, and abolished by Gardiner in 1934, was a superb undertaking, free of politics or profiteering or partiality in the administration of over thirty-five million dollars of relief funds. This was not true under Gardiner or his successor as Premier in 1935, W. J. Patterson. They rejuvenated the Liberal Party machine through the administration of relief. In 1933, during the worst of the depression, when Dr. Anderson offered to step down as Premier to facilitate the formation of an all-party government to meet the catastrophic conditions, Gardiner simply brushed the proposal aside. Like Mackenzie King in Ottawa, Gardiner was prepared to sit back and blame the

Conservatives for the depression, while privately thanking his personal deities that he was out of office for the worst of it.

This extreme partisanship on the part of Gardiner and King generally served them very well. The one occasion on which King was hoist with his own partisan petard was on 3 April 1930, when, baited by Dr. Manion, Harry Stevens, and others on the Opposition front bench, he said that he would not give a five-cent piece to any Tory provincial government for unemployment relief. This statement damaged the Liberal Party during the general election that followed. I recall an interesting explanation of this rare indiscretion on King's part. In February 1931 I was in Ottawa. Rae Manville, one of the most public-spirited citizens Prince Albert has ever known, accompanied Mayor Hugh Sibbald and me to lunch at Laurier House at the invitation of our local Member of Parliament, then Leader of the Opposition. I will never forget the light shining down on the portrait of Mackenzie King's mother, or his statement that her inspiration continued to guide him. During lunch, the conversation turned to unemployment and Rae Manville remarked: "That five-cent speech of yours was not very beneficial to you." King explained at some length that despite the stock market collapse in October 1929 he was not convinced of the seriousness of the situation and doubted the necessity of federal assistance to the provinces for unemployment relief. On the day in question he had entertained Dominion-Provincial representatives at a luncheon at the Royal Ottawa Golf Club. It had been a happy occasion during which a fair quantity of alcoholic refreshment had been consumed. King said: "At about 1:30 I started back to the House of Commons. I invited Howard Ferguson [Premier of Ontario] to ride with me. He was a fine politician. We understood each other and we talked very freely. I said to him: 'Howard, if you were in my position, with these various Tory governments in the provinces making demands on the federal treasury, what would you do?' " There were Conservative governments in British Columbia, Saskatchewan, Ontario, New Brunswick, and Nova Scotia. According to King, Ferguson replied: "Prime Minister, I wouldn't give a five-cent piece to any of them." King went on to describe the circumstances in which he adopted Ferguson's words in the House later that afternoon, and concluded, "If it had not been for the drinks at lunch, I would never have got into that mess." Had King been successful in the 1930 election, no doubt the engineless automobiles with teams of horses hitched to the front would have been known as "King coupés".

No one who lived through the depression in Canada could remain unaffected by it. No group or profession was left untouched. I remember taking a case in Kerrobert, west of Saskatoon, some forty miles from the Alberta border. The District Court Judge looked down at me as the court opened and said: "What are you doing here? This is the first case in ages in which there has been any money for lawyer's fees and now you'll get it." It was an incredible statement for a judge to make, but understandable in the circumstances. Men travelled the entire country by freight car looking for work. Wagons loaded with every earthly possession moved up from the dust bowl through Prince Albert to unoccupied park lands. Families who should have been overwhelmed by hopelessness determined to start anew. It is odd how a small thing will stick in one's mind and at times serve as a symbol for a horrendous event. Considerable quantities of dried salt codfish had been shipped from the Maritimes during the worst of the depression, but few people on the Prairies knew how to prepare it properly. It was not uncommon to see a codfish nailed up on corner posts as a direction guide to the passerby. I often think, when I contemplate the awfulness of those days, that the only reason for our failure to have a rebellion, or the reason that Britain has not had a revolution since 1690, is that under the British parliamentary system we let off our steam in Parliament.

The year 1938 saw two events of importance in Saskatchewan. Rust struck crops in parts of the province, and the Patterson government, despite its dismal record, decided to go to the people. Jimmy Gardiner had gone to Ottawa as King's Minister of Agriculture in October 1935, but he still ran the Saskatchewan show. The election was called for 8 June.

There were fifty-two seats in the Legislature. I had re-established constituency organizations in over forty ridings. In each of them we had candidates nominated in advance of the election writs. Our platform was modest, in the sense that we refused to promise what we would not deliver, and progressive, in that our policies on taxation, the civil service, co-operative marketing, road-building, and relief administration were designed to meet the problems of the ordinary citizen. We also pledged to use whatever influence we might gain at the federal level to re-establish the Wheat Board. We refused to try to outbid the Liberals for the support of the people; to attempt to buy the people with their own money is hardly a commendable, though a frequent, course in politics. It appears nevertheless that our platform was considered left-wing by some who designated themselves "true blue Tories". It is hard to assess the exact effect of the public attacks on the Party's direction by men such as its former Provincial President, Dr. D. S. Johnston of Regina. Heaven knows, they provided plenty of grist for the Grit propaganda mill. Johnston and his cohorts were entitled to their opinions, but our policies were what I had promised on my election as Leader, and, if one may judge by the overwhelming rejection of my offer to resign the leadership at the Party's Convention in Moose Jaw on 26 October following the election, they were also what in fact the rank and file of the Conservative Party in Saskatchewan wanted.

Whatever the cause, however, we were soon in dire straits. I had worked for a year and a half, at my own expense, to rebuild our organization. Now, with the election upon us, we had no money for the campaign. Local contributions ranged from small to nil. Finally, I appealed to friends of the Party in Eastern Canada for assistance. I pointed out that without a viable Tory Party in Saskatchewan, the socialist Commonwealth Co-operative Federation under George Williams, T. C. Douglas, and M. J. Coldwell (the latter two had been elected federally in 1935) would form first the Opposition and then the Government. "Never!" was their reply, and no Conservative money was forthcoming. I got one thousand dollars in outside help, half from an Edmonton lawyer and half from a Calgary businessman. One by one my candidates drifted away. They had lived through the drought, and the vast majority of them did not have enough money to pay their deposits,.let alone to fight an election. With a personal loan from the bank I covered the election deposits of twenty-two of our candidates. Our credibility as a practical alternative to the Patterson government fast diminished in these circumstances. There we were, without enough candidates in the field to form a government if elected, and, to public appearances, divided against ourselves. In the constituencies where we had no candidates, our supporters were placed in the painful position of having to choose between the CCF and the Liberals. But the knockout blow to our chances to establish a core of Members in the Legislature on which to build was the arrival of Alberta's Premier, William Aberhart, and his Social Credit legions.

Social Credit had swept into power in Alberta in the provincial election of 1935. In the federal election that same year, Social Credit had captured fifteen of Alberta's seventeen seats, and had been successful in two Saskatchewan constituencies, Kindersley and The Battlefords. The promise of a major distribution of the wealth of the country through the government's issue of twenty-five dollars each month in dividend cheques (although hardly a novel concept in today's society) was temptation itself in the 1930s, when the sight of a dollar bill had become a rare thing. No one really understood Social Credit's monetary theories, the A-plus-B-equals-C theorem. Perhaps that was the reason for its popularity. In later years, A came to equal BC, when British Columbia joined Alberta's ranks. Premier W. A. C. Bennett's Social Credit had about as much relationship to the theories of the movement's founder, Major Douglas, as I have to the appearance of Hercules. But Aberhart in fact used Social Credit for little more than a designation. His mixture of radical economic theory and evangelical fervour had a powerful impact, none the less. His meetings throughout Saskatchewan in 1938 were tremendously successful. I never saw Aberhart on the stump, but, of course, I heard him on radio. At the time, I thought he was a very good performer; but since he was one of the first, it was hard to judge. His successor, Ernest Manning, a Rosetown, Saskatchewan, boy, was, however, truly excellent as a radio evangelist.

With Aberhart's entry into the Saskatchewan field, the Liberal attack now shifted from the Conservatives to Social Credit. The prospect of a Social Credit victory was very frightening to the established economic interests. Money poured into the Liberal Party coffers. Liberal advertisements depicted the election as a two-way contest:

ATTENTION CONSERVATIVES. Viewing the situation, dispassionately, as it actually exists, it is quite evident that, with only 23

Conservative candidates in the field, they could not possibly form a government without the aid of other groups. The few so-called "unity" candidates whose support your leader counts upon have also sworn allegiance to other groups. Who would they support, if elected, Diefenbaker or Aberhart? Surely with the great traditions of the Conservative party in Canada, its supporters would prefer the stability of the Liberals to chaos as threatened through Social Credit domination.

The effect of Aberhart's invasion with horse, foot, and artillery was to elect two Social Credit Members, and to make certain of the defeat of the twenty-three Conservative candidates.

I ran in the constituency of Arm River. It had been decided that my chances were better there than in Prince Albert. Considering that in the course of the campaign I spent only three days in the riding and taking into account the extremes to which the Patterson-Gardiner machine went to ensure my defeat, I did quite well. It was said facetiously that government inspectors were so numerous in Arm River during the week before the election that they were ordered to wear distinctive ribbons in their lapels, so that they would not waste time asking each other for votes. The Liberal candidate, G. H. Danielson, a fine citizen, beat me by a mere one hundred and sixty-eight votes. Given all the circumstances, I still consider that the Conservative Party did amazingly well to capture what we did of the popular vote. To add insult to injury, the Regina headquarters of the Conservative Party received five thousand dollars from Eastern Party sources the day after the election. I never saw a penny of it; the election debts I had incurred I had to pay myself.

It was more in sorrow than in anger that I now concluded my political ambitions would never be realized. It was not that I was downtrodden in defeat; this I have never been. It was a matter of realistically appraising the situation. I had run federally in 1925 and 1926, provincially in 1929, for municipal office in 1933, and again provincially in 1938. Five successive defeats! My wife was not well. My law practice was suffering. I was the Leader of a Party with no representation in the Legislative Assembly. What I wanted to do was gradually and responsibly to relinquish my political obligations, and to devote the rest of my life to the practice of law.

The provincial election of 1938 was the last in which I crossed swords with my old antagonist, T. C. Davis, Attorney General under Gardiner and Patterson. With the Liberals in power in Ottawa, he was appointed to the Saskatchewan Court of Appeal in 1939. He had an unusual record, the only judge I know who was never reversed on appeal. He never tried a case! In 1940 he was granted leave of absence, which was to last nine years. In that period he was successively federal Deputy Minister of National War Services (a good administrator), High Commissioner to Australia, and Ambassador to China. Following his resignation from the bench in 1949 he continued in the foreign service.

Hardly had the 1938 election concluded in Saskatchewan when the Party was faced with the national Conservative Leadership Convention in Ottawa for July 5-7. I had no desire to attend. I discussed the matter at length with my political colleague, M. A. (Murdo) MacPherson of Regina. MacPherson, a lawyer and a very popular political figure, had been elected to the Saskatchewan Legislature in 1925 and 1929, and had served as Attorney General in the Anderson government. Defeated in the provincial election of 1934, he was called to Ottawa by Prime Minister Bennett for the difficult task of setting up the machinery for the Farmers Credit Arrangement Act. There were no precedents for this type of federal administration. MacPherson did the job with unusual ability. As reward, he was to be a High Court Judge. The appointment instead went to Mr. Percy Gordon, K.C.

MacPherson now took the position that after our abandonment by the national Party in the provincial election, none of us should attend the Ottawa Convention. Major Keown, President of the Saskatchewan Conservative Party, shared this view. I agreed that we had been sacrificed, but I thought it would look strange if no one attended from the provincial Party. In fact, when the Convention had first been announced, in March 1938, I had urged MacPherson to stand for the leadership. With some doubts about the wisdom of our course, I now agreed with my colleagues that none of us should go.

When word of our decision arrived in the East, there was deep concern. There were telephone calls and messages, imploring us to come. We decided to attend. MacPherson decided that he would not only attend but that he would run for the leadership.

MacPherson was a hit at the Convention. His speech accepting his nomination as a candidate was magnificent. He would have won had he entered the field earlier. As it was, he ran second to Bob Manion in both ballots. On the second ballot, the vote was Manion 830; MacPherson 648; Joe Harris (with whom I had gone to school in Todmorden) 49; Denton Massey, 39. J. E. Lawson had dropped out after the first ballot. I admired Dr. Manion. I had never heard him in debate, but his speeches read well in Hansard, and I was impressed by his ability to pick appropriate historical analogies when making his arguments. An Adonis in appearance, he had a distinguished war record and a buoyant personality. First elected to the House of Commons for Fort William in 1917, he had been a Cabinet Minister under both Meighen and Bennett, but had lost his seat in the 1935 election. The 1940 election would see his destruction as Leader.

One amusing incident during the 1938 Convention occurred at the conclusion of R. B. Bennett's farewell address. Seated on the stage while Bennett spoke were the Leaders of the Party in the various provinces plus the oldest and the youngest delegates to the Convention. The youngest was R.B.'s nephew, Billy Herridge, a precocious five-year-old. Billy was sitting between Eric Willis, the Manitoba Leader, and me. Bennett gave a powerful address and as he turned from the rostrum, Billy said to him: "R.B., you sure hit the ball." R.B. stopped short. "Billy, Billy, you should not talk to your uncle that way. You should say: 'Uncle Dick'." "Oh," said Billy, "that's too juvenile."

Billy's father, Major W. D. Herridge, D.S.O., M.C., had married Mildred Bennett, R.B.'s sister, in 1931. He was appointed Canada's Minister to Washington and had been one of Bennett's brain-trusters in working out the details of the Bennett New Deal. He considered the policies adopted by the national convention in 1938 to be meaningless; he defined them in a short word of four letters. Late in 1938, he asked me to meet him in Saskatoon. He wanted me to join his proposed New Democracy Party. He said: "We can launch a party across this country that will truly be a party." I said this didn't interest me, that I wouldn't participate in that kind of thing. Third parties, launched as breakaways from the traditional parties, have never been successful. Shortly after I was nominated in Lake Centre in 1939, he again got in touch with me and wanted to come to Prince Albert. Again we met in Saskatoon. This time he was accompanied by Charles Bowman, the editor of the *Ottawa Citizen*, who, with Herridge, was going to launch this new party. We talked at length. They knew my views, but they spent hours trying to convince me that Saskatchewan would never elect any Conservatives and that therefore what was needed (they claimed they didn't want Social Credit) was the

New Democracy Party embodying the Bennett reform principles modified or extended where necessary on the basis of the United States' experience under Roosevelt in the intervening years. If only I would join, they knew others who would follow. I didn't, and that was the end of that. But I did say to him, "Where are you going to run?" "Kindersley," he replied. I said, "Don't." That was Carmichael country, a Progressive seat under A. M. Carmichael through four elections. Herridge's hopes were based on the fact that in 1935 Kindersley had gone Social Credit. I said, "You have no chance there whatsoever. Why don't you run in one of the Ottawa seats closer to home, where you can build up your organization?" Well, Herridge ran in Kindersley in 1940. He lost, and the Liberals took the seat. (All Social Credit federal candidates ran under the New Democracy banner in 1940; their Members in the House of Commons decreased by seven.) Herridge subsequently retired from politics to build up a tremendous law practice in Ottawa. When I was a Member of Parliament he suggested that I might want to retire from politics and come into his firm. That did not interest me either.

In June 1939, with rumours of war on every hand, a Conservative nominating convention was called in the federal constituency of Lake Centre. It was to be held in the town of Imperial on 15 June at 3 p.m. Imperial was in the provincial riding of Arm River, where I had run the year before. The President of the Lake Centre Conservative Association, Mr. W. B. Kelly, a long-time friend, called me in Humboldt where I was on a very complex case involving arson and fraud charges. "Are you coming down to the convention?" he asked. I explained that I could not, that I was in the middle of a case. He pointed out that many people had worked very hard for me in Arm River during the 1938 election, and for free. It was true. And I might add that in all the years I have never paid political workers, or had to, except, of course, for stenographic staff. I have always tried to mobilize in people that sense of responsibility that leads them to devote some time to public service; and this is what constituency and election work is all about. Kelly wanted me to come down to the convention at Imperial and express my thanks to those who had so lately worked for me. I agreed to talk the question over with J. T. Léger, the presiding Magistrate. He said there was nothing to prevent my absence for a day or two of the preliminary hearing, if someone took my place. I phoned my partner, Jack Cuelenaere, but he was to take a case that day. I then phoned Kelly to inform him that I could not get down. Very late the night before the convention my wife phoned me from Prince Albert to say that Cuelenaere's case in North Battleford had been settled, and that he would be free to take my place at the hearing in Humboldt. Thus, on 15 June, my wife and I travelled to Imperial.

The convention took place in the Town Hall. There was a large turnout. Maurice Western, today a distinguished columnist for the *Winnipeg Free Press*, was one of those attending and was widely spoken of as a prospective candidate. Nominations were called for. Mine was the first name placed before the convention. The others nominated were all local men: W. B. Kelly, George Haggerty, Charles Harlton, F. W. Turnbull, H. J. Burroughs, and C. W. Thurston. Having been the first candidate to have his name put in nomination, I was the first to speak to the convention. I stated that, in my opinion, they should have a local candidate. I added that if it had not been for the number of excellent local candidates whose names had been placed in nomination, I would have welcomed the opportunity to stand as their candidate. My mover and seconder accepted my disclaimer. The hall caught fire after my speech, although I make no connection one with the other. My departure was delayed until the fire was put out. The convention then went ahead with its business. After the first ballot I left.

I got into my car. The motor was running when one of the local farmers hailed me and said that he wanted some legal advice: "I worked very hard for you in the provincial election and I don't want to pay for this advice, but I want it." Some of his cattle had been killed on the CPR right-of-way because the gates had been left open. I told him what I thought his course of action should be. My business concluded in Imperial, I was just starting down the street when out of the hall came Ed Topping. Ed was one of the leading Conservatives in the southwestern corner of the constituency, and a good friend and supporter. He said, "There's a hold-up in the convention." "Well," I said, "the convention has chosen Kelly." He said, "There's a mix-up. We want you inside." I got out of my car and stepped into the hall. As I did, Mr. Kelly said, "I was chosen as the candidate and I therefore move, seconded by A, B, C, D, and E [naming the other candidates], that my withdrawal be accepted and that this convention choose as its candidate John Diefenbaker." There I was—chosen!

Back in the car on our way to Prince Albert, I was silent. My wife couldn't understand this. She said, "What happened in there?" Finally I admitted, "They chose me as their candidate." We decided that I had somehow to get out of it. The next day I was back in Humboldt to continue with the trial. As the preliminary resumed, Magistrate Léger and a number of my colleagues at the bar asked me if we had nominated a good candidate. I said, "Well, not very good." The Saskatoon Phoenix came that afternoon and there was my picture. Everyone had a splendid time at my expense.

At the conclusion of the trial, I returned to Prince Albert. I phoned Mr. Kelly and told him, "I've got to with-draw." He replied that I could not. I was insistent. There was, he suggested, a way whereby, without harming the Party, I could withdraw at the next scheduled executive meeting of the constituency association. It was not to take place, however, until 5 February 1940. I agreed.

The Second World War began in September of 1939. On 25 January 1940, Mr. King made a political turnabout. He had promised that there would be another session of Parliament before dissolution. A new session began. The Speech from the Throne was read and then Mackenzie King announced that dissolution had been asked for and Parliament was no more. That put an end to the executive meeting in Lake Centre for 5 February. I was the candidate in spite of myself!

Parliament had been in session only from 7 September to 13 September 1939, and for a few hours on 25 January 1940, since the outbreak of war. There had been no discussion of war policy in the House, other than whether or not to declare war on Germany. The Speech from the Throne in January 1940 was no more than a Liberal election gambit. Indeed, King, in his pell-mell rush to get rid of Parliament, set the date of the election for Monday, 25 March. He then had to set the election over to the Tuesday, since the 25th was Easter Monday.

When the election was called, I was in Ottawa in connection with a Supreme Court of Canada case, *Studer* v. *Swain*, in which I was for the respondent on an action which I had taken, on behalf of and in the name of the Crown, to have the Crown direct its servants, Ministers, and officials to carry out the law for the benefit of the subjects of the Crown. It was an important case. I had won the trial. I had won the appeal. I lost in a three-two judgment in the Supreme Court of Canada. I returned from Ottawa to find myself in the midst of a murder trial. The accused was the wife of a man of German descent who was an avowed Nazi and a leader in the German-American Bund. His wife was Irish born. They had married by correspondence through some "Lonely Hearts" organization. Although their relationship was hardly cordial, there were a number of children. He regularly beat and abused her. She left him several times, returning only because of the children. Their disputes multiplied following the outbreak of war. This man should have been in an internment camp. Instead he was out. Now he was dead. His wife was charged with murder. She had no counsel. She wanted above everything else that I take her case. The election was on, but finally I agreed. There were no fees, for she hadn't a dollar in the world. At the trial, the Crown produced evidence that she had twice confessed to the crime. I did not call the accused to the stand. I was able to show that one confession had been obtained by the police in circumstances of almost unbelievable duress, and that the other, which was allegedly made to an old neighbour lady, was suspect. I also put on trial the influence of the German-American Bund in Saskatchewan politics. The trial judge ruled out both confessions, and the jury acquitted. The outcome of the trial was considered harmful to the Liberal Party in the election. Strong representations were made and the Crown appealed, I suspect for the wrong reasons. The Court of Appeal ruled that the second alleged confession should have been admitted as evidence by the trial judge; my client's acquittal was set aside and a new trial ordered. I defended her a second time in June 1940, with both confessions in evidence, and the jury brought in a verdict of acquittal. Years later, she sent me one hundred dollars to buy a watch.

Thus, it was about the middle of February before I was able to attend to the business of the election. It was a winter campaign. Except for the main highways, travel was mostly by horse and cutter. I recall on one occasion leaving Kenaston, intending to catch the Prince Albert–Regina CPR train at Nokomis for a meeting the next night in Strasbourg, some thirty miles farther down the line. We drove all night through a storm, and we were about one mile out of Nokomis when the train went through. This meant a further drive in thirty-below-zero weather to Strasbourg. We arrived just before the meeting. On another occasion, I spent one night stuck out on the prairie in a blizzard, a repeat of my narrow escape from freezing to death in 1909 when we were on the homestead. It was not a new experience. I recall campaigning in the 1920s with the late Senator Byron Horner. Again we were stuck in the snow, an eight-mile walk before us, and me with a raging temperature. As we tramped through the sub-zero temperature, Byron insisted that I take his beaver coat. Wrapped in that mass of fur, I began to perspire, despite the freezing cold. By the time we reached Prince Albert, my fever had broken; I was back on my feet the next day. Again, in the winter of 1938 I attended a provincial nominating convention at West Bend. It was held in a hay mow. John Hnatyshyn, later a Senator, another of my long-time political associates and advisers, was with me. After the convention, we set off by team and cutter to catch the train some twenty miles distant. Our driver was of Ukrainian origin. Seated up on the hurricane deck, he entertained us with the songs of the Steppes while he headed off in the wrong direction. After securing directions and righting our course, we overturned twice, escaping unhurt on each occasion. Finally, somewhat unnerved, we arrived at Ituna, where we were to catch our train. It was just pulling into the station. At that point, our driver turned, and in complete innocence inquired of us, "Gentlemen, where did you say you desired to go?"

In contrast to this sort of campaigning, 1940 was the first election in which radio was widely used. The regulations governing its employment, however, were stringent, to say the least. It was war-time. You had to have a full script of your proposed remarks examined in advance by the authorities to determine whether or not it contained any matter that was contrary to the Defence of Canada Regulations or that might in any way be used to encourage or give solace to the enemy. Once it was approved, you had to follow it carefully, without digression. During the campaign, I spoke twice a week for about fifteen minutes. Indeed, I think I used radio more than any other candidate in Saskatchewan. I was able to get through to the homes of many with whom I otherwise would have had no contact. Generally, people will attend only their own Party meetings, but they will listen to the opposition on the radio in the privacy of their homes, where they are not seen by their neighbours and therefore not subject to admonitions for disloyalty or gullibility.

Once, after I had agreed to speak at a meeting in the Bethune area, northwest of Regina, I discovered that the meeting conflicted with my regular broadcast. Since the advertising for the meeting had been published, I could not change plans. Consequently, we went through the then awkward process of phoning James Richardson's in Winnipeg to put my speech on a disc for later broadcast from Regina. The village meeting was a success, some thirty or forty people turning out. It was a strongly Liberal area, but we had hopes that some of them might be swayed. Normally, I always go directly to my home or quarters after a public gathering, but this night it was insisted that, because several of those at the meeting had been present at the marriage of my father and mother in Bruce County in 1894, I should go to one of the homes for tea. As I came in the door, someone was speaking on the radio. I listened for a moment. The loudspeaker was a great horn, similar to those once used on gramophones. I asked, "Who is that fellow? He's the worst speaker I have ever heard in my life. Whoever he's speaking for will certainly be losing votes." Then I recognized two or three phrases that were mine, and this created a great laugh. The story went abroad; I used it myself. It was sent to a radio magazine and received an award for "The most unusual radio story of the year". But the culmination came on election day when the Bethune area gave me a majority.

The chief issue in the 1940 election was whether all political parties should join in a united war effort. Dr. Manion had pledged that if he formed a government, it would be a government representative of all the parties, something similar to the Union Government of 1917. This gave me the opportunity, in speaking to farm audiences, to state that if Dr. Manion formed a government, the person whom I wanted to see as Minister of Agriculture was Premier John Bracken of Manitoba. (I had not the slightest thought that two years hence he would be our new Leader.) In the campaign, most of our candidates ran not as Conservatives but as National Government candidates. I ran as a Conservative, supporting the principle of National Government. Of course, I also pounded away at the question of parity in wheat prices. With the federal government all powerful under the authority of the War Measures Act, marketing and prices came under Gardiner's jurisdiction as Minister of Agriculture, and there was no excuse for the farmer not to get a fair return.

The Liberal candidate, J. Fred Johnson, had been first elected as a Unionist in 1917, then as a Progressive in 1921 and 1925. In 1926 he was elected as a Liberal-Progressive and became Deputy Speaker of the House of Commons. Defeated in 1930, he was re-elected in 1935 as a Liberal candidate. He was a good campaigner, widely known. The CCF had as a candidate W. R. Fansher, who had been elected as a Progressive Member of Parliament in the constituency of Last Mountain in 1925 and 1926. At the time of the 1926 parliamentary crisis, he supported the Conservative Party. These were formidable opponents.

During the campaign, it was alleged against me that I was a lawyer who received high fees, "And why would farmers want a lawyer to represent them in Parliament?", an argument often heard in those days; I am informed that even today there are some who adhere to this view. It was said that there was nothing to equal the low cunning or the deceptiveness of lawyers. It was very difficult to meet this sort of charge, but Jack Anderson did it. I went to Saskatoon one weekend and when I came back on the Monday, everywhere there were posters: "The Liberals Are Right. John Diefenbaker is a successful lawyer and does get large Fees. Farmers, put your case in his hands. It won't cost you anything." They did, and it didn't.

I think, however, that without Fred Johnston's inadvertent assistance, I might have acquired my sixth consecutive electoral defeat in 1940. On 23 March, the Saturday before the election, we both made radio broadcasts from Regina. These were the last speeches of the campaign. He spoke first. In the course of his remarks he said, "Are you going to have me as your Member, or are you going to have a conscript? Diefenbaker was a conscript." The war was under way and emotions were high. It was an appalling statement for him to make. My turn to speak came. My speech had been prepared and approved beforehand. As I read it, I watched the monitor. Jack Anderson was beside me, and when the monitor turned away, I interjected, "I've been in many elections, but this is the first time a deliberate lie has been told by anyone against me. I joined up in 1916 and took my commission. I was invalided home in February 1917. Conscription didn't come in until after the election in December 1917, the Unionist election that I participated in. Johnston's statement reflects on everyone who enlisted in the twenty months preceding conscription." This swung quite a number of votes. And one of the most interesting of those votes was that of a man named Clark, a relative by marriage of Johnston and a dyed-in-the-wool Liberal supporter, living in Bladworth where Johnston was a farmer on a big scale. When he heard what Johnston said, he went to work for me in the two days remaining in the campaign, with the result that I got a majority in Johnston's home area, something none of his opponents had ever done before. There is an inherent fairness in people.

In all, this was a tremendous campaign. I doubt whether there was ever a better organization built than the voluntary organization supporting me. Jack Anderson was my chief organizer and his first lieutenant was Arthur Pearson, later a member of the Senate of Canada, who, in all successive elections, whether in Lake Centre or Prince Albert, has always been in charge of my organization. We covered every nook and corner; icy halls never before opened during the winter were opened for meetings. I went through that campaign without even having a cold. It was full of interesting experiences. At Findlater, a few miles beyond Bethune, a lad of thirteen came to me and said he wanted to make a speech. His name was Jim McDougall. He and his parents had suffered through the depression and his speech was written on discoloured wallpaper. The president of the Association said they could not allow him to speak. I said: "He'll speak." He spoke, and it was an excellent speech. It was the speech of a youth who understood, not clearly, but definitely, that service is essential to good citizenship. He received widespread publicity as the youngest stump speaker in the entire country.

An amusing incident occurred the day before the election. I was in Silton, a village near Last Mountain Lake. I spoke to various people. I make it a rule never to directly ask any person for his or her vote. I have always felt that to do so places that person in an invidious position. Everyone has the right to vote as he or she will. However, on 25 March 1940, I made an exception. There was a woman in Silton who had always been a Liberal, but I was told that if I went to see her she would vote for me. Over I went. I rapped at the door. She welcomed me in and she said, "I'm going to support you." I replied, "That's wonderful, and I see your husband is also on the voters' list. Will he support me too?" "Support you," she said; "he hasn't supported me for the last five years." I lost her vote.

As I look back, I regret that the day of the joint meeting is over. In such meetings the opponents argued their cases before an audience in which each candidate's supporters clustered together in mutually hostile groups. It had all the attractiveness of a prize fight and cost the general audience nothing. The public response to such meetings was overwhelming; they packed the halls to overflowing. I think of one many years ago in a town in northern Saskatchewan. The windows got smashed, the seats got torn up. That meeting may not have changed many votes but it gave a lot of people a chance to let off steam.

I was unable to get outside speakers to come into my riding in 1940, since it was considered that my defeat was certain. I had tried to get one or two, without success. The top-rank speakers, not wanting to ruin their batting averages, went elsewhere. There was one exception, however, whom I shall always remember with gratitude and appreciation, the Honourable H. H. Stevens. He had returned to the Conservative Party in 1938 on the retirement of the Right Honourable R. B. Bennett, and he was a Conservative candidate in British Columbia. When Harry Stevens heard about my situation, he was already scheduled to speak in Regina at an evening meeting. He got in touch with me to say he would be willing to speak for me that afternoon. As sometimes happens, the local organization did not put out the bills. We arrived in the town of Lumsden. The hall was icy cold. The temperature was around thirty degrees below zero. A hurried run around town picked up about twenty-five or thirty people. In the meantime, the fires were put on. Harry Stevens spoke. Of all the speeches I have heard on the stump throughout the years, I doubt that any ever reached the heights of that speech. He gave it everything he had. I went into Regina for his evening meeting. His speeches were always on a high level, but his performance did not even begin to approach the power of that afternoon speech to a handful of people. It showed me something; it revealed more of the Honourable H. H. Stevens than all the write-ups I have ever read about him. He liked the common people. He understood them, and no sacrifice was too much for Harry Stevens if he could bring his message to the average Canadian. That is a test of greatness.

On election night, 1940, my wife and I were at home in Prince Albert. Drs. Lorne and Mabel Connell were with us, as was my law partner, Jack Cuelenaere. Later, Rae Manville and his wife came along. Rae was the Conservative candidate against Mackenzie King in Prince Albert. After his nomination, Rae did everything he could to ensure his own defeat; he actually asked his constituents not to vote for him. Despite this, he reduced King's margin of victory from a high of 5,902 in 1935 to 776 in 1940. During the evening, Jack Anderson phoned in the unofficial results from Lake Centre. At about eleven o'clock, he said, "You're now leading by one hundred and fifty votes. The outstanding polls are sparsely inhabited, so I think you're all right." At midnight, I still had nothing official to go on. For some reason, Lake Centre was the only constituency in Saskatchewan on which there were no regular radio reports. Finally, Jack Cuele-naere, who was President of the Saskatchewan Young Liberals, volunteered to phone his Party's headquarters in Regina. "How are we doing?" he asked. "Fine, except in Lake Centre, and that's a seat we never expected to lose." "You mean to tell me we've lost it?" "Yeah, it's gone." That made it official. In the final count, I beat Johnston by two hundred and eighty votes. Ernest Perley was re-elected in Qu'Appelle. The Conservative Party had doubled its representation from Saskatchewan.

CHAPTER ELEVEN

WHEN THE QUEEN, on 14 October 1957, for the first time in history opened Canada's Parliament, I wanted all Canadians to share this event. In consequence, television cameras appeared for the first time in the House and the Senate. Across the land, people were able to watch the Gentleman Usher of the Black Rod approach the door of the Commons, to see it slam in his face, and to hear him knock three times with his ebony staff and answer, "Black Rod," to the challenge, "Who is there?" The ceremony exactly as my father had seen it in 1891, and as I saw it from the benches to the left of the Speaker on 16 May in 1940, and as those yet unborn will see it in their day and generation.

In May 1940 Canada was in the midst of uncertainty and war. Norway had fallen to the Nazis, the Netherlands had surrendered. The fall of Belgium and France was imminent. There were deep fears, and Members spoke to one another with hushed voices. When I arrived on the Hill that Opening morning, the clock in the Peace Tower had stopped, something unprecedented. It gave the House a strange, almost supernatural aura. Certainly it made more poignant my modest part in that historic ceremony.

After his admission to the Commons Chamber, Black Rod advanced four or five steps to announce the King's command that we go to the Senate. Then, slowly and with dignity, Black Rod moved from the Commons. Led by our Speaker, the Honourable James Allison Glen, we followed. In the forefront of our procession came the Sergeant-at-Arms, the Mace, to symbolize the authority of the House of Commons, over his right shoulder. Never, since the days of Charles I, when the King entered the House to arrest certain of its Members, has the Monarch or, in his absence, the Governor General been allowed within the Commons. Thus, as we stood at the bar of the Senate's Red Chamber, we heard the Speech from the Throne.

No doubt I was somewhat overawed at taking my seat in the House after all those years of trying. Here were the great parliamentarians of their age. Other new Members spoke at once in debate. I did not. I had been on the political stump since 1917. I had been in the courts, but somehow I felt that until I was at ease in my new surroundings, I had best follow the traditional course, to be seen but not heard. I remembered Mr. Bennett's counsel that a new Member was well advised to keep quiet until he had something of the feel and atmosphere of the House of Commons. I also remembered the story I had heard about a young Liberal Member, first elected in 1935, who had been helped by Mr. Bennett over the years. He now came to R.B. for advice: "I want to make my maiden speech." Bennett said, "I would wait." "But," the Member protested, "people are beginning to ask why I don't speak." R.B.'s reply: "Better for them to ask why you don't than why you do."

It has been said that for the first six months a new Member wonders how he ever got elected to such a great institution; thereafter, he wonders how any of the other Members ever got elected. This is a piece of facetiousness, to be sure, but it carries within it an element of truth. All too often, after the initial novelty of a seat in the

House of Commons wears off, Members conclude that they have nothing more to learn; their attendance becomes casual. A Member cannot ever understand the House if he does not devote his time to its business. Mackenzie King practically lived in it; when it was in session, he was continually in and out of the Commons Chamber. I have been a Member for over thirty-five years. I am still learning.

I was the last of the new Conservative backbenchers to speak in 1940. Our ranks were thin; we were thirty-nine in all. Immediately following the election on 26 March, I had received letters from John M. Robb, the Party's Dominion Organizer, and from R. A. Bell, Manion's private secretary, raising the prospect of my being selected as House Leader. Our National Leader, Dr. Manion, had suffered personal defeat in the election. This was not a position that I wanted, but no decision was to be made until just before Opening Day. I could not imagine a greater horror than to make a maiden speech in Reply to the Speech from the Throne.

As it was, I found my maiden speech an awesome ordeal—my nervousness, my anticipation, my hopes, my wondering, as I spoke, whether the outcome would conform at all to what I had in mind. I felt that I was in a great vacuum, surrounded by a material of one-way transparency: I could see the others in the House, but they could not see me; and perhaps they could not hear me. Never before or since have I experienced anything like it.

I have spoken with many long-time parliamentarians who have known a similar feeling. Others were spared. The House of Commons affects different people in varying ways. Naturally, those who read their speeches in the House, or who speak "from very full notes", will not know what I am talking about. There is no nervousness in a manuscript; nor is there any debate! In recent years I have tried to be present when informed that a maiden speech is to be made; and I make it a point, if I hear a particularly fine first speech, to drop a note of congratulations to the Member, whatever his political party.

The Parliament of 1940-45 was particularly blessed with good parliamentarians. Dominating individuals, one might disagree with their views but they would have shown up well in the Parliament of any country. P. J. A. Cardin was a tremendous orator. He was, beyond question, one of the greats in the House of Commons. He invariably spoke in French, excepting in committee. As Minister of Public Works, he was ever a follower and practitioner of the art of ensuring that no contract was ever awarded to anyone beyond the Liberal pale. He broke with King on the conscription issue of May 1942. His speech on that occasion was one not to be forgotten. Jimmy Gardiner I have already mentioned as a seasoned parliamentarian. Ian Mackenzie, Minister of Pensions and National Health, spoke with all the imagery and fire of his Highland blood. He could exercise his mind to such a state of exultation that he could lift you out of your seat.

Mackenzie King was Prime Minister for my first eight years in the House. There are some who will tell you that he was not an able parliamentarian. I do not accede to that view. Although he had the reputation of not paying sufficient attention to Parliament, he certainly far exceeded anything occurring under his Liberal successors as Prime Minister. He had a basic respect for Parliament. On occasion he exaggerated the extent of his devotion, but he was a Commons man none the less. He placed before Parliament what was proper and appropriate, and did not use the war and "national security" to avoid the House. Perhaps he was influenced by the fact that he saw his grandfather, William Lyon Mackenzie, as the great tribune of Canadian freedom, and himself as his grandfather's political heir.

King had an infinite capacity to express one view and within five minutes to express the reverse. In debate, if you quoted some statement of his which you believed to be irregular, he would always clear it up by saying: "Read on." He knew that sooner or later in the speech from which you were quoting he would have said the very converse. He also had a talent for a lachrymose performance when he believed this tactic to be his advantage. Or, he could wrap himself in the garments of righteousness, quote scripture, and condemn the Tories as apostles of darkness. Throughout the years, he did all he could to destroy his political opponents, sometimes not excluding those within his own party, while all the time clasping his hands in pretence that he would never do anything unfair or unjust. No more sublime actor have I ever known.

Prime Minister King did not like me. I presume it was because I took a particular interest in him. I lived and cast my ballot in Prince Albert. He was my Member of Parliament. Of course, King did not like anyone who was not fearful of his ability to devastate in debate. Perhaps more important, King never attacked anyone whom he feared in debate. When he got the worst of a crossfire in the House, he would pick on some backbencher and tear him asunder. I must admit, however, that generally he did not use his large majority to stifle the Opposition's right to play a useful role in the process of government. While I must be critical of the extent to which the King government legislated by Order-in-Council throughout the war, nevertheless when legislation was introduced, the Opposition was invited to make suggestions to improve that legislation. For example, in 1944, even C. D. Howe accepted my suggested amendments to two of the bills for which he was responsible, the War Assets Corporation Act and the Aeronautics Act.

Even in those dark days of war the House was a deliberative body. We did not have some of the stultifying rules we have now. Parliament had a reasonable check on the administrative functions of government through our detailed examination of expenditures. Unfortunately, Her Majesty's Loyal Opposition in recent years has not been jealous enough in guarding hard-won freedoms. If tens of millions of dollars were inserted by concealment of detail into this year's estimates with no basis in statute, it could pass. Today there is a virtual breakdown of the first responsibility of the House of Commons: to examine and control Supply. How are we to be protected from the excesses of our government if the House of Commons is emasculated? I have seen Parliament in all its greatness. I have inwardly wept when its greatness was degraded.

Early in the war, some Conservative and other Opposition Members were made aware of military and other secret developments in private briefings by the Prime Minister and other Members of Cabinet. Normally, the invitation was extended to the Leader of the Opposition, to be accompanied by one Privy Councillor and one Private Member. Howard Green was the Private Member generally chosen. Howard, a front-line soldier in the First World War, was an able, honest, and hard-working person and an exceptionally good debater who was entirely devoted to making his contribution to the defeat of the enemy. He always commanded the respect of the House. Mr. King liked him. In turn, Howard was most respectful to the Prime Minister, in contrast to his criticism of other Ministers. In June of 1940, a radio broadcast announced that Paris had fallen. The Honourable R. B. Hanson, Leader of the Opposition, and the Honourable Grote Stirling, who had been Minister of Defence in the latter days of the Bennett administration, were not able to secure Howard Green's presence that morning, and I was asked to accompany them. We went over to the little office behind the Commons Chamber. Few know of its existence.

It was put there so that the Prime Minister could get away by himself when the House was in session. Within the office was an even smaller room with a wall bunk. A very few minutes after our arrival, King came out wearing a kind of nightshirt. Dick Hanson, who had a distinctive style of speaking, said, "Prime Minister, is it true as reported on the facilities of the radio this morning that the great city of Paris has fallen to the Hun?" I found it strange that the man on whose shoulders rested the security of Canada should reply, "I really cannot say. I have not read my despatches this morning. I worked late on my diary." The despatches were brought in, and King confirmed the radio report. Then, for the first time, I had evidence of that fascination with, and even addiction to, the supernatural he exhibited from time to time, his ability to transmit messages to, and receive them from, those who have long since departed this world. He stepped towards the fireplace on the east wall of the office, his eyes fixed on the mantel clock. There was silence. I was standing beside him. He turned to me, "Diefenbaker, we can't lose. We shall win the war." It was twenty after ten.

The only other occasion on which I accompanied Hanson and Stirling to a briefing was on 24 May 1941. We went over to the Prime Minister's office in the East Block. There were several Ministers present. King was in a state of deep excitement. He spoke to Hanson and Stirling as they entered. Then I came in. He said, "What business have you to be here? You strike me to the heart every time you speak. In your last speech who did you mention? Did you say what I've done for this country? You spoke of Churchill. Churchill! Did he ever bleed for Canada?" And he carried on like that for some minutes, much to the discomfiture of his Ministers. Up to that moment, Hanson had been rather apologetic. I said, "What the hell goes on here?" Grote Stirling said nothing. There were tears in King's eyes. There was rage on his face. Suddenly, the storm blew over and he said with impressive calm, "I regret this, but something awful has happened. The great British battleship, the *Hood*, has been sunk. Where will we go from here?" It had been a very embarrassing time, and with that, the three of us left. This was not, however, to be the end of it. The story got out. I personally think that it came from the Honourable Ian Mackenzie, who considered King's performance disgraceful and said so. One evening not long after, Mackenzie King was speaking in the House. I had retired early to my room in the Château Laurier. The Conservative Party Whip, A. C. Casselman, telephoned me from the House: "You had better get back here. Mackenzie King is taking the hide off you." I dressed quickly and returned. When I came through the curtain into the Commons Chamber, King said, "Here he is." "Yes, he's here," I replied. I demanded he withdraw the suggestion that I had revealed what had taken place; I had not spoken to anyone about it. King withdrew, but only after he realized that I would reveal his inane conduct at the inter-party meeting. His outburst about Churchill, however, told something important about King's normally well hidden nature. Indeed, neither liked the other. Churchill disliked the political opportunism of King. King envied the popularity of Churchill.

On 30 December 1941, Churchill was in Ottawa. He made a deeply moving speech in the House of Commons that morning, and later had a private session with a few Members. When I was introduced to him I said, "Prime Minister, the first time I saw you you were in disgrace." He said, "Will you shay that again." I repeated it. His reply, "Which time was that?" What a tapestry of life he wove. I had always admired him. He was one of the truly great parliamentarians of all ages. I saw him in the House of Commons at Westminster in December 1916 when he was in disgrace following the Dardanelles campaign. It now appears that if his plans had been carried out, the war might have ended much sooner; but apparently the Admiralty and the War Office were in disagreement. They delayed, they postponed. The Turks built up impregnable defences. Churchill was out. He rose to speak. Members who a few short months before had licked his hands like lap dogs now jeered and sneered and left the House. His future, they felt, was behind him. I saw him subsequently in 1936 when he was striving to organize all the King's men to keep Edward VIII on the Throne. Again he was an outcast. Later, I saw him in the House, warning the people of Britain and the free world that Nazi Germany was determined on war. They laughed, they scorned, they ridiculed him as a warlord.

As one looks back, one cannot help wondering why Britain and France were so far removed from reality. In 1936, after being present at the unveiling of the Canadian Memorial at Vimy Ridge, I went to the Olympic Games in Berlin. I saw Hitler, Goering, Goebbels, and Dr. Funk. They were within thirty or forty feet of me. I saw at first hand the curse of militarism renewed in the German people. When I returned home to Prince Albert I made a speech expressing the certainty that war was coming. As Prime Minister of Britain, Churchill roused the legions of free men everywhere with an eloquence that I believe will live as long as freedom lives. He later told me that many of his seemingly spontaneous statements, now part of history, were long in gestation waiting for the event and the opportunity. "Blood, sweat, and tears", first used by Wellington, and later by Garibaldi, needed only the Churchillian touch to make it permanent in both British Empire and Commonwealth history—indeed among all peoples who love freedom.

The afternoon of 30 December 1941, after Karsh had taken his portrait, he came out of the office of the Speaker of the House and started up the hall with Mackenzie King beside and behind him, trying to keep up. Churchill was making his victory sign in response to greetings and good wishes. One of King's more sycophantic backbenchers said to me, "Isn't that wonderful. There is Mr. King making that sign that Churchill has made his. They are together." I replied. "The V has different meanings. For Churchill it means Victory; for King it means Votes."

To illustrate another aspect of Mackenzie King's most complex character, James Sinclair, later Minister of Fisheries in the St. Laurent government, and father-in-law of the present Prime Minister, came into the House in 1940. He was to move the Address in Reply to the Speech from the Throne. Hugues Lapointe, who was the great pride of his father, the Right Honourable Ernest Lapointe, King's right hand in Quebec, seconded the motion. Jimmy made a brilliant speech. King listened with intense interest. Jimmy had his desk on the Opposition side of the House because of the Liberal overflow (184 Members). His closing words were to the effect that if the government continued its uncertain course, the war could be lost. King turned his back on him, and never had anything to do with him from then on. Jimmy and the Liberal Member for Nanaimo, Cowichan, and the Islands, Alan Chambers, were not what one might term intimate friends, and King knew it. Jimmy went overseas with the RCAF, and on his return many months later I met him one morning in the foyer of the House; he was still in uniform. I was glad to see him back. He was a tough debater, but a bonny fighter and a good parliamentarian. One or two other Members came along and stopped to chat. Down the corridor comes King, shuffling along. Jimmy's back is to him.

"Good morning, Diefenbaker." "Good morning, Prime Minister." King turns to see who I am talking to. "Oh, glad to see you back, Chambers." That's how devastatingly fast King's mind worked.

For the CCF, there was J. S. Woodsworth, with all the appearance of a prophet, a leader of men who was a follower of conscience. The respect he enjoyed in Parliament was apparent. When at the outbreak of the war in September 1939 he made a strong speech against Canadian military participation, the House, mainly of the opposite view, applauded him when he sat down. M. J. Coldwell and Tommy Douglas, both able parliamentarians, added eloquent lustre to the institution and have brought honour to Saskatchewan and to Canada. I thought Clarrie Gillis, from Cape Breton South, their most effective Member in the rough and tumble of debate. He had been seriously wounded in the First World War. Unlike some of his Party colleagues, he was dedicated to doing everything he could to assist the war effort. It appeared to me that the CCF found itself corralled by its declaration, during the short session in September 1939, that Canada should limit her contribution to the defeat of Nazism to economic support for Great Britain. Ultimately, they had to back away from it, but they were never able to entirely dissociate themselves from a neutralist mentality; and they continued over the years to experience difficulty because of this. With few exceptions the CCF Members largely restricted themselves to questions of social reform, and their effect, generally, was to spur the older national parties to action on the subject of social security.

Finally, there was Social Credit. Under the Honourable W. D. Herridge's New Democracy banner, they had elected ten Members in 1940, although they soon reverted to their original name. (The CCF, which elected eight in

1940, gradually increased its representation in by-elections.) The Socred Leader, John Blackmore, from Lethbridge, had the second-loudest voice in the House. Joe Harris from Toronto Danforth had the loudest, but Blackmore's was the more penetrating. Regardless of the subject of debate, John always took it upon himself to outline somewhere in his speech the meaning of Social Credit. Certainly, the last thing in the world one ever dared do in private was to ask John about monetary theory. I speak from experience; he would begin an hour-long verbal barrage from which there was no escape. One day, out of devilment, I said to John, "The trouble with you is that you always deal in generalities. You never give the House enough detail about Social Credit." "Well," he said, "I'll fix that." He did. Week after week, everyone was out of the Commons as soon as John started in.

In referring to the Opposition, I might point out that the present designation of "Official Opposition" is a fiction, and in my view has no constitutional basis. When I hear references made in the House to the Leader of the Official Opposition, I begin to wonder whether those who use this term have studied the meaning of "Her Majesty's Loyal Opposition", or the circumstances under which that term emerged. Also, although I sometimes err in this direction myself, Members opposite you are never "my honourable friends". "Honourable friend" refers to a Member within one's own Party. "The honourable gentleman" or "the honourable lady" is the proper appellation for those opposite. It is a distinction worth maintaining since it describes the relationship that in fact exists in the House of Commons; and it ought not to be confused with personal friendship. As I mentioned earlier, some of my closest and most intimate friends have been amongst my most critical political opponents. And, in over thirty-five years, only one Member has ever broken a confidence with me. The House of Commons is a place that I revere. It is too great an institution to permit bitter personal antagonisms. Unless a Member's personal integrity is attacked, it is feckless to take offence at what is said in debate.

The Honourable R. B. Hanson was, I think, the best rough-and-tumble debater I have ever heard in the House. He had been Minister of Trade and Commerce in the Bennett government, following the resignation of the Honourable Harry Stevens in 1934. Member for York-Sunbury in New Brunswick, he was Conservative House Leader and Leader of the Opposition from 1940 until early 1943. But there were very definite limits to Hanson's effectiveness. Whenever he made any particularly strong attack on government policy, King, pointing his finger, would say, "I've had enough," and immediately Dick would be silenced. Why this was so, I cannot say. But the Prime Minister could be cruel (and often was) to those too weak or unable to defend themselves. It has been my experience, however, that the quality the House admires above everything is courage. No matter how you may disagree with a viewpoint expressed, when there is sincerity marked by courage, the House will never treat a Member with contempt. I don't know why some Members never understand this. Sometimes they speak the words well, but if a Member has no backbone, he might just as well be yelling down a rain barrel.

On the day when Richard Burpee Hanson was welcomed in the House as Leader of the Opposition, King praised him. Coldwell praised him. Blackmore praised him. The saccharine matter poured out. Now, Dick Hanson had a tremendous paunch. When he stood up, it served as a guide as to how long he was going to speak. If he just put his hands around his tummy, he was up for ten or fifteen minutes. But if he laid his stomach on his desk, you knew the House was in for a long speech. On the day in question, Hanson was just preparing to lay it on his desk to reply to his well-wishers when up jumped Jean François Pouliot, the Liberal Member for Témiscouata. Pouliot was the parliamentary wit of his day, and the best that I have ever known. He could be nasty and irresponsible, but he had about him a way of expression and a manner of delivery that captivated the House. We knew when he got up that the impossible was about to be said. And Hanson he did not like. "There he sits, Leader of the Opposition. All he has is the initial [an allusion to R. B. Bennett]. Richard Burpee, R.B., he's got the initials. That's all. Nothing else. Mr. Speaker, the words of the poet come back, 'But O for the touch of a vanish'd hand, and the sound of a voice that is still!' R.B. Every time I look at the honourable gentleman, I think to myself of Ferdinand the bull with a flower in the mouth." Hanson was livid. It was obvious that the Speaker was going to ask Pouliot to withdraw. And Pouliot, without delay, said, "Mr. Speaker, I withdraw the bull, nothing else."

An example of King's control over Hanson was shown in the debate on the Hong Kong Inquiry in July 1942. Chief Justice Duff's Report was a whitewash of the government's action in sending untrained Canadian soldiers to Hong Kong, when everyone knew it would be overrun by the Japanese. The debate began on 27 July. I came into the House shortly before noon, the House having opened at eleven. Howard Green was speaking when I came in. I knew nothing of his amendment, which he had stated I would second, when I took my seat. Unlike Wellington during Quatre Bras—"Give me night or give me Blücher"—Howard almost immediately dropped into his seat. I was forced to start in not knowing what the motion was, although I realized that it had to do with Hong Kong. I had before me a series of lectures entitled "The Battle of Brains" which, since June 1941, had been given to officers and men of the Canadian Expeditionary Force to teach them the meaning of democracy. Lecture IX, "Our Precious Freedom", set out in some detail the various steps in man's climb to the heights of freedom. I began to read to them from this book: number one, Leonidas and the Spartans at Thermopylae; two, the Barons at Runnymede. King was particularly fond of the Barons at Runnymede, and often likened his fight against what he described as "malignant Toryism" to the nobles in their stand against King John. I had often twitted the Prime Minister about his sense of historical analogy. Number three was Bishop Latimer and the religious martyrs at Smithfield Market. And what was number four in this book to instruct servicemen on what they were fighting for? It was the grandfather of the Prime Minister, William Lyon Mackenzie. It was obvious to all that I found it passing strange that he should have been included along with the greats. Imagine, William Lyon Mackenzie! Well, King lost his customary sense of proportion. I have never seen him more annoyed, and his voice rose to a level that I imagine has only been equalled in the days when the buffalo roamed the Western plains. I cannot exaggerate what took place. You have only to read, not Hansard, but the newspaper reports the following day. The Speaker informed me that my time was up. I suggested that I had not even started, that most of the time had been taken up by others on points of order and interruptions. The Speaker said I could continue, providing I had unanimous consent. King indicated to the Speaker by a wave of his hand that he was in favour of my being permitted an extension. However, a group of private Members sitting to his right, comprising what was called "Little Chicago", did not get the message. These were French-Canadian Members who were regarded as the protectors of everything the government did. The Speaker asked whether I had unanimous consent. "Little Chicago" yelled "No, no, no." King silenced them in an abrupt way. He then directed the Speaker to try once more. Unanimous consent was obtained. That is where the trouble really began. I said I didn't see any reason for all this contention, and went on to tell the story that I recounted in Chapter One about my grandfather chasing William Lyon Mackenzie across the United States border. Well, if anyone thought that there had been a noisy, uncontrolled, raucous House before, it was silence beside what happened afterwards. King was completely out of control; he screamed and referred to the Conservative Members as a "mob", a term he later had to withdraw.

When the House adjourned for lunch, King told Hanson that he wanted the entire incident expunged from Hansard. Hanson agreed. The next day when Hansard came out every portion that might have been embarrassing to the Prime Minister was out. I wish that I had had a better understanding then of my rights. The debates recorded in the House of Commons are not to be changed in any substantive way before their publication in Hansard. Every Member has the right to review what he has said and to make grammatical alterations, but not to change the sense of what was recorded or excise any portion thereof.

To continue for a moment on the subject of Hansard, changes sometimes do happen, with humorous results. In February 1942 there was a by-election in York South, when the Right Honourable Arthur Meighen, who had again become Leader of the Conservative Party, resigned from the Senate to seek a seat in the Commons. Mr. King announced that there would be no Liberal opposition to Mr. Meighen, but in the House of Commons it was clear that Mr. King's publicly expressed view would not deny dedicated Liberals the responsibility of defeating Meighen by any means, not excluding voting for the CCF. Liberal backbenchers came to the House with speeches

26. Mr. and Mrs. Diefenbaker chat with a delegate at the Conservative
Leadership Convention, October 1948.

27, 28 & 29. *(Right)* John Bracken and George Drew. *(Below)* The candidates and their wives exchange greetings. *(Far right)* Addressing the delegates

30 & 31. *(Above)* Two seasoned campaigners meet at the Opening of Parliament in January 1949. Mackenzie King had been succeeded as Prime Minister in November 1948 by Louis St. Laurent, and this was his last session as a Member of the House of Commons. *(Below)* Frequently honoured by the native peoples of Canada, Mr. Diefenbaker was made "Chief Eagle" at Duck Lake Saskatchewan in August 1953.

32 & 33. *(Above)* John Diefenbaker and the former Olive Freeman Palmer were married in Toronto in December 1953. At a reception in their honour in Saskatoon, the couple chat with the groom's aunt, Mrs. Sadie Bridgeman. *(Below)* The candidates for the leadership of the Progressive Conservative Party, December 1956: Davie Fulton, Donald Fleming, and John Diefenbaker.

34 & 35. *(Above)* Supporters of the three candidates march around the convention hall before settling down to hear the nomination speeches. *(Below)* Acknowledging the cheers of supporters before making his speech accepting the nomination.

36 & 37. *(Above)* Mr. Fleming and Mr. Fulton congratulate the newly elected Leader, 14 December 1956. *(Below)* Mr. and Mrs. Diefenbaker receive an enthusiastic ovation from the delegates after his victory on the first ballot.

38. A few days after his selection as Leader, John G. Diefenbaker returned to Saskatoon where he visited with his mother, who is obviously very proud of her distinguished son.

extramurally prepared, portraying Meighen as an ogre and a dangerous person. These they read with great gusto. One day, the Member for Northumberland, W. A. Fraser, was reading one of these diatribes. The Postmaster General was the Honourable William Pate Mulock, whose grandfather, Sir William Mulock, had done so much for Mr. King. It was he who had taken King on as Deputy Minister of Labour. If you really wanted to please Pate, you asked a question; it gave him such obvious joy that we never denied him the happiness that came to him on finding his name in Hansard. On read Fraser about the awfulness of Tory tyranny, of those powerful interests who, from the days of the Family Compact, had trampled on those who stood for right and justice. Then he came to the punch line of his speech. "No longer will the Canadian people allow themselves to be dominated by the *Mulocks* of finance." In his manuscript, it was the *Molochs* of finance. He apparently had never heard of them. In his pronunciation, it was the *Mulocks* of finance. When Hansard came out the next day, it was the *Murdocks* of finance.

Tommy Church, Conservative Member for Broadview in Toronto, was dependent on a helpful Hansard staff to rewrite every speech he made in the House. Tommy was a lovable character. He had been Mayor of Toronto, an office to which he was re-elected more times than anyone before him. As Mayor during the First World War, he met every troop train, coming or going. He was held in affection by the people without regard to political persuasion. But Tommy couldn't make a speech. No one, including the Hansard reporters, could understand what he was saying when he spoke. The best speech he ever made was when Bob McGregor, the Member from East York, who was quite a practical joker, took Tommy's notes, those uneven, torn bits of paper that he piled one on top of the other on his desk, and shuffled them while Tommy was out in the lobby. It was the only speech in which Church ever showed any signs of unified thought. In Hansard, his speeches read unnaturally well. But they do reflect his sentiments, which were always well defined. He loved the British Empire. He had no use for the suggestion that Canada have its own armed forces, particularly its own navy. Sir Adam Beck, the father of Ontario Hydro, was his deity. Those three subjects became intertwined in almost every speech he made.

I will always remember him at the Leadership Convention in Winnipeg in 1927. It was held in a rink. The delegates were on the floor, the visitors in the seats surrounding. It was the first time that I had seen loudspeakers. The sound was amplified through horns in the corners of the rink at the point of intersection between wall and roof. The subject under discussion was agriculture. Tommy got up. "I'm against that. There's been too much done," he said. "We must not have this navy forced on us. The *Rainbow* and the *Niobe*—where are these ships? One is in a garage in Halifax, another's in a garage in Esquimalt." The English-speaking chairman said, "You're out of order. We're not dealing with that." Tommy said, "I'm against that too." (Tommy's hearing was not good, I need hardly add.) "I just want to tell you that the time has come when action should be taken to determine this question once and for all, a tariff that protects, not a tariff that does not protect." The chairman said, "We're not dealing with that." Tommy ploughed right ahead, "I'm against that too." With that, Senator Beaubien, the French-speaking chairman, who had a great stentorian voice, stood up. He said, "You're out of ordaire. Sit down." His voice simply echoed from the horns up in the galleries. Tommy turned, stared at the gallery, and said, "Shut your damn mouth. You're not even a delegate here."

I do not think proper credit has ever been paid to the

Hansard staff and to those connected with the House of Commons in other capacities. I have had more courtesies extended by them than I can ever adequately repay. From the very beginning, there were those in the Library who took an interest in me; when books came in that I might like to read, these came to my desk. That has continued through all the years. When Olive has been ill, often the first messages received have been from the members of the Security staff. I can never say how much all this has meant to me.

When I first entered the House, our more experienced Members were helpful to me. Joe Harris, from Toronto Danforth, had been in the House since 1921. He regularly gave me the benefit of his views. "Don't endeavour to put too much into one speech," or, "When you've been in Parliament a while you'll find that every speech prepared can be used ten years later without many changes!" His basic principle was, "Be sure of your facts." It was advice that coincided with my experience at the bar. The pages of Hansard show most clearly what happens to those who are not careful with their facts. It is a simple truism that you do not have to be concerned about what you have said if it is true. One thing that I am particularly proud of is that in all the years I have been in the House of Commons, I have never been checked by the Members opposite, or in my own Party, as to the truth of a statement that I have made. That does not mean that the House will agree with the conclusions to be drawn from a given set of facts. Differences of opinion on events as they occur, or of matters as they take place, are essential to the House of Commons and are basic to its needs. For out of the crucible of discussion should result the best in legislation.

Another who helped me was my one Conservative colleague from Saskatchewan, Ernest Perley, who was first elected in 1930. Perley spent hours with me giving me sound counsel. And then there was Billy Esling. Billy was the oldest man in the House of Commons—in his late seventies. He was almost blind. Most mornings, he would stop by my office to discuss that day's editorial comments (he paid someone to read the Toronto and Montreal newspapers to him each morning). He represented British Columbia's Kootenay West. A very kind, dearly beloved person, he loved all mankind, except Doukhobors of the radical Sons of Freedom sect, who every now and then resorted to bombings, burnings, and nude parades. The Sons of Freedom represented but a small minority of the Doukhobor population. The orthodox Doukhobors from the earliest days have been law-abiding, worthy citizens, excellent farmers, and often no less averse to the antics of their more fanatical brethren than most other Canadians. Enforcement of the law against the Sons of Freedom seemed only to increase their efforts to break it. I had seen a few of them on the march during our homestead days. Many years later, a number of Sons of Freedom women in my audience took off their clothes at an election meeting in Trail. That was a scene to be remembered by many who were there.

It was before my election to the House that Billy had inspired one of the very few witty exchanges in the Commons involving Mackenzie King, one that Hansard does not adequately record. Bennett was Leader of the Opposition. Billy was concerned and shocked over the way in which the Sons of Freedom were carrying on. As Billy spoke this day, he heard that not unfamiliar snicker of Mr. King. Billy could identify the voice of every Member who regularly spoke in debate. He said, "The Prime Minister laughs. I ask him a question. What would he do some morning out at Kingsmere if he were to arise, go out and find on his verandah a half a dozen Doukhobor women totally devoid of all clothing. What would he do?" Mackenzie King asked something to this effect: "Is that a question or a rhetorical one?" "It's a question. I want an answer." King said, "I would immediately call in the Right Honourable Leader of the Opposition." Bennett rose to reply. "As usual, the Prime Minister exaggerates. Dispensing patronage outside of his own party has never been characteristic of him at any time."

Parliament without wit would be a tiresome institution. What I mean by wit is not buffoonery, but the ability to laugh at oneself, to laugh when the proceedings of the House become boring or hard to bear. And wit springs up under unusual circumstances. Early in the 1940 session, wheat was debated and debated. It went on and on. Some of us were acquiring a new understanding of eternity. Ian Mackenzie was the Liberal House Leader. He sent me a note which read:

> To the mating bird, the dearest word
>   is tweet, tweet, tweet;
> To the orphan lamb, the saddest word
>   is bleat, bleat, bleat;
> To the maid in love, the dearest word
>   is sweet, sweet, sweet;
> But the blank-damndest word I yet have heard
>   is wheat, wheat, wheat.

Ian and I became close friends. Born in Sutherland, a few miles from where my great-grandparents had lived, he was the son of a poor tenant farmer. A brilliant student, he became an outstanding scholar of Gaelic languages at Edinburgh University. In 1948, when he learned I was going to be a candidate for the Conservative leadership against Drew, he worked for several days on a draft of the kind of convention speech he thought I ought to deliver. I did not use it, but that was the kind of relationship we had.

The House used to sit on Friday evenings. It was time

for fun, and matters were brought up that were not regarded as controversial. The only M.P.s regularly present
were the Maritime and Western Members. While I refused, when I was Prime Minister, to permit the opening
of bar facilities, or indeed the serving of liquor, in the
Parliamentary Restaurant, I must say there were often ex-
ercises in oratory on those Friday evenings not otherwise
heard in the House, and much of it resulting from a judi-
cious admixture of intoxicating liquors. On one such evening, our job was to hold up the Public Works estimates
of the Honourable Alphonse Fournier, who had replaced
Cardin as Minister. Fournier was the Member from Hull.
Opposition Members criticized several items, relevant
and irrelevant. I contended that there had been altogether
too much political consideration in awarding contracts,
and that certain changes should be made. Mr. King came
in, sat down, and chatted with the Minister while I was
speaking. Shortly thereafter, Fournier announced that he
had listened to the arguments advanced by the Opposition, and said, "I am impressed by them, and I intend to
look into the questions raised with favour." This was met
by some jeering. Fournier said, "There's no need to jeer.
It is from my heart; I have that intention in my heart."
And with that the Member from Calgary South, Art
Smith, Sr., observed, "The road to Hull is paved . . ." On
yet another Friday, Ian Mackenzie wrote the following
epigram during one of Fournier's speeches: " 'Twixt hill,
Hull, and hell, the difference is only one letter. If he were
in hell or Hull this bill would be better." Spontaneous,
witty, and unwounding. The House was tremendously
alive. The Honourable James Ilsley, King's Minister of Finance, never could understand these frivolities. An able
Member, he was without a vestige of humour.

On the other hand, the Honourable James Layton Ralston understood and enjoyed the atmosphere of the
House. He was a forward-looking, determined gentleman,

but tough in debate. He had a magnificent record in the First World War. As Canada's Minister of National Defence from 5 July 1940 to 1 November 1944, he did everything possible to make full our contribution to the war. I used to see him regularly on Sunday mornings at the Ottawa First Baptist Church. At times after the singing of a hymn when everyone else in the congregation had sat down, he would still be standing; lost in meditation, he might stand there for fully a minute before he realized where he was. I had a great regard for him, and it has not diminished with the years.

I talked to Ralston within two hours after he was fired by Mr. King on 1 November 1944. He told me the story. On an inspection tour overseas, he had found that our battalions, because of heavy losses, were depleted and without needed reinforcements. He concluded that those who had been conscripted for home service in Canada must be sent to fill the gap. What he advocated meant his immediate destruction by King. Overseas conscription was to King a political, not a military, consideration, and he feared its consequences for the Liberal Party in Quebec. Ralston told me that in Cabinet that afternoon King had said, "You are no longer Minister of National Defence; I accepted your resignation this morning." "But I didn't resign." "Oh, yes, you did. You submitted a letter of resignation on 7 July 1942 and I've just got around to it." The irony was that within a month King had to reverse himself and bring in conscription anyway.

I, of course, supported Ralston in the House. What I had been demanding in debate since 1942 had been a One Canada policy on conscription, with equal rights and equal shares of service for all. I rejected flatly the concept that Confederation could be based on the right of a minority to dictate to a majority; there could not be one law for eight provinces and a different law for Quebec. Even for home service, the draft was inequitably distributed.

216 / Diefenbaker: One Canada

Statistics were juggled to account for what I described as "a lost legion of men". Political expediency, not national security, dictated the government's course on everything.

General A. G. L. McNaughton replaced Ralston as Defence Minister, a position he held until 20 August 1945, without becoming a Member of Parliament. McNaughton, born in Moosomin, Saskatchewan, in 1887, came from a Conservative family. Deeply annoyed at being shoved out of his Command of the Canadian Army in Europe because of Montgomery's antipathy toward him, he first considered running as a Conservative. Then he heard King's call. King, in the finest biblical fashion, must have said to him, "Follow me." McNaughton was installed as Minister. He then sought election in Grey North. I took part in that by-election campaign.

The by-election was set for 5 February 1945. The Conservative candidate was Garfield Case, Mayor of Owen Sound. Mr. Bracken was insistent that I speak for Case. I agreed. In those days, flying overnight from Saskatoon was a hard, hard trip. When I got to Toronto, there was a big snowstorm. Despite this, we started out by car for Owen Sound. We finally got stuck near Arthur. After many hours, we arrived in Owen Sound. I had never met Garfield Case before. Immediately on my arrival, he undertook to drive me to Thornbury, some fifteen or twenty miles distant, where I was to speak that evening. During the drive, I said to him, "You've become quite a figure in this campaign." His wife interjected, "I've been telling Gar that he's a national figure." Case turned to look at her: "I'm an international figure," and with that the car swerved into a snowdrift. In getting the car out of the bank I disappeared through a crust of snow into a six-foot ditch. Fortunately, my hat served as a guide to Case in finding me and helping me out. Back in the car, he picked up the conversation where it had left off: "Let me make this clear. You don't seem to realize that yesterday I was on the front page of the London *Times*." I said, "I don't think advertising over there would pay." I had to explain what I meant. He said, "Well, by gosh, I'm glad you told me because I was going to use that tonight."

That evening in Thornbury, Case gave one of the most unusual and effective speeches that I have ever heard on a political platform. I was to speak; Gar was only to introduce me. His introduction went on for about an hour and a half. When my turn came, I said a few words and concluded, "At this late hour I should really limit my address to Prince Albert, Saskatchewan." Gar had already said it all. His message was to this effect: "What is McNaughton doing here? Why isn't he abroad with the Army? These are the questions your old friend, Gar, has been asking himself. Why did he come back to Canada? And where is that dagger, the one in General McNaughton's hand on Victory Loan Bond No. 1, the dagger at the heart of Berlin? I've asked myself that question over and over again. Some say that dagger was left in Italy. Others say McNaughton lost the dagger on his return trip home. But ladies and gentlemen, do you know where you'll find that dagger? In my considered opinion, it is lodged between James Layton Ralston's shoulder blades!" A tremendous speech. He beat McNaughton by 1,236 votes.

I had had my day with McNaughton when, as Minister of National Defence, he was granted permission to sit on the floor of the House on 23 November 1944 to explain his position on conscription. My questioning was anything but pleasing to him. In the general election of 1945, McNaughton ran in Qu'Appelle. Ernest Perley lost his seat, but not to McNaughton. The riding was taken by the CCF. McNaughton was in good company, though. Mr. King lost Prince Albert to the CCF's E. L. Bowerman in the same election, defeated by the soldier vote.

CHAPTER TWELVE

IN MY FIRST SPEECH in the House of Commons, I supported the Defence of Canada Regulations, the internment of enemy aliens, and a stronger course of action
against Nazi subversion, especially in Saskatchewan.
However, I condemned those government practices that
divided us as a nation. Certainly, I have never advocated
that we depart from the principles of Confederation, nor
have I ever suggested any alteration in the guarantees of
language provided in Section 133 of the British North
America Act. Quite the contrary. But I have always considered the official policy of separating our country into
various racial groups to be a curse on the realization of a
united Canada. One Canada, one nation, my Canada,
your Canada, cannot be a hyphenated Canada. In my
maiden speech, I spoke of all those who were proud to
wear "Canada" on the shoulders of their uniforms in the
First World War, and of the sense of nationhood, the concept of citizenship that developed. What distressed me
was the shallowness of official vision that forced these
Canadian men and women on their return from service to
register by their paternal racial origin in the federal census in 1921 and in successive censuses. (Under Section 8
of the B.N.A. Act, provision is made for a federal census
every ten years.) In 1940, we were again at war. Canadi-

ans of all racial origins had once more trooped to the colours. Their sense of nationhood was intense. I did not want this invidious practice of forcing them into national sub-categories carried into the 1941 federal census. The government was unmoved by my plea.

This was the darkest period of the war. From the fall of France in 1940 until the German invasion of Russia and the Japanese attack on Pearl Harbor in 1941, Britain, Canada, and the other members of the Commonwealth stood alone against Hitler and his Axis partners. Some five hundred thousand of Canada's eleven and one-half million people were of German descent. Another one hundred thousand were of Italian parentage, and twenty-three thousand were of Japanese origin. Where was the provision in the Criminal Code or elsewhere that a Canadian citizen whose racial antecedents were German was a less worthy citizen than any other Canadian? How could this Canada of many racial origins survive and prosper if we could not conceive a common nationality; if a John Stoneburner, the direct descendant of United Empire Loyalists, had still in 1941, or in 1971, to classify himself as a German-Canadian? I have never registered as requested in any census. I am a Canadian, and I register as a Canadian. When I was Prime Minister, I made certain that the 1961 census contained the question "Are you a Canadian?" Although the change was disapproved by the Liberal and bureaucratic establishments, and in consequence discontinued after I left office, hundreds of thousands of Canadians answered this question, "Yes," and with ringing pride.

In time of war, civil liberties must be placed in pawn, held as security for victory. In Canada, the War Measures Act of 1914, reinvoked in 1939, gave the federal government authority to make such orders and regulations as it deemed "necessary or advisable" for the safety of Canada and the prosecution of the war. The Cabinet could rule by Order-in-Council, and legislative authority could be re-delegated to those in administrative positions. In theory, and too often in practice, the individual Canadian stood at the mercy of his government and its servants. In these circumstances, Parliament was the court of last resort for the protection of fundamental freedoms.

I was privileged during the Second World War to sit on the Commons Committee on the Defence of Canada Regulations. It was one of the finest committees I have ever served on. Of the seven or eight others who sat with me, all save the CCF's M. J. Coldwell were lawyers, and outstanding lawyers. Our task was to make certain that those interned were detained because there was evidence to suggest that they were in fact a threat to the security of the state, and not because the regulations had been too rigidly or improperly applied. So broad and comprehensive were these security regulations that the most loyal could unwittingly contravene them. So overheated were popular emotions that the most outrageous slanders might be believed by those in authority. Mistakes were made, and the person interned deserved the right to demand, "Now, why am I here?" I recall the case of a contractor of Italian origin who had been unmercifully slandered by business enemies; they had had a field day at his expense. When we examined his case, we found not one scintilla of evidence, other than hearsay, against him. Finally, to secure his release, I threatened to bring the matter before the Commons. I am reminded of another instance where a loyal Canadian of Italian origin was interned for some months on the basis of hearsay. While it would have been understandable had he harboured hatred and a desire to revenge the wrong done him, he accepted his lot in a spirit of forgiveness. Some twenty years later, he was elected as a Member of Parliament. In other cases, our Committee enjoyed a more immediate success in assuring that the rights of the individual were not forgotten, even in the midst of a world war. There were, however, some people we could not help at all.

The treatment of the Jehovah's Witnesses during the war can never be justified. They were a small group. The 1941 census listed their number at 7,007, although I suspect that they numbered more than this. In any event, their religion was banned under the Defence of Canada Regulations in July 1940. To be a Jehovah's Witness was an offence. I believe that the King government was not motivated simply because the Witnesses refused to serve in the war, or because their interpretation of the scriptures envisaged a kind of theocracy in which they were responsible only to God. To proscribe the Jehovah's Witnesses was worth votes among some people.

I took the stand that their religious views should be recognized, that the ban against them should be removed, and that they should not be required to serve in the armed forces in any combative capacity. Conscientious objection is not questioned today, but during the early days of the Second World War it was difficult to get the message across to those in authority, despite the fact that there was provision for it. I supported every man's right to take his stand on the basis of his conscience, on his personal concept of his relationship with his Creator. I was not prepared, however, to support the Jehovah's Witnesses' contention that their ministers were being denied the right provided ministers of all other religious faiths to exemption from compulsory military service. I asked for figures on the number of their ministers involved, suggesting that if one were to allow for a normal congregation of a hundred, this might give at least an approximate number of those who should be exempted. The Witnesses who had approached me on this question replied that they were all ministers. I considered that a completely unreasonable proposition.

If policies leading to a general discrimination on the

basis of racial origin were a bane to the development of a united Canada, if an official act of religious intolerance was worse, the English language does not have words to condemn adequately the treatment of the Canadian Japanese. On 26 February 1942, the King government by Order-in-Council decreed that all people of Japanese ancestry on the West Coast (the Fraser Valley, Vancouver, and Steveston) be uprooted from their homes and businesses. It did not matter whether they were Japanese nationals, naturalized Canadians, Canadian-born, First World War veterans, even heroes. They were driven out, ostracized; their means of livelihood were taken away, their properties taken over. Many of the Japanese lost everything they had built up through their years of citizenship, loyalty, and hard work. Even today there are Canadians of Japanese origin who are still suffering the effects of this action. This situation was made worse by the fact that the more rapacious of their Occidental fellow Canadians realized large profits from an unconscionable government action.

I did not question the proposition that, in war, security and survival are paramount. But to take a whole people and to condemn them as wrongdoers because of race was something I could not accept. The Conservative Party took its stand, not officially but in fact, in favour of the government's plan for immediate forced displacement and the eventual deportation of the Japanese, regardless of place of birth or loyalty. Feelings were running high and were not confined to any one party or to the members of any one party. The Independent Member from Comox-Alberni, A. W. Neill, an able parliamentarian, had been long warning not only Parliament but the people of his province and of the country as a whole that unless measures were taken to prevent the Japanese from acting so as to undermine Canada's security, there were dark days ahead. He played upon the general fear that Japan, instead of being our ally as in the First Great War, would be our enemy. Among the people of British Columbia there were increasing demands that action be taken to force the Japanese from the coastal areas, so as to guard against the possibility of their engagement in Fifth Column activities.

The situation was more or less similar to that prevailing in 1916 and 1917, when there was so much antagonism in our country against those of German birth and origin. There were those who, during the First World War and its immediate aftermath, demanded the forced removal of all Germans and Slavs from Canada, their deportation *en masse*. In British Columbia, however, there was, coupled with the almost irresistible force of racial hatred, a jealousy over the economic success of the Canadian Japanese. When war broke out with Japan in consequence of its dastardly and unprincipled attack on Pearl Harbor, there was a revulsion across the country against Japan and all things Japanese. Only those who lived at that time can fully appreciate the depth of this revulsion.

The course that was taken against Japanese Canadians was wrong. I said it over and over again. It was considered unbelievable that I would take this stand. Concern for the security of the state caused many otherwise reponsible people to translate fear into evidence, and to regard those who took the opposite view as disloyal. I was strongly criticized. I doubt whether there are very many today who would dare to stand up to defend what was done—and I am speaking of the most vociferous in favour of the action taken.

At the war's end, the King government was forced to admit that there had not been one case of sedition, proven or even established in part, concerning a person of Japanese extraction. This is not only an answer to one of the cruellest episodes in our history, but evidence of the fact that overheated popular feelings are a poor basis on which to determine the course of government.

Over and over again, I took my stand in the House of Commons, often alone, against any attenuation of the rights of the citizen by the state. Government, however, had found the easy way. Rule by Order-in-Council, rule through regulations against which the courts could provide no redress, the spending of money without parliamentary consent—these had become a way of life to the King government, and Parliament was demeaned in the process. The transparent excuse was that Orders-in-Council were needed because Parliament acted too slowly. During the war, we reached the point where Orders-in-Council were chasing one another; their number reached ninety thousand. In July 1942, on my motion, a Return was made to the House of Commons listing the Statutes which had been amended, abrogated, or suspended by the King government. The record, at that early point in the war, ran to three hundred and sixty pages. It was reported that the Governor General, the Earl of Athlone, said he would no longer sign them one by one. Consequently, he signed the top one of each pile placed before him; the ink was supposed to penetrate through the pile. This process continued under Prime Minister Louis St. Laurent. Parliament came to be regarded as hardly more than a decorous necessity to the operation of government. The House of Commons was to be tolerated. This became a basic viewpoint, part and parcel of the attitude of mind of certain higher civil servants in the Liberal tradition.

We were no sooner out of the war than we were into a new crisis to test the mettle of our freedom. In September 1945, Igor Gouzenko, a cypher clerk in the Soviet Embassy in Ottawa, defected. He carried with him evidence of extensive Soviet espionage activities in Canada. The last thing that Mr. King wanted to do was to get into any controversy with the USSR, but he was finally forced to act. I was greatly concerned over the Royal Commission set up to look into the Gouzenko charges; I took strong objection to the procedures followed. Every vestige of individual rights was swept aside. I am not speaking simply of the process of arbitrary arrest, but of the police state methods employed against those in custody. They were held incommunicado for days on end, denied the right to communicate with counsel, constantly interrogated, their sleeping quarters continuously under bright lights. What was done had no possible justification on the basis of security. Supposedly, our purpose in breaking the spy ring was to prevent the spread of Soviet totalitarianism, not to adopt its most vicious practices. Anything that an NKVD might have done, short of individual torture, was legalized by Order-in-Council under the provisions of the War Measures Act. Habeas corpus was swept aside. The incarcerated individual could not insist on being brought up before a court within a set period of time; he was simply the pawn of his captors. Many even in the Conservative Party felt this was something that should not be mentioned in debate. I dealt with it. I condemned the wrongdoers but, as I stated in the House in March 1946, "There is only one liberty, namely the liberty based on law and under law. So long as the War Measures Act is on the statute books there is no reason why governments, if they so choose, might not create emergencies real or apprehended, thereby permitting them to commit arbitrary acts under its powers." Unlike the situation in October 1970, the spy ring in 1945 and 1946 was a legitimate crisis. But in my view even this was not sufficient to justify the flagrant denial of basic and fundamental rights. Of course it was argued that those involved were a dangerous group. There is always a pretext when the rights of the citizen are trampled on; those who participate in the destruction of liberty invariably profess the highest of purposes.

I never could understand Louis St. Laurent, as Minister of Justice, countenancing what was done. A habeas corpus application calls upon the captor to show cause why the individual is being held. The government argued that habeas corpus had not been done away with. How palpably false was that argument; the Order-in-Council provided that each person taken into custody should be deemed to be lawfully held. It was a disgraceful performance. Canada became the only country in the British tradition where habeas corpus could be suspended other than by Parliament.

Among those who spoke against the government's methods in the Gouzenko investigation was Charles Gavin Power, Minister of National Defence for Air until he resigned from Mackenzie King's Cabinet over the conscription issue on 26 November 1944. "Chubby" Power had been a most effective Minister, one who approached the tasks of administration with a determination that belied the benign reputation that was his. It was alleged that he drank heavily, but it was argued that if some of the other Ministers had done the same, Canada's war effort would have benefited immensely. This was reminiscent of Abraham Lincoln's response to those who, knowing that Lincoln was a temperance man, argued that General Ulysses Grant drank to excess. Lincoln inquired what brand of liquor Grant consumed so that he might have it provided for his other less successful generals.

During the First World War, Chubby Power went overseas as a private. His father was the Liberal Member of Parliament for Quebec West. When the Minister of Militia, Sir Sam Hughes, heard that Chubby was a private, he immediately ordered that he be given a commission. Chubby rose rapidly to the rank of Captain and Acting Major, and won the Military Cross. Power was a French Canadian through and through, although his paternal origins were Irish. He told me that while on leave in England in April 1916 he thought that he would take the opportunity to visit Dublin. He arrived just in time for the Easter Rebellion. He took off his Canadian uniform and fought for the Republicans during the five days of revolt against British rule. He then returned to his unit. Invalided home, he was elected to the House of Commons for Quebec South in 1917, a seat he was to hold for thirty-eight years.

During the Second World War, there were some thirty-four M.P.S who had served in the First War: Ralston, Power, Ian Mackenzie, LaFlèche, Gillis, Turgeon, Howard Green, myself, and so on. We formed an informal old soldiers' club, meeting from time to time for lunch or dinner. There was a fine spirit of camaraderie that was apparent even in debate. Our concern was the veteran and his welfare. We wanted to make certain, so far as we could, that those serving in this war would get a better deal on their return than their predecessors in the First War. We were, of course, concerned equally that the First World War veterans also secure justice. When the office of Minister of Soldiers' Civil Re-establishment was created in May 1918, there was no basic experience to serve as a guide. We now had the experience of the Pension Act and the Pensions Board, the Land Settlement scheme and the Soldier Settlement Board, and other programs designed in 1918 and 1919 to absorb half a million returned men and women into the peace-time economy. We had as well the experience of Britain and the United States on which to draw. Over the years, I had been greatly disturbed by the strictness of some of the decisions of the Pensions Board. Many a veteran, anxious to get his discharge, anxious to do anything that would speed up his demobilization, had been willing to ignore or even to cover up a lingering physical injury. He signed statements to the effect that he had no disability. In consequence, he could not get a pension when he later needed help. What

I wanted was a more equitable pension scheme, including a scaling down of the differences in benefits among the ranks. I supported a government-sponsored national life insurance plan for our soldiers, and loans for veterans to go into business or return to school, a "first in, first out" demobilization plan, grants for war widows, and a better deal for RCMP officers returning from overseas service. I was pleased with the results, as they represented the fruits of co-operation between Members of all parties. When, in the summer of 1944, the Veterans' Charter was introduced by the three Service Ministers, Colonel Ralston, Chubby Power, and Angus L. Macdonald, tribute was paid to my contribution to this legislation.

Angus Macdonald came into the House bearing a high reputation. He had been Premier of Nova Scotia for almost seven years. He had built his political image on his Scottish name and his paternal Highland ancestry; indeed, he spoke the Gaelic. Curiously, when Britain's Ramsay MacDonald came to visit Nova Scotia, and he a Highlander from Lossiemouth, he could not understand why Gaelic had been so jealously preserved among the people of Nova Scotia, particularly those in Cape Breton. I found Angus L. an interesting man. When Norman Rogers, Minister of National Defence, and a man generally regarded as a future Prime Minister, was killed in an accident on 10 June 1940, Macdonald was elected in the by-election that followed in Rogers' Kingston, Ontario, seat. Macdonald became Minister of National Defence for Naval Services. He had difficulties, however, in getting used to the House of Commons. Like the vast majority of former provincial premiers who have sat in the Commons since the turn of the century, he could not overcome his provincial point of view. Among the exceptions to this have been Fielding, Dunning, and Gardiner. Macdonald simply could not adjust to his new situation. I remember his first speech in the House, given in that lilting manner

of his. A word eluded him and he paused to look heaven-
ward. Karl Homuth from Waterloo South interrupted to
comment that it was the first time he had ever known
words to be written on the ceiling. Nevertheless, I formed
a liking for Macdonald. He was truthful and unevasive in
answering questions. Macdonald returned to Nova Scotia
politics at the war's end, and was again Premier. By then
he had come to hate Mackenzie King with a passion exceeding even that of Ontario's Mitchell Hepburn.

The Honourable Milton Gregg was another of King's
Ministers from the Maritimes for whom I have always
had the warmest admiration. His service to his country in
war and peace has been distinguished. His appointment
to Mr. King's Cabinet, however, was the result of a curious confusion. Gregg came from a New Brunswick Tory
family. In the First World War, he won both the Victoria
Cross and the Military Cross. In 1934, the Right Honourable R. B. Bennett had him appointed Sergeant-at-Arms in
the House of Commons, a position he held until the outbreak of war. In the Second World War he rose to the
rank of Brigadier. From 1944 to 1947 he was President of
the University of New Brunswick. Here fate intervened.
Francis Bridges, the member of King's Cabinet from New
Brunswick, died in office on 10 August 1947. The question
arose as to who should be his successor. Bridges had a
brother whose Christian name was Gregory. Apparently
Ilsley, who at the time was Minister of Justice and the
senior member of Cabinet from the Maritimes, suggested
to Mr. King that "Greg" would be a worthy successor.
King didn't comment immediately, but when he returned
to his office, he telephoned Milton Gregg, not Gregory
Bridges, and much to Gregg's surprise offered him a Cabinet post. It was only after it was announced that Gregg
was to be appointed as the new Minister of Fisheries that
the mistake was realized. Errors of that nature could not
happen to anyone with a name like Diefenbaker! Never-

theless, Gregg did well as the Minister and was highly regarded by political friend and foe alike.

I am reminded of a book, *Out of the Mouths of Babes*, written by my friend Austin Cross. Most of the parliamentarians of the day were in it. As the consequence of a hunting experience we had enjoyed together, he referred to me as "the Buick Nimrod". He had very strong likes and dislikes, and his biases were reflected in his descriptions of the Members he mentioned in his book. I said to him one day after the book's publication, "Almost all the Members are very angry with you." He agreed, adding, "The angriest of all is Paul Martin." "That's odd," I replied, "I didn't see him mentioned." Cross said, "That's why." I suppose that Paul, always a fine parliamentarian, had reason to be upset, but Cross for some reason did not include him.

An organization that interested me long before I entered the House of Commons was the Empire (now the Commonwealth) Parliamentary Association. This was the creation of Sir Howard d'Egville, who served as its Secretary-General during both its Empire and its Commonwealth phases from 1911 until the 1950s. Until after the Second World War, conferences were limited to parliamentarians from Britain, Canada, Australia, New Zealand, and South Africa. Today, these meetings bring together repesentatives of all parts of the old Empire and the new Commonwealth. Delegates have a chance to secure so many diverse viewpoints. In consequence, one realizes something of the motivations of the new members from Asia and Africa, as well as those of the old members. In other words, one can realize something of the meaning of the Commonwealth, of the fact that while each nation may belong to a different race or colour or religion and may hold different ideas on problems peculiar to its own situation, in the warp and woof of discussion there is a golden thread of pride in the fact that all belong to a world-wide organization that is dedicated to freedom and, above all, to world peace.

On becoming a Member of Parliament, I argued strongly that it would be an important step forward if, at least occasionally, we could include in its meetings representatives of the United States Congress. I thought that we would greatly benefit from the exchange of ideas and the personal association that would result. After the United States' entry into the war in December 1941, I considered it urgent that we have the opportunity to meet together. In fact, I wrote to two or three leading members of the United States Senate and House of Representatives suggesting that nothing would establish the unity of the English-speaking world more than these gatherings of democratically elected representatives. In 1943 a breakthrough was achieved. An arrangement was approved whereby the United States Congress would send representatives to Ottawa to meet with members of the Empire Parliamentary Association. This was a remarkable gathering. Indeed, of all the conferences I have attended of a parliamentary nature, none developed the close personal relationships that were the consequence of that gathering. One United States Congressman, Dr. Charles A. Eaton, brother of Cyrus Eaton, the financier, was a former Canadian. (Incidentally, the Eatons were cousins of my wife Olive.) As a little boy I had once or twice attended his church, the Walmer Road Baptist Church in Toronto. Our formal discussions, of course, were mainly concerned with the war and the survival of freedom. I acted as joint chairman, along with Lionel Chevrier, afterwards a Minister in the King, St. Laurent, and Pearson governments. The speeches were of great distinction, and everyone agreed that without victory over Germany and Japan, there would be a recession to the Dark Ages. A plaque in Room 16 of the Parliament Buildings commemorates that historic gathering. This was the first of many such meetings between Commonwealth and United States parliamentarians. Three years later, in 1946, we met again, both in Washington and in Bermuda. The Bermuda meeting was not largely attended—I think twenty-five would be the outside figure—but among those who were there, three, within a very few years, were to become Prime Ministers within the Commonwealth: the Right Honourable Anthony Eden, the Right Honourable Keith Holyoake, and myself. Among the American representatives was Senator J. William Fulbright, a member of the Foreign Relations Committee of the Senate, the Committee of which he later became Chairman. Perhaps it was the small attendance at this meeting that favoured it, but I have always felt that our discussions there contributed, perhaps more than at any other of these joint meetings, to bringing about an understanding between the United States and the Commonwealth as a whole.

It can be said that Mr. King was largely responsible for Canada's foreign policies. He considered foreign policy to be his own prerogative, and he did not like to have our external relations discussed in Parliament. Those debates that did take place under his administration tended to be extremely general in context, and they were few and far between. Before the war, King refused to allow Britain to establish in Canada the foundation for the Commonwealth Air Training Scheme. He thought he had brought about peace when he visited Hitler in 1937. He came back and reported how disturbed Hitler was during their discussions. He said, "I looked him right in the eye when I told him, 'If you don't watch out, you'll have Canada against you in the event there is war.'" King came back convinced that all was well. From the outbreak of war until its end, he followed the course from time to time of making speeches on foreign affairs and the progress of the war. One could get more out of the Sunday *New York Times* than from a whole week in our Parliament.

I was a student of foreign affairs long before becoming a Member of Parliament, and I was particularly interested in the emerging United Nations Organization. It appeared to me that Canada, in consequence of her position as one of the most important Allies in the war, should and could have an equally important role in any new League of Nations that might emerge from the war. As early as 1943, I argued in the House of Commons that we should support and contribute to the establishment of an International Police Force. In the debate that preceded the San Francisco Conference, I was in favour of giving up some of our sovereignty to the proposed United Nations, in the cause of stemming the sources of war. I pointed out that if our commitment to the new United Nations were as limited as it had been to the League of Nations, the United Nations could not last. Central to my thinking was the role which the Commonwealth might play in this new world order. I judged an active Canadian role in a strengthened Commonwealth to be a prerequisite to any effective broader international association. When I considered our inability to solve the problems of Empire Defence in the 1920s and 1930s, however, I wondered how we could hope to secure universal collective security if we could not first secure it within our own family of nations.

It was with these thoughts in mind that I agreed to act as advisor to my friend Gordon Graydon, the Conservative member of Canada's delegation to the San Francisco Conference. For me, the Conference was an inspiring experience, one of the great experiences of my life. There in that hall in San Francisco were gathered the leaders of the free world, dedicated to the achievement of peace on earth, good will to all men. Even the USSR spoke in fulsome terms through Molotov, its foreign minister. That opening day will never be effaced from my memory. I sat in the centre of the hall, the third seat behind Field Marshal Jan Christian Smuts. He was the only person present in a representative capacity who had been present at and had contributed to the establishment of the League of Nations. Over the doorway of the hall in which the Assembly took place was this epitaph: "This edifice, eloquent of hopes realized and dreams come true." The building had been erected to honour the soldiers of the United States who had given their all in the First World War. And here we sat, twenty-seven years later, having failed to do what that epitaph envisaged, trying once more to bring about an international organization for peace. I saw the United Nations as man's last chance. I was enthusiastic over the results. I felt that for the first time in all history the various nations would provide forces to a strong international army which would serve under the aegis of the international organization to ensure that whenever and wherever aggression took place, it would be met and defeated. This dream has not been attained and I doubt whether it will be attained in generations to come. The reason was simply that the Great Powers were entirely opposed to doing that to which they gave their vocal support. Like most people, I suppose, I hoped against hope, while aware of the weaknesses in the United Nations Charter from the very beginning. As I said in the House when we debated the u.n. Charter:

The Charter provides the basis to end war, but it does not terminate the prerogative of any of the great Powers to wage war. It prevents aggression among small nations. In theory it allows powerful nations, who alone have the power and resources to make war, to go unpunished if any of them commit acts of aggression.

An amusing memory of the Conference was when one evening Gordon Graydon and I went down to a fine restaurant on the famous Fisherman's Wharf for dinner. The head waiter looked us up and down and inquired, "You boys just in from the country?" This served to remind us that not only did we both represent rural constituencies, but we had to return from the San Francisco Conference to fight the 1945 general election, which had been called for 11 June.

Louis St. Laurent, who was to become Secretary of State for External Affairs in 1946, had entered Mackenzie King's Cabinet soon after the death of the Right Honourable Ernest Lapointe on 26 November 1941. He was elected in Mr. Lapointe's old seat of Quebec East in a by-election in early 1942. Like Lapointe, St. Laurent was a firm believer in constitutional democracy, although I do not think that he ever fully understood Parliament. When speaking in Parliament, he spoke as a constitutional lawyer arguing an appeal case.

St. Laurent I had known through the years. A *grand seigneur* in appearance, I met him first in 1930 at the Canadian Bar Association Annual Meeting in Calgary when Mr. Bennett was elected President. It was a memorable occasion. The Prime Minister had arranged lavish entertainment for the delegates and guests, among whom were the British Lord Chancellor and the President of the American Bar Association. One event took place at the Pat Burns ranch. Pat had started as a cowboy in the 1880s and had built a successful meat-packing empire. He was a rough diamond, and Bennett was very fond of him, which explains why Pat, a Liberal, became a Senator when Bennett became Prime Minister. Pat Burns cut quite a sartorial figure dressed in morning clothes as he welcomed his guests from the Bar Association. He said, "This sure is a great occasion. Never did I ever think that ever it would be a time when I would welcome so many distinguished people coming from all over the university." He then proposed there be a milking contest before the barbecue. To see the Lord Chancellor of England, Lord Hailsham, and the President of the British Probate,

Divorce, and Admiralty Court, Sir Boyd Merriman, trying
to milk wild heifers with little or no success and much
personal embarrassment was something much beyond
description.

St. Laurent was one of the anointed of the Department
of Justice on constitutional cases. He acted as counsel for
the Dominion when the constitutionality of the Bennett
New Deal legislation was brought before the Judicial
Committee of the Privy Council. Mackenzie King, while
paying lip service to the Bennett reforms to keep the Liberal Party out of political trouble, was not prepared to seriously defend that legislation in the courts. St. Laurent's
arguments, in consequence, reflected the government's
point of view, and the Bennett reform program, unhap-
pily from the perspective of the welfare of the Canadian
people, was thrown out, declared *ultra vires* of the Dominion Parliament by the courts. Nevertheless, I was
much impressed by St. Laurent as a polished gentleman
and an able lawyer. It was our destiny to follow each
other in our public careers. When he was President of the
Bar Association, I became a member of the Association's
Council. Later on, I became Vice-President for my province, one of the nine vice-presidents. When St. Laurent
came into the House in 1941 as Minister of Justice, I became Opposition critic on Justice. Later, in 1946, when he
became Secretary of State for External Affairs, I became
Opposition critic. He was Prime Minister when I became
Leader of the Opposition. When I became Prime Minister, he became Leader of the Opposition.

We always had a pleasant relationship, and a number
of judicial appointments were not made because St. Laurent, when Minister of Justice, asked me what I thought
of them. There is always a certain amount of political
pressure surrounding appointments to the bench, the
Senate, boards, and commissions. But over the years, the
basic principle laid down by Sir John Macdonald has

been generally accepted: that no amount of political pressure should be sufficient inducement to appoint an incompetent or unworthy judge. However, the best of counsel are sometimes the worst of judges, in that they are apt to forget that they are on the bench and to too great an extent examine or even cross-examine as though they were counsel at the bar. But, again, often enough lawyers who were quite indifferent at the bar become outstanding judges. Most important is the attitude of the judge to the counsel before him. Good judges demand good counsel and treat them with respect. A poor bar means a poor bench. Thus, I have always been inclined to another of Sir John's rules: "First he must be a gentleman. Then, if he knows a little law, I will not hold it against him." That may sound frivolous, but it is not.

Every Prime Minister knows what it is to be importuned by those who desire appointment. For example, the craving of people to serve their country in the Senate knows no bounds. The only exception I encountered as Prime Minister was that of Fred Hadley, my long-time friend and political supporter in Prince Albert. I wanted Fred to be a Senator. He deserved it and he would have made a good Senator, but he refused. He said, "No one is ever going to say that I worked for you because I had any personal object in mind."

The Senate of Canada is one of the high institutions of patronage in this country. In my experience the only time the Senate seemed to catch something of the original concept of the Fathers of Confederation was between 1932 and 1942 when the Conservative Leader was Arthur Meighen and the Liberal Leader, Raoul Dandurand.

On the subject of those who aspire to government appointment, there was a certain Colonel who lived near Smiths Falls. He had served in the Indian Army and was most anxious to secure a position from Sir John Macdonald. He was always around the Prime Minister's outer office, badgering Sir John at every opportunity. He had been in the British Engineers, he was proud of his contribution, and at the least provocation he was prepared to set out in accumulated detail what he had done. He bothered Macdonald so frequently that finally Macdonald said, "Now look, don't come around here any more. If I never see you again, it'll be too soon." One afternoon about three weeks later Macdonald came out of his office with his friend Sir John Carling. There was the Colonel. The story is recounted in E. B. Biggar's *Anecdotal Life of Sir John Macdonald*: " 'God bless my soul, Col. Playfair, is that you!' exclaimed the prime minister, grasping him with both hands, 'How are you? I'm so glad to see you. By-the-bye, colonel,' he went on, after the greetings were over, 'we have just been discussing in council a military matter that we cannot decide. Now you, with your great military experience and your memories of Salamanca and Talavera will be able to solve the question.' The colonel drew himself up and looked grave. 'The question is,' said John A., 'how many pounds of powder put under a bull's tail would blow his horns off?' And John A., who had been edging towards his office, disappeared through the door and could be seen no more. 'And is this the result of all I have come for?' ruminated the disgusted and disheartened colonel as he drove his old mare home with the mail (for he held amongst other offices that of mail carrier from Perth to Playfair); and with muttered imprecations he sat down on arriving home to open the mail bag. The first letter he took out was an official one addressed to himself, and it contained the appointment he had despaired of. He had been the unconscious carrier of his own appointment."

I might add a story on the personal side of my relationship with the St. Laurents. This is a story that began in February 1953 when the incomparable Dr. Charlotte Whitton, Mayor of Ottawa, called me to ask whether I would accompany her to the National Press Club Ball. I was a widower; Charlotte was a long-time acquaintance, and I acceded, even though I am less than skilled in the terpsichorean art. I was in Prince Edward Island the day before the Ball and I wasn't sure that I would get back to Ottawa in time. Luck was not with me. I was in plenty of time. When I came into the Château Laurier where I was staying, the first person to meet me was one of the bell-boys. He smiled and remarked, "You're on the front page of the *Journal* this evening." I saw nothing that would disturb me too much in that. As I got up to my room the house detective came along and he said, "Ha, ha, you're on the front page." I didn't get the joke until the next morning when I turned up for breakfast at the Parliamentary Restaurant. All the girls who worked in the restaurant stood in line and sang Lohengrin's Wedding March. It was then that I saw a copy of the *Ottawa Journal*. I had phoned Charlotte from Prince Edward Island to tell her that I would be back to take her to the Ball. I asked, "What are you going to wear? I want to get you an orchid." She said, "If you get me an orchid, I'll provide the Cadillac." The headline in the *Journal* was something like this: "Orchid traded for Caddy." It set out in detail our entire conversation, with suitable embellishments. Charlotte denied having anything to do with the story. But the publicity that surrounded our supposed romance was frightening. Olive saw our picture in the Toronto *Globe and Mail*. Never was there anything to equal the unenthusiastic appearance that I portrayed in that photograph. In all, it was quite a night. During the course of the evening, Charlotte lost her heel. Jimmy Gardiner assisted her in putting it back. Had it been anyone other than Charlotte, my observation would have been, "From one heel to another." Shortly after the Ball, I went to the United Nations as an observer on the Canadian delegation. Madame St. Laurent got in touch with me to invite me to lunch. There were about six or seven there, members of the family and close friends. Afterwards, she asked me to stay behind for a moment. She said, "The reason I got in touch with you is to give you some warning. Don't ever marry Charlotte Whitton. You are too much alike to ever get along."

I need not pretend that I was not concerned when St. Laurent trounced Gardiner at the National Liberal Leadership Convention in August 1948. But while I had been distressed by St. Laurent's pallid rationalization of the trampling of individual liberties during the Gouzenko investigation, the prospect of a Canada-wide Gardiner political machine—well, that was more than even the Liberal Party was prepared to accept. What I realized at the time was that, as Prime Minister, St. Laurent would fall heavily under the influence of the Right Honourable C. D. Howe. Howe was the genius of Canada's war production, and he deserves full credit for a magnificent achievement. However, he thought of Parliament in much the same manner as Trudeau does. The Cabinet was a kind of board of directors; the shareholders had the right to know something of what was going on but had no inherent right to examine carefully or question the policies that had been decided. If one was a Member of the Liberal Party he had few rights, other than to vote for whatever the gods of wisdom at the time determined the course would be. Such measure of party discipline is the very antithesis of my action when I was Prime Minister; I always made it clear in caucus that on matters of principle we had to stand together. But when a Member felt that he could not conscientiously support a measure, he was entitled to do as he pleased, providing he gave the Whip advance warning. I used to tell a simple story when on the stump to illustrate the high degree of obedience of private members in the Liberal Party in the 1950s. It concerned a Western Liberal Member, home during the Easter vacation. I could see him walking down the main street in this small town, screaming at the top of his voice: "No, no, no, no, never!" The police warned him to be quiet, that he was creating a disturbance. But on he went. Finally, the police picked him up, asking, "What's the idea? What are you trying to do?" The Member said: "Don't give me any of your lip. I'm one of Howe's yes-men on vacation."

Howe stood like Gibraltar. Parliament was to be made efficient. But Parliament is not a joint stock company where the President, who has the largest number of shares, says: "Now gentlemen, I called you together for the purpose of discussing items one, two, three, and four. Do I have general approval? Of course. Motion passed." Parliament does not work that way. C.D. and I had many, many battles in the House. His attitude of "La Chambre des Communes, c'est moi" made him an obvious and important target for those interested in preserving, indeed restoring, the rights of Parliament. One has only to examine his powers and those of his Cabinet colleagues as they moved from the Emergency Powers Act to the Transitional Powers Act to the Defence Production Act to conclude, as I did in the House, that there was an "inexhaustible appetite on the part of this Government for unnecessary powers". We did battle over the War Assets Corporation Act, the Aeronautics Act, the Trans-Canada Air Lines Act, the Foreign Exchange Act, the Combines Investigation Act, and many more. Howe and I clashed in debate almost as often as did Gardiner and I. What he hated most about me was that in the midst of debate I would point my finger at him, a habit from my days at the bar. He told a mutual friend that I did it only because I knew that it enraged him. I did not. Had I known the effect of my action upon him I would not have done it, his equanimity in the House, of course, being one of my principal concerns. Only recently did I learn that Sir John Macdonald used to irritate the Opposition with his pointing finger. On one occasion a Liberal front-bencher arose on a Question of Privilege to ask protection of the Speaker against the words used by Macdonald, "accompanied by pointing his finger at me". Macdonald immediately replied, agreeing to withdraw his finger.

Yet, despite our differences, often bitterly expressed, I never ceased to admire C. D. Howe for his contribution to Canada. The extent to which he reciprocated is perhaps shown by the letter I received from him the morning I became Prime Minister.

Personal and Private
Dear John:

I have waited until my last day in office to send you a note of congratulations. I am confident that you will lead a Government that will be a credit to Canadian tradition and that you yourself will establish a record as Prime Minister that you will be proud of.

My defeat after twenty-two years in the Ministry seems to me to establish a point where I can drop out of public life without being missed and I propose to do so. I have enjoyed every minute of my Government service and it will be hard to find an equally interesting occupation outside Government.

If at any time you think I have any information that may be of use to you, please do not hesitate to call on me. We have been friends for many years and I hope you will always regard me as a personal friend.

My wife joins me in wishing for Olive and yourself good health and happiness in the years ahead.

When I came into the House in 1940, the normal practice was that a backbencher share an office and a secretary with another M.P. There was no research assistance of any kind. Even a good stenographer was hard to find, and harder to keep; they were paid only for the time when the House was actually in session. I have mentioned elsewhere that the parliamentary librarians and their staffs were a boon to a hard-working M.P. But even so, there was a great deal of digging that one had to do on one's own; one had to work diligently to keep the government on its toes. It is very important to an M.P.'s effectiveness that he build up a chain of associations with experts in various fields and with those who are politically attuned to what is happening in various parts of the country. I began this practice immediately following my election in Lake Centre in 1940. From personal experience I knew that farmers were enduring economic hardship. Following the outbreak of war, the government assumed control of wheat markets and prices. To do this, the Wheat Board, a Conservative creation brought into being by Prime Minister Bennett but emasculated by Mr. King, was brought back into operation because the King administration feared that the price of wheat would climb to inordinate limits. Rather than being used to secure the best deal possible for the farmers, the Wheat Board was now used to prevent the Western farmer from reaping the benefits that should have been his, as was the case in all other industries, during the days of war. To jump ahead, the Wheat Board was later used to the detriment of the Western farmer when the Canadian government, at the war's end, decided to present the British government with wheat at prices below market level. My contention was, "Fine, help Britain; I'm all for it. But if gifts are made to Britain of aircraft, war material, or anything else manufactured, the cost doesn't come out of the manufacturer's pocket. You are treating the farmer unfairly." Eventually, as these practices became increasingly understood in the West, many Liberal farmers came to oppose the King government.

To get back to 1940. If I was going to criticize effectively what seemed an obvious fault in Jimmy Gardiner's Ministry of Agriculture, then I needed to be certain of my facts. The greatest authority on wheat marketing in

Canada was John I. MacFarland in Calgary, who had been in charge of the Wheat Board during the Bennett régime. It was arranged that I spend several hours with him, getting the wheat market situation as he saw it. If you read all that you can on a subject and discuss it with as many good people as you can find, there is a reasonable probability that you will be able to see most, if not all, the facets of whatever proposition you are debating.

In 1940, all that we had as Members of Parliament, in addition to our four-thousand-dollar indemnity, was free transportation on the railway and the right to frank our letters. We had no additional assistance for expenses, and we had to pay our own telephone accounts. I decided that I would write to various people with whom I was acquainted and whose views I regarded as worth having. I built up a large correspondence. And, of course, I protected their identities when I made use of their materials. These people gave me their best views, sometimes very critical ones, but always helpful. I have never objected to criticism; constructive criticism is essential to anyone who would properly represent the people of Canada. I reply to all letters, and I still answer critical letters in detail, if they are based on honest disagreement. I do object, however, to some persons who, because of their position in life, believe that whatever they think should be acceptable to everyone. It is most often they who write the bitter letters of personal criticism. When I receive one of those letters, I reply: "Dear Mr. so-and-so, I have just received from some crackpot who is using your stationery, even forging your name, a letter. I know how shocked you will be to know that your name is being used in this way. If you would like to have the letter in question returned to you so that you can use it and take such action against the wrongdoer as counsel may advise, I will be glad to send it by the next post." With only one exception over the years, this has ended the correspondence.

I have always followed the course of paying no attention to letters written to me without names attached, or to information that is surreptitiously given to one of my secretaries by someone hiding behind his anonymity. There was, however, one occasion on which I made an exception to my rule. In 1956, someone called me regularly during the Pipeline Debate. He had a gravelly voice like mine. The first two or three times he called, I advised him that if he did not identify himself, I could not use his information. He said, "I can't." But I found that what he gave me was quickly borne out by events. I came to rely on this anonymous voice. How angry Mr. Howe would get! I had the information. I knew what the next government move would be and I was able during the last week of that debate to make my colleagues ready.

I shall never forget those awful days. The Government of Canada from 1953 to 1957 might just as well have been composed of one man. C. D. Howe made what he liked and unmade what he did not like. The Pipeline Debate was not a sudden expression of a disregard of Parliament in respect of one bill. This was the culmination of a process that had continued virtually unabated from the days of war. No one can completely reconstruct what happened during those days in June 1956. The Speaker of the House of Commons, René Beaudoin, had established for himself a very good reputation. That reputation disappeared without trace because of the fact that whatever Howe wanted, or Pickersgill wanted, the Speaker decided was right. Jack Pickersgill, with the knowledge of Parliament he gained in the office of Mr. King, must have realized the harm that was being done to the institution of our freedom, but he gave no indication of that, bobbing up and down like a jumping jack. I can still see the St. Laurent Cabinet and the Liberal Members—arrogant, overbearing, condescending in their attitude to the Opposition, sneering at suggestions that they were becoming

246 / Diefenbaker: One Canada

all-powerful. Finally, it came to the point where the Speaker made a ruling on a Friday which upset the guidelines that the government was following in respect of that legislation. We in the Conservative Opposition knew something was going to take place on the Monday, for Pickersgill's car was parked outside the home of the Speaker at Kingsmere for some hours on the weekend. Events subsequently established that he must have wrestled with the Powers of Darkness, for on the Monday following, the Speaker ruled that Friday's events had not taken place, indeed that Friday never was.

There were valiant fighters in the Opposition: Drew, Fleming, Fulton, Green, M. J. Coldwell from the CCF, and others. They stood. Coldwell was a person who normally gave an appearance of detachment. He became more and more furious as the debate went on. We saw re-enacted what had happened in the Long Parliament during the reign of Charles I when Coldwell rushed up to the Clerk's desk saying, "You can't do this." And he grabbed the Mace, the symbol of the House of Commons' authority to sit. I thought he would carry it away. Parliament at its worst and Parliament in its greatest hour, that is what we saw. Speaker Beaudoin made a ruling against Donald Fleming that could not be justified in any way. Beaudoin was so highly regarded as an authority on the rules that he was writing a book on them. That book has never been published. It was torn asunder and the pages removed as he performed his duties, a puppet of the government. The Ministers smiled in approval at what he was doing. They derided the Opposition. The juggernaut rolled on. Donald Fleming was ordered ejected from the House. As Donald walked by, I said, "Farewell, John Hampden." The government won its victory by applying closure.

Howe strode across Parliament like a colossus; the others followed. What of Mr. St. Laurent? Day after day he sat, taking part, as I recall, only once, and then but a short interposition. He sat huddled and in obvious discomfort. He knew that what was being done to Parliament was wrong. I predicted that sooner or later the government would find an excuse not to proceed with the bill. There was a viable alternative to the Trans-Canada Pipeline, the all-Canadian route proposed by McMahon, without Texas financing. I could not believe that stubborn stupidity would be carried to the limit and that the bill would be engineered through the House regardless of consequences. The government trod on the Opposition and, in doing so, they trod on the rights of the people of Canada. The House of Commons: what does this mean? It is the House of the common people; and the common people must not be forgotten by the institution to whom they have given their name. The Liberals, to their chagrin, would discover this in 1957.

CHAPTER THIRTEEN

MY FIRST INSIGHT into what now seems a predisposition on the part of Canadian Conservatives to self-assassination came with the political destruction of Dr. Robert Manion. Manion, who had become Leader in 1938, was unceremoniously heaved out when he failed to lead us to victory in 1940. There had been such high hopes. Manion was the happy warrior. Big business liked him. His wife was a Desaulnier and he was a Roman Catholic; he was going to sweep Quebec. Now, the very people who had been instrumental in making Manion Leader said, "Shouldn't have had him in the first place. Very damaging. Lost because he was a Roman Catholic with a French-Canadian wife." This was the kind of nonsense that was prevalent in May 1940 when we met in caucus for the first time following the election.

Dr. Manion had left his resignation with the Chairman of our caucus. I regarded this as the formal act of an honourable man who felt that the Party should have the opportunity to replace him if it chose to do so. He had been defeated personally; the Party had sustained a serious defeat. As soon as the caucus opened, Manion made one appearance, said little except that he was sorry that the election had gone as it had. The Honourable Earl Rowe, who claimed to be Manion's friend and supporter, said,

"Oh, don't worry about that, Bob. We know you did your best." Manion left. Led by Rowe and Hanson, one after another argued that we should accept his resignation without delay.

To me their attitude was completely unfair. Manion had no foreknowledge that we were even going to consider his resignation. There were only four of us who stood by him: George Tustin, Bob McGregor, Joe Harris, and I. We stood. We argued all day. About five p.m., we were finally overwhelmed; Manion's resignation was accepted and the Honourable R. B. Hanson became our House Leader. The most callous, damnable thing was that not one of the Party old guard was prepared to tell Manion that his resignation had been accepted. Dick Bell, Manion's Private Secretary, was to notify him. Apparently he did not. Late that night, Manion got in touch with one of his so-called friends to inquire about what had happened. This was how he learned that he was out.

The powerful who had pushed Manion aside so cavalierly soon had the opportunity to give a practical demonstration of their own qualities of leadership. The Reverend W. G. Brown, the Independent Unity Reform Movement Member for Saskatoon, died shortly after the 1940 general election. Those who now ran the Conservative Party decided we should not contest the by-election. It would cost too much. I took strong exception to their position. Finally, a small amount of financial assistance was forthcoming. A strong campaign was mounted, and our candidate, Alfred H. Bence, was elected.

By 1941, there was a general feeling that what the Conservative Party needed most was a strong leader. The decision on who our new Leader would be, however, was not to be made by a National Leadership Convention as in 1927 and 1938. In view of the emergency of war, caucus, together with an assemblage of the Warwicks or king-makers of the Party, would choose. The Toronto and

Montreal groups supported the proposal to bring back Arthur Meighen. Meighen had been appointed to the Senate by Mr. Bennett in 1932. Certainly, after Manion's political demise, Meighen came to be widely regarded as our *de facto* Leader. During those early days of war, he did a consummate job in prodding the government into action. I thought he should stay in the Senate. So, in fact, did he. I did what I could to prevent his leaving it. I remember rising in this leadership meeting to state: "My admiration for your qualities as a parliamentarian and as a man of integrity, Arthur Meighen, is unbounded. But your superb abilities are having full sway in the Senate. If you resign to seek a seat in the House of Commons, King, who hates you with a hatred that is apparent whenever your name is even mentioned in debate, will destroy you. I don't want to see you sacrificed."

The proponents of Meighen's leadership argued to the contrary. They said it would be an easy election. Mackenzie King would not permit the nomination of a Liberal candidate. Colonel A. Cockeram, Member for York South, had agreed to resign his seat to make way for Meighen. The war was believed by some to have become a solvent to the tremendous antagonism that pervaded King's mind. In the end, only Heber Hatfield, father of the present Premier of New Brunswick, held out against Meighen's selection as our Leader. The Liberals, as promised, did not run a candidate in the by-election; but of all the certainties of life, the position that I had taken was borne out. Meighen ran a bad campaign. He centred his attack on King. King's arch enemy within the Liberal Party, Ontario Premier Mitch Hepburn, came out in support of Meighen. The federal Liberals described Meighen as a dangerous man who would upset the equanimity of the House of Commons and, in consequence, weaken the war effort. On election day, many of the Liberals in York South voted socialist and the CCF candidate, J. W. Noseworthy, won. I will never forget the night of 9 February 1942. I was in the House of Commons when the returns came in. King sat there, his face sombre, almost sad, but all the time rubbing his hands with invisible soap. When the final count showed Meighen to be badly defeated, King was so happy. He laughed uproariously. That which he feared was not going to happen. Meighen was no more. Pointing his finger at the Opposition, he said, "Diefenbaker and Hanson, you have your answer." Why he named me first I could not understand. The cheers and merriment in the government lobby were loud and long that night.

Pressure now mounted for the calling of a National Leadership Convention. No longer was the war considered a sufficient excuse to avoid this. Something had to be done to secure a Leader who would be successful. The Party power brokers in Montreal and Toronto, and these included Mr. Meighen, decided that they would give a public imitation of Pharaoh's daughter. "Was not Moses found in the bulrushes; why should not we go out and shake those bulrushes to find ourselves a leader?" They did; they concluded that the politician above all who filled the needs of the hour was the Honourable John Bracken, Premier of Manitoba. There was one difficulty. Although it was rumoured that his mother, before women had the right to vote, appeared to think as a Conservative, Mr. Bracken had never evinced even slight interest in being a Conservative. He had been a Progressive, a Liberal Progressive, and, finally, a Liberal. But he had never lost an election. He had been Premier of Manitoba since 1922. And it was said on every hand that if Mr. Bracken were chosen, he would be able to do what he had done in Manitoba: secure the support of French Canadians. The Province of Quebec would turn to the Conservative Party; it needed only this chance to translate its innate philosophic conservatism into electoral support.

252 / Diefenbaker: One Canada

Conservatives from Toronto and Montreal, with the assistance of some from Ottawa (particularly Gordon Graydon at the behest of Arthur Meighen), made pilgrimages to Winnipeg almost with the same dedication as others go to Mecca. Bracken viewed the matter. He looked at it. He discussed it. He gave no direct answer. The convention was called in the city of Winnipeg for 9-11 December 1942. Nominations were to begin at eight p.m., 10 December. Eight o'clock came, but Mr. Bracken wasn't present. Ten minutes later, he was rushed to the platform and received a tremendous ovation. The galleries were filled with Brackenites. My brother Elmer, stationed in Winnipeg as an officer in the RCAF, described the popular mood as, "How dare anyone stand against John Bracken?"

I agreed to contest the leadership of the Conservative Party, knowing full well that I had no opportunity to win. Most of my colleagues in caucus had taken Meighen's lead and were supporting Bracken. But my organizer, Jack Anderson, was most anxious that I stand. So were Bill Brunt and M. J. (Mickey) O'Brien, who became two of my most stalwart supporters. They accepted the fact that I would not have much chance, but felt that my views ought to be placed before the Convention and, thereby, before the country as a whole. I wanted to plant at least the seed of my ideal: "This is one nation, one Canada." I recall very well one of the joint chairmen at the Convention, a lawyer and financier from Edmonton who had known me through the years, mispronouncing my name in every reference he made to me, making it as strongly German as it was possible to make it. It is interesting that his attempt to play on anti-German feelings aroused by the war did not get the reaction he sought from the crowd. I would have dropped out after the first ballot had it not been for this. A Leadership Convention, in any circumstances, is one of the most difficult audiences for a speaker. Over the years, I have heard only a few out-standing speeches made by leadership candidates. Within the time allowed, it is impossible to develop a thesis. It is difficult to interest a large group of delegates in propositions that consist of more than simply stating that we are on the way to victory and that whoever is chosen at the Convention will be the next Prime Minister. In 1942, I tried the impossible:

We meet in Winnipeg, the beginning of the plains. One hundred and thirty years ago my mother's forebears came to this very spot. Since then men and women of all races and creeds have had liberty and opportunity under the protecting fold of British institutions in Canada. We can never build a united Canada which permits discrimination against loyal Canadians, whatever their origin. Canada cannot be made great on a policy of hyphenated Canadianism. It will take courage for me to plead tonight for an end of that viewpoint....

It had been in Wakaw, some twenty years before, that I began to draft a Canadian Bill of Rights. It became my abiding purpose to see every Canadian not only secure in his liberty, but secure in the knowledge of his fundamental rights and freedoms. It distressed me that those who were neither British nor French in origin were not treated with the regard that non-discrimination demands. I was even more distressed that many contended they would never become Canadians. My determination to see the Bill of Rights a reality was increased by experiences during and after the Second World War. Even now, I am still somewhat amazed at the opposition I encountered in trying to forward a Canadian Bill of Rights. In 1946, when the House debated the Canada Citizenship Act, an act that I very much favoured, I endeavoured unsuccessfully to have a Bill of Rights included in its provisions. If the support for this concept in the House of Commons was less than overwhelming in 1946, at the 1942 Convention my plea did not so much as receive an honourable mention in the press.

My nominator at the Winnipeg Convention was my close and devoted friend David J. Walker of Toronto. Dave had come to Winnipeg to place in nomination the name of Sidney Smith, President of the University of Toronto. Smith was the Toronto group's reserve candidate. When at last Bracken decided to stand, Smith did not allow his name to go forward. In consequence, Dave was free to support me. The seconder of my nomination was R. L. "Dinny" Hanbidge, from Kerrobert, Saskatchewan. I had read Dave Walker's speech on behalf of my candidature and had approved it. As he stepped forward to speak, however, he looked towards Mr. Bracken and, to everyone's surprise, led off with words to this effect: "What are you doing here? You're not a Conservative. You're just like the camel who got into the Arab's tent." Hundreds of Bracken supporters booed in response. Dave said, "You can boo. You don't bother me." His was not exactly the type of speech that I would recommend in nominating anyone. He and I often joke about this event. Not that it did any real harm; I had no chance anyway.

Bracken ran first on both ballots. I ran third. M. A. MacPherson repeated his 1938 performance, running second. Between the 1938 Convention and the 1940 election, MacPherson had been something of a twelve-day political wonder in the Conservative Party. He was one of the Party's most popular political speakers in 1940, but his personal defeat in Regina marked him as someone who was not going to secure for the Conservative Party its millennium. MacPherson and I had been friends for many years. But our personal relations were never to recover from my decision to stand as a candidate in 1942. My action was heresy, and a cardinal sin.

Of the other leadership candidates in 1942, the Honourable Harry Stevens received only twenty of the eight hundred and seventy votes cast on the first ballot. He stood unforgiven for his contribution to the schism in the Party that was blamed for the disaster of the 1935 election. He was not in the position of Mr. Trudeau, who in 1963 condemned without qualification the Liberal Party and all its works, only to become Leader of that Party five years later. Stevens' speech, however, was a superb effort and by far the most inspiring at the Convention. It must have caused some momentary apprehension among some British Columbia Conservatives who had engineered his defeat as an M.P. in 1940, lest he re-establish his influence in the Party and diminish theirs in the process.

Howard Green, the only other contender, had been the first to enter the leadership race. He was able, fearless, and honest, and was expected to do well, but he also dropped out after the first ballot. Howard's nomination experience emerged as an unmitigated disaster. He had just begun his speech when he began to repeat a single sentence. Then he collapsed in a dead faint; he had to be carried from the platform on a stretcher.

Bracken made the adoption of the Port Hope Report, a relatively forward-looking document on social policy, a condition of his nomination. By the 1945 election, however, he and his advisers had all but forgotten their pledge to reject some of the more doctrinaire and reactionary of Conservative beliefs or shibboleths. Perhaps more important was Bracken's demand that the Party change its name to Progressive Conservative. The sense of this move escaped me. From its inception as Canada's first national political party in 1854, the Party had been called Liberal-Conservative. The name was changed under Dr. Manion. In the 1940 election, Conservative was nowhere mentioned; the Party became the National Government Party. I have always preferred the name Conservative.

My father was deeply disappointed when I was not elected Leader in 1942. I tried to tell him that I had no chance, but this did not lessen his hope and expectation. He used to tell the people he worked with in the Saskatoon Customs office that sooner or later his son would be Prime Minister. When he was teased about this, he would reply, "Well, some day. You'll see."

I had known John Bracken at university. During my first term, he came to the University of Saskatchewan as a Professor of Field Husbandry. I was a frosh-sophomore, than which there is none wiser. Waiting for the streetcar at the university one day, I took Bracken to be a student. I asked how he was enjoying his first year. He said he found it very interesting, and then added to my surprise and discomfiture, "Of course, I'll have to reorganize the department." I followed his career. I watched him on the stump; he had an amazing capacity for meeting people. I do not think I have ever known anyone more effective with a farm audience. He understood their problems, and the farmers knew it. No one in public life knew more about agriculture, both theoretical and practical. John Bracken was a man of good character; his word was his bond. He was also blessed with a wonderful wife who ably assisted him through his years of public service.

In 1943, I had him speak for me at a small town between Regina and Moose Jaw. It was the first and last time that I invited him to speak on my behalf. In 1940, I had had to fight the criticism that a lawyer should not represent an agricultural constituency. Bracken forgot that I was on the platform; his message to my surprised constituents was that farmers had no need of lawyers as M.P.s! His Secretary, Mel Jack, one of the most brilliant, reliable, and practical politicians whom I have ever known, and Victor Mackie, of the *Winnipeg Free Press*, were present and had a hearty laugh at my expense.

To return to the Leadership Convention. At its conclusion, Mr. Bracken called a meeting of caucus in Winnipeg, at which he assigned various duties to the Conservative M.P.s and Senators. He then announced that he felt that he ought not to try too quickly to find a seat in the House of Commons. There were one or two constituencies available, including Souris, Manitoba, where the sitting Member, Colonel James A. Ross, was prepared to resign. But our new Leader thought that he ought to be free to travel, to meet people, and to acquire a first-hand knowledge of the country and its problems. His decision meant that we would have to select a new House Leader, since Dick Hanson had indicated that he did not wish to carry on. Bracken asked that caucus vote by letter, each Member designating that person who in his opinion should be the Leader of the Opposition *ad interim*. The Member whom Mr. Bracken had in mind for this position was Gordon Graydon, Member for Peel, a fine gentleman, a good parliamentarian, and one of the most popular Members of the House of Commons. At the Convention, it was Graydon who nominated John Bracken.

Even though Bracken did not want me as House Leader, I knew that I had enough support in caucus to make my selection a distinct possibility. The letter vote was taken in early January, 1943. About the middle of the month, Mr. Bracken visited Saskatoon to see his mother. He telephoned me to meet him. We chatted for two hours or so. Since nothing was said about the choice of a temporary Leader, I naturally concluded that someone else had been chosen. I learned later that Bracken had decided to ignore the results of the letter ballot and to put the issue of the House leadership directly before caucus when it met on 27 January, the day before the Opening of Parliament. As a consequence of our talk, I considered myself free to take on a very complicated civil fraud case involving much time and research. Other lawyers had turned down the suit as impossible. After considerable study, I concluded that we might succeed, provided we had a jury trial. The case was set down for the sittings in Saskatoon. It was after all the preparations for trial had been completed that Mr. Bracken insisted that I be in Ottawa for the meeting of caucus on 27 January. I explained that I could not be there. He continued to insist. When my clients learned that there was a chance of my becoming Leader of the Opposition, they insisted against my advice to the contrary that I return to Ottawa, even though in so doing they had to give up the jury.

Fate moves in its peculiar way. When I arrived at caucus, it was obvious that I still had very good support, despite the strong efforts of the Toronto group of Members to ensure a Graydon majority. But I was now in the middle of the case, and I had given my word to my clients that I would carry it through. When the final voting took place, I defeated myself, a novel experience for me considering that I usually did not require any such help. I showed my colleagues my ballot marked "Gordon Graydon". "Now," I asked, "is that convincing evidence of my determination not to be Leader of the Opposition?" Graydon defeated me by one vote. I returned West to win my client's case. As I look back, I consider my decision to have been a fortunate one, for being Leader of the Opposition during the last part of the war in a House of Commons dominated by Mr. King might well have meant my end. If you read Pickersgill's "selectivities", which masquerade as Mackenzie King's own record of events, it is amusing to note King's comment that "The Tories seldom choose a decent man. They are likely to take Diefenbaker." He was apparently greatly relieved when Gordon Graydon was selected.

The 1945 election was called for 11 June. The war in Europe was over. The war in Asia was still at its height. Enlistment in the armed forces from the Western provinces had been very high. Those near and dear to the soldiers and sailors and airmen were anxious to have their loved ones return home at the earliest possible date. During the campaign, I received from a friendly donor, who was trying to assist my re-election, a pile of highly decorative election literature for distribution in my constituency. It was costly, it was attractive. Arthur Pearson, who replaced a seriously ill Jack Anderson as my campaign manager, turned his home into a workshop so that this material could be stuffed into pre-stamped envelopes and addressed for mailing. Some seven thousand were ready for mailing before I had an opportunity to read what they contained. The message therein was that at the earliest possible date, those serving in the European theatre should be sent to fight in the Pacific. Seven thousand stamped envelopes went into the fire that day.

Because of my personal experiences as a candidate, when I was Leader of the Party I insisted that I approve all national advertising. I consider ninety per cent of the professional advertising produced in election campaigns less than beneficial. In the election of 1949, the advertising campaign produced pages of material in fine print, with endless detail, its value non-existent. When I received my share of it for Lake Centre, Jack Anderson, Arthur Pearson, and I read every piece thoroughly. It had no message at all for the voters on the Prairies. We decided that the only people who stood to benefit from its distribution were the optometrists and oculists. We must have had almost a ton of it. Our problem: what to do with it? It was like the national campaign literature in 1945; to distribute it would have cost us votes. The constituency of Lake Centre derived its name from having Last Mountain Lake down its centre. It was a fairly deep lake at one time but continual droughts had reduced its level. When I tried to secure the King government's agreement to divert waters into it, my arguments met the usual reaction: "We'll have that looked into." At the hour of midnight, one night in June 1949, we left the summer resort town of Regina Beach. Arthur Pearson and I were about to provide a unique solution to a double problem. We had loaded the Party's national advertising into a borrowed boat; at a respectable distance from shore, we dumped it. It must surely have raised the level of the lake.

Regularly at election time, Liberal governments would promise early action on the proposed South Saskatchewan Dam. People had been debating the pros and cons of this since the 1860s. The Honourable James G. Gardiner, Minister of Agriculture, would announce that the fullest possible investigation was taking place to ensure that the tremendous flow of water on the South Saskatchewan River be made available for irrigation purposes, so that the curse of drought would finally be removed. But it was obvious that Mr. Gardiner did not have the support of his Cabinet colleagues. I recall the by-election in Rosthern in 1948 when the government slogan was "Vote for Boucher and get the dam". The people got Boucher but the government didn't give a dam.

At the time of the election in 1945, my brother Elmer was on his retirement leave from the RCAF. He, Jack Anderson, Arthur Pearson, and I were travelling through a part of Saskatchewan that the proposed dam would serve. A heavy rain had fallen during the night. We turned off the main road to find ourselves stuck in the mud. A quarter of a mile away, a farmer was working with his team of horses. He unhitched them and came over. While helping us, he kept up a stream of conversation, taking advantage of the opportunity to advance all his socialist CCF ideas. It was obvious that he did not recognize me as I was wearing dark glasses. Two or three times when the wheels were out of the mud, we slipped back into it. When finally we were out, the farmer was covered with mud from his efforts. I asked, "How much do I owe you?" He demanded, "Are you going to vote for

Diefenbaker?" I said, "Never." Of course, I had no vote in Lake Centre; I lived in Prince Albert. He said, "Then it's been worth while altogether; I'm not going to charge you a cent." As we proceeded on our way, Elmer observed that a regular supply of water would, as had the recent rain, change the whole countryside. There and then, he coined one of the most effective election slogans I have ever had: "It'll be a dam site sooner if John is elected."

Under the terms of the 1905 Autonomy Acts creating Alberta and Saskatchewan, there was to be a redistribution of seats in the House of Commons from these provinces every five years to allow for increased representation as immigrants filled the West. In the rest of Canada, redistribution took place every ten years. By the 1940s, rapid changes in the distribution of the West's population had long since ceased. Redistribution, however, still took place every five years. One result was that my constituency was regularly gerrymandered by order of Mr. Gardiner. In 1940 I got in by 280 votes, and of my total vote, one thousand was secured in an area from Lumsden south, east, and west. Without support from that area I would have been hopelessly defeated. Before the 1945 election, redistribution removed that area from the boundaries of Lake Centre.

I was inclined to agree that Gardiner's move would achieve my defeat. Indeed, on the night when the House of Commons was dissolved in April 1945, I walked up to Parliament Hill and stood for a few moments on Wellington Street to look at the House of Commons for the last time. I had promised myself that if defeated I would never return. Despite redistribution, my plurality in 1945 increased to a thousand and nine. Mr. Gardiner was distressed at his failure to get rid of me.

He apparently concluded that he must go further in the next redistribution. This was a little difficult because it seemed that people were voting for me without regard to

Party. Thus, in what I called a "Jimmymander", he simply had chopped off those areas that gave me my largest returns. He then added on to Lake Centre areas that were overwhelmingly CCF, including the area around Wynyard, Kandahar, and Dafoe that had never been directly or indirectly connected with Lake Centre. Mr. Gardiner did not care who defeated me as long as my defeat took place. If one took the 1945 election returns as a basis for calculation, I was faced in 1949 with an adverse majority of some three or four thousand votes.

The feelings that must have been Gardiner's I can only imagine when in 1949 I was elected by 3,432, for he had done everything that the mind of a machine politician could envisage, short of destroying my constituency altogether. I did come close to getting into serious trouble during the 1949 election though, when I stated over the radio that all the Communists in Lake Centre were going to vote for my CCF opponent. I was challenged by the Premier of Saskatchewan, T. C. Douglas, to name them. I could have, for I had in my possession the Communist Party list of members and contributors. A Communist Party official had tried to make a success of the newspaper in the village of Semans in my constituency. When his endeavour failed, and he had to clear the premises, he loaded up the big old stove with Party materials, including this list, but forgot to put a match to them. My response to Tommy Douglas, however, was to point out that it would cost too much money to read out all the names on the radio (I think there were three hundred and ninety) but that if he wanted to give me a list of the Communists who were not going to vote CCF, I would read that. Everyone was amused, and this was the last I heard from Tommy Douglas on the question. A further consequence was that the Communist Party then instructed its members to spoil their ballots by writing "peace" on them; some had difficulty with the spelling!

In 1945, I had been surprised by the success of the CCF, particularly by its share of the soldier vote. I did not consider the CCF stand on the war as one that would attract many votes. Yet, in Saskatchewan the CCF elected eighteen, the Liberals two, and the Conservatives me. The standings nationally were: Liberals 125; Conservatives 67; CCF 28; Social Credit 13; Independents 11.

Following the 1945 election, Mr. Bracken entered the House of Commons as the Member for Neepawa, Manitoba. Over all, the Conservative Party did very well, if compared with 1940 and 1935. Of course, Bracken had expected to do better. So had the Party hierarchy. Their anticipation of success was no doubt heightened by the overwhelming success of the Ontario Conservatives under George Drew in the provincial election that took place the week before the federal election. What the federal leaders of our Party failed to realize was that Drew, in beating back the CCF threat in Ontario, had exhausted the Party's resources at a time when they were most needed federally. Bracken was now labelled a loser. The Liberal argument that Mr. Bracken did not have the knowledge of national affairs so necessary for one occupying the position of Leader was widely disseminated through the press, and was even widely accepted among Conservative Party supporters. Mr. Bracken had covered all of Canada during the period from 1943 to the general election of 1945, and had worked hard to acquire a full appreciation of domestic issues. He went abroad, visited the troops, met with the leaders of the Allied Armed Forces, and made an intensive study of international affairs. In addition, he had as his Secretary-in-Chief Rod Finlayson, who had an unusually wide knowledge of public affairs. However, the pressure was on. George Drew was a winner. Bracken must go.

The Warwicks (I should not call them that for Warwick was successful) within the Conservative Party seem to

264 / Diefenbaker: One Canada

coalesce when it comes to the question of leadership, and they set out to remove Bracken. He became exasperated and frustrated, and he finally resigned "for reasons of health". A race for the leadership of the Conservative Party was again under way.

My friends and supporters across the country joined in a renewed effort to bring about my election as Leader. As usual, we had no money; I do not think our total expenditures in the leadership campaign exceeded five thousand dollars. Among those who worked the hardest to secure my election was the late William R. Brunt of Toronto, of whose abilities I cannot say enough. He was one of the wisest, most knowledgeable, and most practical politicians I have ever known. He had a feeling for the public mood, and he always gave his best to me. He was with me in the leadership contests of 1942, 1948, and 1956, and in every election until his death in July 1962. When I was Prime Minister, he was to me what Colonel House had been to President Woodrow Wilson of the United States. It is my firm conviction that, had he not been killed in a tragic automobile accident, those events that shook the Conservative Party following the June 1962 election would not have taken place.

I had toured the country before the 1948 Convention and I was encouraged by the rank-and-file response to my message. I even concluded that we might beat the Liberals when they next went to the country. What I underestimated was the staying power of those who controlled the organizational apparatus of the Conservative Party. It was impossible to convince them that under their direction the Party had nowhere to go. Yet the facts were there for all to see. From 1896, we were in office from 1911 to 1917, when the Unionist Government was formed, a period of six years. We again became a Conservative government in July 1920 and stayed in office until December 1921. We returned to government for a couple of months in 1926. We were in from 1930 to 1935. That was only some thirteen years out of a period of fifty-two years. Conversely, by 1948 we had spent thirty-nine years out of office. There must have been some reason for this record. It should have been obvious that certain reactionary policies had no national appeal.

By 1948, my views on social issues were well known. The Party was gradually moving my way. Indeed, when the convention was over, the "interests" were so concerned over the fact that I had received more votes than they expected possible that their outbursts knew no limits. I had made my position clear in 1944 on the issue of Family Allowances. That was the first time this minority of one became a majority. In consequence, the reactionaries described me as "Western populist". I once asked one of them to define the term for me. He thought it was some kind of erratic radicalism. When pressed further, he wasn't certain what his new term encompassed, except that it did encompass those things he disapproved of. Mr. Drew was a Leader the establishment could warm to. He had openly condemned the whole principle of Family Allowances; indeed, he went on radio to condemn it as a scheme to breed slackers in the Province of Quebec. Dr. Bruce had been ejected from the Commons Chamber when he refused to withdraw a similar remark. Both men were encouraged in their stands by McCullagh of the Toronto *Globe and Mail*. Although Drew later recanted on this view, he incurred a double political disadvantage by flatly denying having made the speech in question.

I believe in the right of the individual to make his best in life. I have nothing but contempt for those who regard profits as being dangerous. Without them there is no advance, nor would there be the free society that is ours. But I believe that there must be a minimum for all. There is a profound division between those who believe that the State has no legitimate role in determining the course of the individual, and those who believe that the State has responsibilities as a referee, and so must have the power to protect the weak and the less privileged. I am not against big business. Bigness today is essential as never before; but I am against bigness when it permits the few to destroy or undermine the welfare of the many. I made that clear when the Combines Investigation legislation was before the House. I took the stand that the penalties provided were preposterously lenient. To steal a million dollars and face a ten-thousand-dollar fine, if one was caught, was an invitation to the potential wrongdoer. My stand was, and it has remained unchanged, that a corporation as an artificial person is not punished by picayune penalties of that kind; and I further contend that the directors of companies who deliberately break the law in order to achieve unjust, unconscionable gains should be subject to jail as would the ordinary wrongdoer. I see nothing in my stand of antipathy to the large corporations, but in some circles these views were bitterly condemned as evidence of the fact that I did not have that appreciation of economic matters that was essential so as to realize that the welfare of Canada was secondary to the benefit of the few and the powerful.

The 1948 Convention was an enthusiastic one. The galleries were filled and were strongly in support of me; there the average Canadian was represented. The outcome, however, came as no surprise. George Drew won on the first ballot. I was second. Donald Fleming was a distant third. Once I saw the line-up of the delegates I knew that Mr. Drew would win. He had a record for winning, they said. The press generally supported his candidature. Brilliant, a fine parliamentarian, a man with wide knowledge and a distinguished record of war service, he had been a successful Premier of Ontario and had given good government. At conventions, the one question above all that is naturally in the minds of the delegates is

"Who is most assured of victory?", a question intensified in 1948 by the fact that we had been in the political wilderness then since 1935.

In 1948, it was said that if Mr. Drew were chosen, Premier Maurice Duplessis would throw the entire weight of his Union Nationale behind the Conservative Party in Quebec. It was going to be a sweep. We had Quebec behind our Party. They did not say how far behind us. In 1935 we elected thirty-nine Members, of whom five were from the Province of Quebec. In 1940 the number we elected was thirty-nine, with one Independent from Quebec. In 1945 we elected sixty-seven Members, one from Quebec. Everything was in shape for 1949.

As far as the organization of the Convention was concerned, it was in the hands of those who, if not absolutely opposed to me, were one hundred per cent dedicated to ensuring that Drew would be Leader. Delegates are divided into two classes. Generally, delegates are elected by constituency organizations. But often the selection of these delegates is less than democratic; in some parts of the country where constituency associations are no more than pieces of paper, their selection is an offence to the whole idea of a popularly elected leader. Then there is provision for delegates-at-large who are chosen by the National Organization itself. They are supposed to be outstanding men and women of the Party. In 1948 there were delegates-at-large who had never made any contribution to the Conservative Party. I do not mean financial contribution, but the work that citizenship demands. They were there to vote. They had only one objective in mind, and that was to elect Mr. Drew. Anyone suspected of supporting me was removed from the list of authorized delegates-at-large. For that purpose, there were people stationed outside my hotel suite taking down the names of my visitors. This created needless bad feelings between my supporters and Drew's. The method of choosing a Leader by means of a National Convention is something that we have borrowed from the United States. One reason why it is less than perfect in our system is that a Leader must primarily have the support of his colleagues in Parliament, and not simply the support of those who try to manage the affairs of the Party from their luxurious offices on the outside.

On the night of Drew's victory, I went up to his suite in the Château Laurier. They were celebrating. I was an intruder. I went to congratulate him. I walked into that gathering and it was as if an animal not customarily admitted to homes had suddenly entered the place.

As the 1949 elections approached, a sense of victory was in the air. We had won several by-elections and hopes were high. On the Saturday before the election, in anticipation of a Conservative victory the *Ottawa Journal*, whose editor, Grattan O'Leary, was an avowed Drew supporter with naught but antipathy for me, offered its readers a preview of the new Conservative government. I was relegated to the portfolio of Solicitor General, a position it was expected I would refuse. When the ballots were counted on 27 June, however, these speculations proved as chaff to a hurricane. St. Laurent had been returned with one hundred and ninety seats. The Conservatives had forty-one members, two of whom were returned from the Province of Quebec.

I can only shake my head in wonder at some of the schemes devised to win Quebec back to the Conservative Party. By 1948, the Cold War was at its height. Western defences against Soviet-directed international Communism were being consolidated; the North Atlantic Treaty was signed in April 1949. The spy-ring revelations of Igor Gouzenko made Canadians aware of the seriousness of Soviet espionage activities in our own country. In the United States anxiety over the threat of Communist subversion had resulted in a witch hunt under Senator McCarthy. Some of those who directed the Conservative Party saw in all this a chance to make large political gains, especially in Quebec. At our policy meeting in the Château Laurier in March 1949 it was proposed that the Party should adopt the policy of outlawing Communism in Canada. This, they claimed, would make the Conservative Party irresistible in Quebec. One after the other spoke in favour of it. Finally, I arose to speak. I contended that if the law covering sedition and treason did not encompass some of the dangerous activities of the Communist Party, "change the law, put teeth in the law, but do not outlaw Communism." I suggested that experience had shown that if we outlawed them, we would make martyrs of people who deserved no such glorification. We would drive the Communists underground only to have them emerge later as a stronger and more dangerous force. I was booed to the echo by the majority of my fellow-Conservatives. However, I did gain some support among young men and women of our Party who realized that one cannot outlaw an idea. To outlaw an idea is the antithesis of every principle of democracy. Political expediency is the weakest of reeds. I pointed out that I had sat cheek by jowl with Fred Rose, Labour Progressive Member from Montreal's Cartier constituency, in the House of Commons. Rose had gone to jail for his part in the Soviet spy-ring. Was I now expected to take the stand and swear, as a consequence of that association, that I was not a Communist, or that I had not been ideologically contaminated by my reading of Marx and Engels? I told these assembled Conservative policy-makers that there was no way I would ever be forced to such a declaration. I have been credited with stopping this suicidal foolishness.

Some have criticized George Drew for being difficult to

work with. He had strong views, and he expressed them strongly. Although he was intensely proud and resented criticism, he was prepared to consider the other person's viewpoint and often took it. He was a debater of unusual ability, his speeches well-prepared and delivered in a true parliamentary fashion. His principal political weakness was that he was never able to divest himself of the popular image that strongly associated him with the big business interests of Toronto and Montreal. There were press articles stating that Drew was subject to my challenge within the Party. This was not so. I had no reason to feel in any way unfairly treated by him. Our relations were strained at the time of the 1948 Convention. They continued to be rather formal after his entry into the House of Commons as the Member for Carleton in a by-election in December 1948. After the election of 1949, things went along very well. There was still apparent among some of the palace guard a feeling that I should in no way be "preferred", to use the expression that was bandied around by two or three of them. I wasn't preferred. But George Drew as Leader of the Opposition had me lead in debate from time to time, not by my request, but by his own decision. I was on no black list that would prevent my being a delegate to the Commonwealth Parliamentary Association, to the NATO Conferences, or to other organizations abroad. He insisted that I should be included, even though sometimes it was felt by others that it would be better if I were not. When International Kiwanis invited him to speak in Seattle, Washington, he asked me to take his place. I inquired what he intended to deal with. He said that Canada–United States relations was his subject but that the content was for me to decide. I chose to develop the thesis of Canada co-operating with the United States, but at all times demanding and requiring that Canadian policy be made in Canada. I could use the same speech tomorrow. I know that Mr. Drew found the House of Commons difficult, the atmosphere disturbing, because of the studied decision in the Liberal Party to treat him with contemptuous indifference.

As always, I followed the course of speaking on behalf of the Party wherever the opportunity offered itself. I spoke in several provinces through the 1949 campaign. In 1953, I spoke across the country. I might interject that although I have had various members of the Party speak for me, I have always followed the course of insisting that no one come into my constituency except by my invitation. This has meant that if an election turned out badly, I would have no one to blame but myself. Too often alibis are created after elections that it was the injection of A, B, or C into the campaign that brought about the defeat of the candidate.

Before I leave George Drew, I should mention his first election to the House in December 1948. Russell Boucher resigned his Carleton seat to make way for Drew. The CCF candidate was Dr. Eugene Forsey, now a member of the Senate. An outstanding authority on the Canadian constitution, a delightful personality, a fine raconteur, he has made a good Senator. During the 1948 Carleton by-election, a joint meeting was held and all hell broke loose. Drew and Forsey became involved in a wrestling match for the loudspeaker. I forget who won the microphone that evening, but Drew won the election.

I would have retired from politics in 1952 if my constituency had not for the third time running been gerrymandered in the redistribution. Mr. Drew was fit and in the prime of life; it seemed unlikely that he would soon retire from politics. I had been in the House of Commons for twelve years. It seemed that those things for which I had striven politically would not be realized. I was seriously considering offers from law firms in Ontario. I loved the courts, and I was greatly tempted to end my years therein. It was at this point that the Honourable James G. Gardiner decided that Lake Centre constituency was to be dismembered. He trifurcated it; he added parts of it to constituencies on the east and on the west and tacked its remnants onto Moose Jaw. It was then that I determined I would show him and the Liberal government that they could not do this to me. If it had not been for that redistribution, 1949 would have been my last campaign. It has been said that "Though the mills of God grind slowly, yet they grind exceeding small;" the determination of Mr. Gardiner and his associates to obliterate me had the result of intensifying my determination that they were not going to achieve their objective without a fight. The question was—where was I to fight?

In July 1952 I motored home to Prince Albert. En route, I attended the Republican Convention in Chicago. Davie Fulton was with me. I was attracted to the candidature of Senator Robert A. Taft. Taft had always been to me the embodiment of what I wanted to be in politics: a person who, regardless of the ups and downs and uncertainties of political life, had strong principles and stood by them. Taft had everything except a vital personality, and this lack he revealed clearly in the Convention. The delegates admired and respected Taft, but they loved Eisenhower.

General Eisenhower I later came to know as a friend, on a first-name basis. I found him a delightful person and an amazing personality. He could become easily aroused, particularly at any suggestion that Communist China should be recognized, and when he was, there was down-to-earth clarity in his language. But no matter what the provocation, suddenly he would burst into that familiar grin. I could understand how he successfully handled all the prima donna generals of the Western Allies in the Second World War.

When I arrived home after the Republican Convention, I met Fred Hadley, one of Prince Albert's leading Liberals, on the street. He was much concerned about what had happened in the "Jimmymander" of Lake Centre, but suggested that we forget about politics and go fishing up at Lac La Ronge. We went. No one has ever had to ask me twice to go fishing. My brother Elmer and E. T. (Tommy) Martin, a well-known businessman and leading Social Crediter, were in the party. One evening on Lac La Ronge we were sitting listening to the Democratic presidential nominations on radio. These also took place in Chicago, ten days after the Republican Convention. Adlai Stevenson was the Democratic choice. We were listening to his acceptance speech: "Let's talk sense to the American people. Let's tell them the truth, that there are no gains without pains." Suddenly, Fred Hadley said to me, "Why don't you run in Prince Albert?" "Oh," I said, "the idea is ridiculous." Tommy Martin said he would work for me. Naturally, my brother said he would give all his time; he always did in every election in which I participated. Elmer was a pillar of strength to me through all the years. He knew people. He was always able to secure the support of those who, if left to me, would have proven obdurate. We spent the next couple of days fishing, and very little more was said about my contesting Prince Albert.

I returned to Ottawa, promising only to think about running in my home constituency. When the Session recessed in December, I went West. I was met at the airport by Fred Hadley and Ed Jackson (a leading CCFer). Without my knowing of it, Hadley, Martin, and Jackson had been instrumental in organizing a series of Diefenbaker Clubs, made up of members or supporters of all political parties except the Communist, in Prince Albert constituency. The executive reflected the membership at large; it was a mixture of well-known Liberals, CCFers, Social Crediters, and Conservatives. Their slogan, "The North Needs John".

During the holidays I met with a number of people from various parts of the constituency; they were full of enthusiasm, except for the Conservatives, who felt I had little or no chance of being elected. Most were very anxious to have a nomination convention. I was not. Throughout the winter of 1953, under Hadley's leadership, these men and women in the Diefenbaker Clubs worked unceasingly. When the Easter recess came, I was again met on arrival at the Saskatoon airport. Hadley and his group gave me the picture of what had been achieved. I think their work one of the most extraordinary examples of citizenship in action that I have ever known. They had built an organization without regard to party, determined to elect me the Member for Prince Albert. They knew my views on northern development. They knew my views on agriculture. They knew my ideal of an unhyphenated Canadianism. When a Convention was called in May 1953, the hall which seated eight hundred people had standing room only. The election was in August. The Diefenbaker Clubs were entirely responsible for my electoral victory. In a riding where I had been defeated three times, I was elected by over three thousand votes—one over.

With the exception of Fred Hadley and Drs. Lorne and Mabel Connell, no one in Prince Albert knew at that time that Olive and I had become engaged. We were to be married in December 1953. Olive and I had been acquainted for years. I had met her first when I came back from overseas in 1917. She was a young teenager—too young for me; we went our separate ways. I was married in 1929 and she in 1932. Her husband, Mr. Harry Palmer, a lawyer, died in Toronto within three years of their marriage, leaving her with their daughter Carolyn. When we met again after all the years, we started to talk about the things we talked about so many years before. We became engaged, and married, and have lived in abiding happiness.

After the nomination meeting in Prince Albert, I flew to Toronto. Olive was Assistant Director of Counselling Services for the Ontario Department of Education. One day I was waiting for her at the Royal York. Bill Brunt was with me. He afterwards told me that I suddenly said,

"I've got to go, I've got an appointment," and rushed for the main door. He went home and told his wife, Helen, "There's something on. I don't know what it is, but there's a girl somewhere." And he added, "I did everything I could to find out and failed." When I left him, he apparently rushed out the west door of the hotel. Olive had an Austin car. Bill was looking for someone with a large car. We passed by not three or four feet from him. A little later on, David Walker, who had assumed the role of matrimonial adviser, found out that Olive and I met from time to time. He and his wife, Bunty, invited us for a weekend at his summer place. On our return to Toronto, Dave phoned Bill Brunt: "There's nothing to it. They're not even close friends."

The day I arrived in Toronto from the nomination convention in Prince Albert, I told Olive that I could not understand why I had agreed to run as a candidate in Prince Albert. Experience, I explained, should have taught me that the only thing a Conservative candidate could expect there approached extinction. I had an invitation to the Coronation of Queen Elizabeth, and I intended to accept it. Olive argued against this. She pressed me to reconsider. She said, "Go back to Prince Albert and to work." I agreed. If I had not I feel sure that I would not have been elected.

It is impossible for me to convey what I owe to all those people in Prince Albert who, in the face of bitter criticism from their respective parties, worked so hard for my success. During the campaign they visited most if not all the homes in the city of Prince Albert, and in the towns and villages outside. Never have I seen anything to approach their election-day organization, planned by Hadley and Brunt. Rows of telephones, someone manning each one and seeing to it that everyone in his particular poll got out to vote. When anyone voted, our outside scrutineer at that particular poll phoned this information in immediately. This person was then checked off the list. Those who were thought favourable to my candidacy, and who had yet to vote, were reminded by phone. They were provided when necessary with transportation from one of the largest car pools I have ever seen. Our vote was mainly out by two o'clock that afternoon. When our victory was assured, everyone who had joined had every reason to feel, as each one did, that he or she was responsible for the victory.

When Mr. Drew took ill and resigned in September 1956, the Honourable Earl Rowe became House Leader of the Party, at George Drew's request. Rowe called me in Prince Albert to advise me of Drew's resignation and suggested that I come East at once to learn at first hand something of what was taking place. I was shocked; a man who had been as strong physically as Mr. Drew would have led anyone to believe that he had years ahead. After the 1948 Convention, I was fully convinced that I would never have another chance to become Leader. After the 1949 and 1953 elections, when I was approached by Members of the caucus who claimed that I had majority support and could challenge the leadership, I spurned the suggestion. I gave loyalty and support to George Drew to the very limit of my capacity.

A leadership Convention was called for December in Ottawa. I had no exact idea of the support I might expect. A comment in the press on the day of my arrival in Ottawa was that there were five or six potential candidates, and that a preliminary poll among Members of the Conservative Party in the House of Commons gave me the lead. I met with three or four of my friends. Bill Brunt and David Walker came to Ottawa at once. I stayed in Ottawa for a couple of days, then returned to my home. I knew I had a solid base of support in Saskatchewan and Alberta. Duff Roblin was supporting me in Manitoba. M. J. O'Brien of Vancouver considered my support in British Columbia substantial, despite the fact that Davie Fulton had already indicated that he would be a candidate. The next few days I spent in looking after some matters that required attention in my law office. Then, I decided to make my campaign headquarters in Ottawa. I determined that I would try, so far as I could, to go across the country and meet with friends and supporters.

Passing through Winnipeg on my way east, I did not feel that I should approach Gordon Churchill, one of the most outstanding parliamentarians and authorities on the Rules of the House of Commons of the present century. I have remarked before that I have always followed a practice not to solicit votes in either election or leadership campaigns. I didn't want to embarrass Churchill by asking him what he was going to do. He, nevertheless, met me during the stop-over. He reported that eighty per cent of caucus was with me. Without giving any indication that he personally was supporting me, although he claimed afterwards that his support should have been very apparent, he decided to travel part of the way with me so we could discuss matters further. He did not leave the train until we reached Ottawa, where he stayed to become my number one adviser on general national campaign strategy, and one of my closest friends.

Allister Grosart, who had managed Drew's campaign in 1948, offered to support me. I accepted with enthusiasm, knowing his capacity for organization. I would place him among a very select two or three organizers in all the political parties. He was a person whose advice I was happy to accept, and whose determination to secure results was confined entirely to what was fair and honest.

My close friend through the years, Paul Lafontaine of Montreal, provided me with his estimate of the situation in Quebec from time to time. He was a Canadian in the finest sense of the word, a descendant of the family that gave Canada the Baldwin-Lafontaine administration, and a man who asked nothing for himself, except to serve his Party. It will always be one of the regrets I'll carry to the end of my life that I did not make him a Senator, as I should have done. The Convention was fought fairly, with the exception of those from Quebec who lined up with Léon Balcer, the Member from Three Rivers, and three or four of the old guard from Ontario and the Maritimes. Their objective was to annihilate me. When I went to Quebec City to meet with the leaders of the Party, with only one exception the message they gave me was that under no circumstances should I stand. This was underlined in Montreal, in the Windsor Hotel, where I was approached by a man still prominent in the Conservative Party in Quebec, a tall, heavy-built individual. He came to my suite. He said that he had a message for me and would not take no for an answer. He handed me a document signifying my resignation as a candidate. He said, "You sign that now. I won't leave here otherwise." He left a lot faster than he had expected. The story he told afterwards was, as I heard it: "That Diefenbaker, he is a dangerous man. He was very angry with me. He called me names. He told me, 'You get out of here, you baboon-face, or I'll throw you out that window.' " In fact, I was fortunate that he left before anything started: I would have been the one thrown out in any physical contest.

Following the Convention, I participated in a radio program with a group under the chairmanship of Grant Dexter, one of the icons of Canada's Liberal press establishment. Dexter opened the broadcast by stating that I had made a fatal mistake at the Convention in not having a French-speaking mover or seconder to my nomination. I answered him to this effect, "What about Mackenzie King? He did pretty well, didn't he? You have always regarded him as having been the epitome of success. I'm not saying this in a critical way or satirical way, but you were always one of the worshippers at his throne. Who moved and seconded his nomination in the 1919 convention? You were there." He could not recall. He thought it might have been Sir William Mulock. I had to inform him that Mulock had been on the bench since 1910. The fact was that Sir Allan Aylesworth and Sidney Fisher had moved and seconded King's nomination, and although Fisher was from Quebec, he didn't speak in French. I do not know what King's reasons were, but I was certain as to why I didn't have a French-speaking mover or seconder. I wanted this convention to be one not dominated by Toronto or Montreal. If I had chosen a mover from Ontario, I would have had to have a seconder from Quebec, or *vice versa*. This would have meant that all of the other provinces would have been forgotten. Therefore, I decided I would have one nominator from the Pacific and the other from the Atlantic region: General George Pearkes, v.c., from British Columbia, and the Honourable Hugh John Flemming from New Brunswick. Several Quebec Conservatives warned me against this. I chose to rely on the advice of Paul Lafontaine: "Don't worry about these fellows who still preach the kind of stuff learned with their mother's milk and the Liberal Party as to what has to be done and what has not to be done in order to win Quebec."

I felt that, except for Quebec, support for my candidature was general, although I had no idea for whom the Nova Scotia delegates would vote. There were some individual delegates supporting me, but George Nowlan, M.P., leader of the delegation from that province, gave no indication as to what his people were going to do. Even at the convention, few of these delegates wore badges of any of the candidates.

A few weeks before the convention, when in Toronto, Premier Leslie Frost called me and suggested we have a chat in his suite at the Royal York. With him was Oakley Dalgleish, the editor of the *Globe and Mail*. The generalities that were indulged in convinced me that he just did not want to tell me he was not supporting me. But as I started to leave, he said that he had decided that his support was going to me. From that point, things started to move in Ontario. No one ever did more than he did. He threw himself into the campaign. He was an amazing politician, of high ability and political acumen. I have heard him say that he viewed everything from the perspective of the barber chair in Lindsay. He was a man of and for the people. He had no ambition to become federal leader; he made that clear to me on several occasions. If he had been a candidate I would have supported him. After my government came into office I asked him to join the Cabinet. Later, when he had ended his Premiership of Ontario, I offered him a Senatorship. He said, "No." Only then did I say: "Well, at least you should be a member of the Queen's Privy Council in Canada." He said he would be very happy to have that.

The emergency debate in the House of Commons on the Suez Crisis in November 1956 had an effect on the convention. My wife and I had been in Israel in 1954; I always had a particular interest in the Middle East. On 31 January 1956, in the course of a debate on external affairs, I suggested that ultimately there would be war unless something was done to set up an organization under the United Nations, a watching force, a presence between the Israeli and Arab forces. Hansard records what was said. Later in the year, in the United Kingdom, one of the greatest British foreign ministers of all time, Prime Minister Anthony Eden, suggested such a force. The Right Honourable Selwyn Lloyd, his foreign minister, pressed for such a force. It was only when things came to a head later in the year that Mr. Pearson, speaking on behalf of our country, brought the idea of such a force before the United Nations.

I recall those dark days very well. All of us feared international war. That fear must still be in the hearts of men and women everywhere in the world today, as a solution to the Middle East problem seems so uncertain. For some reason, and it has never been explained to my satisfaction, Prime Minister St. Laurent made a most bitter speech. It must have been produced by the Department of External Affairs. He stated that no longer would powerful nations be able to dictate the course of history. The days of Britain and France were over, they were past. He put Britain, France, and the Soviet Union on the same level. It seemed obvious that Nasser had been handsomely aided and abetted by the Soviets in his moves to cut off Britain's lifeline, the Suez Canal. St. Laurent's remarks were totally out of keeping with his general philosophy and, although he never offered any alibis for the speech, I know it caused him a great deal of heartache. Certainly, it was an element in the Liberal Party's loss in the general election of 1957.

I did not speak for the Conservative Party when I spoke in that debate. My speech was far removed from "Me too", or "Ready, aye ready". I endeavoured then, as I always have on international affairs, to bring about a non-partisan unity. But I could not help being critical of Canada's failure to vote on key resolutions in the General Assembly. It would appear that the Government of Canada continues to this day to be afflicted with the malady of abstention on key votes. I pointed out that if Nasser could control the United Nations Emergency Force, UNEF, it did not augur well for the future of any international police action. My speech received general support from the influential press across the country, and I think favourably influenced many delegates at the convention.

The 1956 convention was the first since 1927 that saw a real and effective determination on the part of the rank and file of the Party to be represented, rather than to have the leadership determined by a small clique who, having control over the Party machinery and the operation of conventions, had been able, in earlier conventions, to direct or at least to guide the delegates, by various means, to the object of their choice. The delegates knew me well; they knew where I stood. I carried 774 of the 1,284 votes cast on the first ballot. Donald Fleming and Davie Fulton shared the balance. It was 14 December 1956. I was the Leader of my Party.

It is always difficult to reconstruct one's feelings, particularly on such occasions. It had been such a long, long trail. I was calm, more so possibly than usual. The opportunity that I had looked forward to was now given me, the opportunity to bring about, not a Canada of principalities, but a Canada in unity. I thought of the millions of Canadians who wanted someone to give them a vision of the kind of Canada worth trying to bring about, that Canada to which so many of their sons and daughters had contributed in two world wars. All through the defeats, I had never lost faith. Faith does not deny realities, but it generates hope. Faith carries one on. In achieving the leadership of my Party, I had a deep sense of thankfulness to Almighty God, and appreciation for those who had stood with me through the years. There was no exultation on my part, but there was a humble determination to do my best to achieve the Canada of my dreams. I do not know how to express it further. I told the assembled delegates, and all Canadians, "We will be the next Government. We have an appointment with Destiny." Of that I never had a doubt.

APPENDICES

APPENDIX ONE

For the more specialized readers a representative cross-section of my reported law cases is given below.

Boutin v. *Mackie*, [1922] 2 W.W.R. 1197 (Sask.).

Savidan v. *Laplante*, [1924] 2 W.W.R. 1222, [1924] 3 D.L.R. 1089 (Sask. C.A.).

Cherry v. *Bredin*, [1927] 2 W.W.R. 314, 22 Sask. L.R. 24, [1927] 3 D.L.R. 326 (C.A.).

Farrell v. *Sawitski*, [1929] 3 W.W.R. 23, [1929] 4 D.L.R. 289 (Sask.).

R. v. *Olson*, [1929] 1 W.W.R. 432, 23 Sask. L.R. 321, 51 C.C.C. 122, [1929] 2 D.L.R. 300 (C.A.).

R. v. *Wysochan*, [1930] 54 C.C.C. 172 (Sask. C.A.).

Bondholders Securities Corpn. v. *Manville* [1933] 3 W.W.R. 1, [1933] 4 D.L.R. 699 (Sask. C.A.); [1935] 1 W.W.R. 452, affirming [1933] 3 W.W.R. 677 (Sask. C.A.).

Marshall v. *Hett & Sibbald, Ltd.*, [1933] 2 W.W.R. 315 (Sask. C.A.).

Hazlett v. *Ross (Van Ross)*, [1934] 1 W.W.R. 252, 62 C.C.C. 192 (Sask.).

R. v. Smith, [1935] 2 W.W.R. 433, 64 C.C.C. 131, [1935] 3 D.L.R. 703 (Sask. C.A.).

R. v. Harms, [1936] 2 W.W.R. 114 (Sask.).

Hackworth v. Baker, [1936] 2 W.W.R. 622, refusing leave to appeal to Privy Council from [1936] 1 W.W.R. 321 (Sask. C.A.).

Kwasnica v. Porter [1938] 1 W.W.R. 802, affirmed [1938] 2 W.W.R. 14, [1938] 2 D.L.R. 805 (Sask. C.A.).

Prince Albert Agricultural Society v. Dobson, [1939] 1 W.W.R. 719 (Sask.).

Re Belaney ("Grey Owl") Estate: Belaney v. Perrier and Dawn, [1939]3 W.W.R. 591 (Sask.).

R. v. Hutchinson, [1939] 1 W.W.R. 545, 71 C.C.C. 199, [1939] 3 D.L.R. 189 (Sask. C.A.).

R. v. Emele, [1940] 2 W.W.R. 430, 74 C.C.C. 76 (Sask. C.A.).

E. Swain et al. v. R. Ex relatione Adolph Studer, [1941] S.C.R. 40.

White Fox Alfalfa Seed Growers Co-op. Marketing Assn. v. A. E. McKenzie Co., [1942] 1 D.L.R. 45, [1941] 3 W.W.R. 919.

White Fox Alfalfa Seed Growers Co-op. Marketing Assn. v. A. E. McKenzie Co., [1944] 3 W.W.R. 173 (Sask.).

Re Hicks, 7 C.R. 59, [1948] 2 W.W.R. 400, 92 C.C.C. 154 (B.C.). [Further abridged under Part xx, infra.]

R. v. Irons, [1949] 1 W.W.R. 475.

Davidson Co-operative Association Limited v. Minister of National Revenue, [1953] 9 Tax A.B.C. 369.

R. v. Cathro, [1955] 22 C.R. 77, 15 W.W.R. (N.S.) 541, 112 C.C.C. 154 (B.C. C.A.).

APPENDIX TWO

The second volume of the Diefenbaker Memoirs will deal with some of the achievements of the Diefenbaker Government in the context of the stirring years from 1957 to 1962.

The posture of the Government in domestic and international affairs bore the stamp of John Diefenbaker's convictions, tempered and nurtured over the years. He proposed a new vision of Canada for Canadians. His phrase "the New Frontier" (an expression that was three years later appropriated by President John F. Kennedy) captured the hearts of Canadians.

What was the hallmark of the Diefenbaker years—years of conviction and responsibility in international and national affairs? Canada carried out her responsibilities, maintained her defence forces, wholeheartedly supported NATO and the principles of collective security, and upheld and preserved our sovereignty in the Arctic. Canada called on the U.S.S.R. to grant self-determination to the captive nations—the Ukraine, the Baltic States, and the countries of Eastern Europe.

The policy of a "colour-blind Commonwealth", given new shape and texture by Diefenbaker's convictions, represented new hope for millions of black, yellow, and brown human beings in the Commonwealth. He held firmly to the principle of Canada's right to make her own decisions in all questions affecting Canada's interests.

Parliament's supremacy in national affairs was recognized and reinforced; through the use of simultaneous translation Parliament became in fact bilingual. Mrs. Ellen Fairclough became the first woman federal Minister, and the first woman named to Her Majesty's Canadian Privy Council.

Under the Diefenbaker Government the Arctic became a known part of Canada. Roads were built to resource areas. Aid was provided to the provinces and to regions, particularly the Atlantic provinces. Great projects such as the Columbia River development, the South Saskatchewan Dam, the Pine Point Railway, and the Manitoba Flood Control were hallmarks of that Government's dedication to national economic development in all parts of our country.

Parity prices, cash advances on farm-stored grain, and crop insurance were elements in a program to bring Canadian agriculture into the twentieth century and to provide for the farmer the security enjoyed by other segments of our industrial society.

A vast program of technical training was launched from coast to coast, and the results of that are still apparent in every part of industry. Tens of thousands of young Canadians received training they would otherwise have been denied.

A special concern of the Government was physical fitness, and the structures set up under the Fitness and Amateur Sport Act have shown results in Canada's improved performance in international athletic competitions since that time.

Social justice and health policies placed Canada in the forefront of modern nations.

In the fundamental areas of citizenship and individual freedoms, the real meaning of being a Canadian, Mr. Die-

fenbaker raised issues which other governments had by-
passed; he wrote large on the scroll of public policy a
warning against tolerating concepts leading to a kind of
second-class citizenship for those of neither English nor
French background. He granted new recognition to the
Indian population by providing them with the right to
vote.

Breaking new ground, he was subject to criticism and
controversy; yet he never faltered. His vision of Canada,
rejected by many at the time, has come full circle and is
now accepted by the vast majority of Canadians. Future
historians in an attitude of calm objectivity will not find
his legacy in a sterile enumeration of legislative enact-
ments but in an enhanced citizenship, a fuller compre-
hension of individual rights as embodied in his Bill of
Rights and the body of jurisprudence which has grown
up around it, and a new pride in being a Canadian.

Gregor Guthrie
Thomas Van Dusen

INDEX

INDEX

Aberhart, William, 174-76
Advertising, political, 259-60
Aird, Hugh, 80, 86, 90
Almighty Voice, 28-29
Anderson, J. T. M., 150, 157, 166
Anderson, Jack, 164-65, 189, 191, 252, 259-60
Anglo-Japanese Alliance (1921), 148
Arm River, 176, 180-81
Athlone, Earl of, 224
Automobiles, 12-13, 134-36

Baby bonus. See Family Allowances
Baker, Colin, 137
Baker, Fred, 58
Baker, George, 58-60
Balcer, Léon, 278
Bannerman, Duncan, 19, 42
Bannerman, George, 2, 5-7
Bannerman, John, 5
Baptist Church, 5, 73-74
Barr, Rev. Isaac, 22
Batoche, Battle of, 25, 32
"Battle of the Brains, The", 206-07
Beaudoin, René, 245-46
Bell, R. A., 195, 249
Bence, Alfred H., 249
Bennett, R. B., 58, 95, 152, 155-56, 161-66, 177-79, 194, 212-13, 235, 236, 243
Bennett, W. A. C., 175
Berlin (Kitchener), 7
Bethune, 186-87
Biggar, 68
Bill of Rights, 110, 252-54
Blackmore, John, 204
Bladworth, 189

Blizzards, 49-51, 184-85
Boer War, return of Canadian Contingent from, 13-14
Bonnar, R. A., 95
Borden, Sir Robert, 74-75
Boucher, Russell, 271
Bowerman, E. L., 217
Bowman, Charles, 179
Bracken, John, 187, 216, 251-52, 254-58, 263-64
Branion, S. J. A., 139
Bridgeman, Rev. E. J., 14, 73-74
Brown, C. Roscoe, 70
Brown, Rev. W. G., 249
Brunt, Helen, 275
Brunt, William R., 252, 264, 274-75, 276
Bryant, J. G., 130
Bryant Charges Commission, 129-30
Buffalo, Aaron, 29
Bureau, Jacques, 146
Burgess, David L., 160-61
Burns, Pat, 235

Calgary Eye-Opener, 72, 95
Campbell (great-grandfather), 2
Campbell, Flora (grandmother), 2
Canada Citizenship Act, 253
Canada–United States relations, 270
Canadian nationalism, 75, 218-19, 282
Canadian Northern Railway, 21
Canadian Pacific Railway, 19-21
Canoe River case, 111-16
Capital punishment, 6-7, 96, 106-07, 123-24
Cardin, P. J. A., 196
Carlton, 23-24, 55

Carlton House, 24
Case, Garfield, 216-17
Casselman, A. C., 200
CCF. See Co-operative Commonwealth Federation
Census regulations, 218-19
Chambers, A., 202
Cheadle, Dr., 24
Chevrier, Lionel, 231
Church, Tommy, 209-10
Churchill, Gordon, 277
Churchill, Sir Winston, 199-202
Churchill, Manitoba, 4
Civil liberties, 219-26
Clark, J. G. ("Champ"), 75
Cold War, 268-69
Coldwell, M. J., 174, 203, 220, 246
Colonist cars, 19-20
Combines Investigation Act, 266
Commonwealth, 140, 230-31, 233
Commonwealth Air Training Scheme, 232
Commonwealth (Empire) Parliamentary Association, 230-32
Communist Party, 262, 268-69
Confederation, 7, 39
Connell, Drs. Lorne and Mabel, 191, 274
Conscription (1917), 91, 126, 188-89; crisis (1944), 215-17
Conservative Leadership Conventions: (1927) 155; (1938) 177-79, 248; (1942) 251-57; (1948) 263-68; (1956) 276-82
Conservative Party, 7, 28, 57, 64, 74-75, 125-26, 140-44, 145-67, 177-80, 187, 195, 198, 205-06, 216-17, 248-82; House Leadership (1943), 257-58; Leadership (1940-42), 248-51; philosophy, 140-41, 153, 255, 264-66, 268-69, 282
Constitutional crisis (1926), 146-48
Co-operative Commonwealth Federation, 174, 203-04, 250-51, 262-63
Cousins, F. C., 137
Crerar, T. A., 53, 133
Cross, Austin, 230
Crow's Nest Pass rates, 142
Cuelenaere, J. M., 138-39, 181, 191-92
Culloden, Battle of, 2
Cumming, J. Douglas, 89
Customs Scandal (1926), 146-47

Dalgleish, Oakley, 279
Dandurand, Raoul, 237

Dardanelles campaign, 201
Davies, Robert, 16
Davis, T. C., 131, 136-37, 139, 143, 150, 168, 177
Davis, T. O., 55, 136
Defence of Canada Regulations, 186, 218-23
d'Egville, Sir Howard, 230
Depression, 169-73
Derksen, Gerhard, 40
Dexter, Grant, 278-79
Diefenbacker (grandparents), 1-2
Diefenbaker, Edna Mae, 111-12, 165-66, 181-82
Diefenbaker, Edward L., 40-41, 44, 49-50, 67, 77, 80
Diefenbaker, Elmer, 10, 16, 23, 33-34, 39, 41-47, 48, 49-54, 69, 71-73, 98, 128, 252, 260-61, 273
Diefenbaker, Henry, 51
Diefenbaker, John George: family background, 1-18; move to West, 18-23; homestead, 35-37, 38-54, 66-67; education, 10, 14-15, 34, 44, 67-71, 77-85, 91-92; childhood ambitions, 66, 71, 95; real estate venture, 73; teaching experience, 81-82; book-selling, 84-85; military service, 85-91; war injury, 90-91, 156-57; law career, 91-124; reported law cases, 103-24, and see Apperdix One; public speaking, 54, 70-71, 78, 91, 143, 157-60, 195-96, 252-53; leadership of Saskatchewan Conservative Party, 166-67, 169-77; retirement considered (1952), 271; elected Leader of federal Conservative Party, 282; fishing and hunting, 14, 33-34, 43, 48-49; music, 10-11, 33, 47-48; religion, 5, 10, 32, 44, 47-48, 282; sports, 44-46, 70
Views on: one Canada, 140, 218-23, 252-54, 282; perspective in politics, 138-39, 204-05; political advertising, 259-60; political parties, 83; public service, 17-18, 66, 125-26; racial discrimination, 16, 126-27, 140-41, 218-23, 252; social welfare legislation, 151; tariff, 127, 140; unhyphenated Canadianism, 140, 218-19, 274
Diefenbaker, Mary Florence (née Bannerman), 5, 9-18, 19-23, 32-33, 34-35, 42-47, 51-52, 66-69, 74, 77, 83, 95
Diefenbaker, Olive, 239, 274-75

Diefenbaker, William Thomas, 7-18, 19-23, 33-37, 38-54, 66-71, 74, 77, 83-84, 95, 193, 256
"Diefenbaker schooners", 51
Discrimination, racial, 16, 140-41, 218-23, 252
Donaldson, Sam J., 58-64, 143
Douglas, T. C., 174, 203, 262
Doukhobors, 35, 36, 40, 212
Drew, George, 165, 246, 263-71, 276
Duck Lake, 28-29; Battle of, 25-26
Dumont, Gabriel, 25-26
Dunning, Charles, 132

Eaton, Charles A., 231
Eden, Sir Anthony, 232, 280
Ehman, Alex, 137
Ehman, Gerry, 137
Eisenhower, Dwight D., 272
Election, Prince Albert (1933), 168-69
Elections, federal: (1911) 74-75, 126; (1917) 91, 126; (1921) 126, 133; (1925) 126, 139-44; (1926) 129, 145-54; (1930) 163; (1935) 163; (1940) 180-92; (1945) 235, 258-63; (1949) 262, 268; (1953) 271, 275-76
Elections, joint meetings, 57, 190
Elections, Saskatchewan: (1925) 128; (1929) 150-51; (1938) 173-77, 180-81
Elizabeth II, 193, 275
Empire Parliamentary Association. See Commonwealth Parliamentary Association
Ens, Gerhard, 58
Esling, W. (Billy), 212-13

Family Allowances, 152-53, 265
Fansher, W. R., 187-88
Farmers' Institute, 53-54
Fees, legal, 116-17, 184
Ferguson, Howard, 171-72
Fielding, W. S., 131-32
Finlayson, R. K., 163, 263
First World War, 82, 85-91
Firth, Wally, 30
Fish Creek, Battle of, 25-26
Fitzpatrick, Charles, 27
Fleming, Donald, 246, 266, 282
Flemming, Hugh John, 279
Flynn, J. H., 97, 132
Forsey, Eugene, 271
Fort Carlton, 18, 24
Fort Walsh, 30

Fort William, 5, 20
Fournier, A., 214
Freedom, guarantees, 93
Frost, Leslie, 279-80
Fulbright, J. William, 232
Fulton, E. Davie, 246, 272, 276, 282

Gardiner, James G., 64, 128-30, 150, 157-59, 170-76, 187, 196, 239, 240, 243, 260-62, 271-72
German-American Bund, 184
Gerrymandering, 261-62, 271-72
Gillis, Clarrie, 203
Gladstone, Chief James, 30
Glen, J. A., 194
Godfrey, R. B., 137
Gordon, Percy, 178
Gould, "Fighting Bob", 128-29
Gouzenko affair, 224-26, 269
Grain marketing, 52-54
Graydon, Gordon, 233-35, 252, 257-58
Green, Howard, 198, 206, 246, 255
Greenwood, 10-12
Gregg, Milton, 229-30
Grey Owl, 118-20
Grosart, Allister, 277
Guthrie, Hugh, 155-56

Hadley, Fred, 272-73, 275
Hague, 38-40
Hailsham, Lord, 235
Halcyonia, 40-54
Hall, Emmett, 92
Halley's Comet, 68-69
Hamilton, C. M., 157
Hanbidge, R. L., 166, 254
Hansard, 208-11
Hanson, R. B., 198-200, 205-08, 249, 251
Harris, Joe, 204, 211, 249
Hartney, Russell, 85
Hatfield, Heber, 250
Haultain, Frederick W. G., 56-57, 127
Hawkesville, 1-2
Haydon, Rev. A. Eustace, 73
Heaps, A. A., 151
Helmsdale, 3
Hepburn, Mitchell, 229, 250
Herridge, R. "Billy", 179
Herridge, William, 163, 179-80, 203
Hicks, Calvin Knox (case), 108-10
Hitler, Adolf, 201, 232
Hnatyshyn, John, 185
Hoffnungsfeld, 40

Holyoake, Keith, 232
Homestead regulations, 38
Homuth, Karl, 229
Hong Kong Inquiry, 206
Horner, Byron, 185
House of Commons, 7-8, 193-98, 204-05, 212-14, 240-47
House of Commons Committee on the Defence of Canada Regulations, 220-21
Howe, C. D., 139, 197, 240-47
Hudson Bay Railway, 142-43
Hudson's Bay Company, 4-5
Hunter, J. Kelso, 92
Hyphenated Canadianism, 140, 218-19, 274

Ilsley, James, 214, 229
Immigrants, 20-21, 22, 43-44
Imperial (Sask.), 180-82
Indians. See Native peoples
Isaacs, Sir Rufus, 116-17

Jack, Mel, 256
Jackson, Ed, 273
Jamieson, Duncan, 81
Japanese Canadians, internment of, 222-24
Jehovah's Witnesses, 221
Johnson, D. S., 173
Johnson, J. Fred, 187-88, 192
Judges, appointment of, 169, 236-37
Jury system, 100-01
Justices of the Peace, 93-94

Kelly, W. B., 180-83
Kenaston, 185
Keown, H. E., 155, 159
Kerrobert, 172
Kildonan, 2-3
King, William Lyon Mackenzie, 6, 8-9, 131-32, 133, 144, 145-50, 171-72, 183, 195, 196-97, 199-200, 202, 205-08, 212-13, 215, 232, 236, 243, 250-51, 258, 278-79
King-Byng affair (1926), 146-48
Kinistino, 133
Knox, Andrew, 60, 133, 139
Ku Klux Klan, 150
Kyle, David, 97

Lafontaine, Paul, 277-78
Lake Centre, 156, 180-92, 261-62, 271-72
Lamont, John H., 56
Langley, George, 58, 131,
Lapointe, Ernest, 202, 235
Lapointe, Hugues, 202
Laurier, Sir Wilfrid, 7, 55-56, 74-77
Lavergne, Armand, 154
Law, concept, 93, 95-96, 108, 121-24; criminal, 11, 104, 110; punishment and rehabilitation, 121-4
Lawyers, 11, 93-95, 103, 188
Léger, J. T., 181-82
Lemieux, F.-X., 27
Liberal Party, 7, 55-58, 62-64, 74-75, 93-94, 125-33, 145-59, 184, 187-89, 219-20, 224, 236, 240-47, 250, 270-71, 271-72, 278-79, 281
Lilburne, John, 65
Lincoln, Abraham, 65-66
Lloyd, Selwyn, 280
Lloyd, George David, 87
Luchkovich, Mike, 133-34
Lukacsffy, Count, 135-36

McCheane, W. C., 47-48
McCraney, George E., 58
Macdonald, Angus L., 228-29
McDonald, Charles, 139-44
Macdonald, Sir John A., 3, 7, 70, 159-60, 236-38, 241-42
MacDonald, Ramsay, 228
McDougall, Jim, 189
MacFarland, John I., 244
McGee, Thomas D'Arcy, 7
McGregor, R., 209, 249
MacKay, A. G., 95
McKay, Gentleman Joe, 25
MacKay, Ira Allen, 79-80
McKay, James, 58-59
Mackenzie, Ian, 139, 196, 200, 213-14
Mackenzie, P. E., 95
Mackenzie, William Lyon, 6, 196, 207-08
Mackie, Victor, 256
Mackie v. Boutin, 121
Maclean, Donald, 80
McLorg, E. A. C., 92
Macmillan, Allan, 80, 86, 89-90
McNab, Archie, 58
McNaughton, A. G. L., 216-17
MacPherson, M. A., 177-78, 254

Makaroff, Peter, 37
Maloney, J. J., 150
Manion, Robert, 171, 178-79, 187, 195, 248-49, 255
Manning, Ernest, 175
Manville, O. B., 154
Manville, Rae, 171, 191
Marchand, Leonard, 30
Martin, E. T., 273
Martin, Paul, 139, 230
Martin, W. M., 131-32
Marty, Rev., 47
Meighen, Arthur, 126, 141-44, 145-55, 208-09, 237, 250-51
Mennonites, 23, 33, 41-42
Merriman, Sir Boyd, 236
Métis, 25-28
Middleton, General, 26
Mighton, Stanley, 84
Milton, Viscount, 24
Mock Parliament, 82-83
Morgentaler, Henry, 79
Moxon, Arthur, 80
Mulcaster, Richard, 154
Mulock, Pate, 209
Mulock, Sir William, 209, 279
Murray, Walter C., 78-79

National Government Party, 187
Native peoples, 28-30, 117-18
Nazis, influence in Saskatchewan, 184, 218
Neill, A. W., 222
Neilson, James W., 69
Neustadt, 9-10
New Democracy Party, 179-80
Newsboys' Association of America, 72
Nisbet, Rev. James, 59
Nokomis, 185
Nolan, P. J., 94-95
North West Company, 4-5
North West Mounted Police. See Royal Canadian Mounted Police
North West Rebellion, 25-28
Northern Crown Bank, 69
Noseworthy, J. W., 250-51
Nowlan, George, 279

O'Brien, M. J., 252, 276
O'Leary, Grattan, 268
Olympic Games (1936), 201

Order-in-Council, government by, 197, 219-20, 224
Ostrovsky, A., 139

Palliser, Captain John, 24
Palmer, Carolyn, 274
Paris, fall of, 198-99
Parliament, 7, 193-98, 213-14, 240-47
Patrick, J. M., 164
Patterson, W. J., 170-76
Pearkes, General George, V.C., 279
Pearkes, John, 115
Pearson, Arthur, 180, 259-60
Pearson, L. B., 280
Pennefather, P. W., 31, 145, 154
Perley, E. E., 166, 192, 211, 217
Perley, Sir George and Lady, 86-87
Petrofka, 36-37, 40
Philion, Alexis, 137
Pickersgill, Jack, 245-46, 258
Pipeline Debate, 245-47
Plains Road School, 12, 14-15, 18
Pook, Sergeant, 25
Port Hope Report, 255
Pouliot, J. F., 206
Power, C. G., 226-27
Prince Albert, 37, 55-56, 59-60, 137, 168-69, 197, 273-76
Prince Albert Club, 60
Progressive Party, 133-34, 145-46
Progressive Conservative. See Conservative Party
"Provincial Righters", 57
Public meetings, 55-57, 103-04, 157-60

Quebec, 25-28, 148, 248, 251, 267-69, 277-79

"Rabbitskin Election", 62-64
Racism, 148-51, 218-23, 252
Racjcs, Count von, 22
Radio, election use, 185-87
Radisson, 13, 52
Ralston, J. L., 214-17
Rebellion of 1837, 6
Reciprocity (1911), 74-75
Reconstruction Party, 163-64
Red River carts, 24-25
Red River Settlement, 3-5
Redistribution, 261-62, 271-72
Regina, 21

Republican Convention (1952), 272
Rex v. *Harms*, 104-06
Rex v. *Smith*, 117-18
Riel, Louis, 25-28
Robb, J. M., 195
Robinette, J. J., 11
Robinette, T. C., 11
Roblin, Duff, 276
Rogers, Norman, 228
Rose, Fred, 269
Rosthern, 22, 32
Rowe, Earl, 150, 248-49, 276
Royal Canadian Legion, 91
Royal Canadian Mounted Police, 25, 30-31
Rutherford, A. C., 57

St. Henry, Lucky, 47
St. Laurent, Louis, 124, 224, 226, 235-36, 240, 246-47, 268, 281
St. Pierre, Joe, 98
Samletski, Joe, 33
San Francisco Conference, 233-35
Saskatchewan, creation as a separate province, 39, 57; early politics, 55-64
Saskatchewan Grain Growers' Assoc., 53, 127
Saskatoon, 21-22, 68
Saskatoon Phoenix, 39, 72
Scott, Walter, 57, 127, 131
Second World War, 193-232
Selkirk, Thomas, fifth Earl of, 3
Senate of Canada, 237
Shorncliffe, 88-89
Sibbald, Hugh, 171
Sifton, Sir Clifford, 22, 74, 126
Sikorski v. *Lozinski*, 103-04
Silton, 189-90
Sinclair, James, 202-03
Skelhorn, 13
Smith, F. E., 116-17
Smuts, Jan Christian, 233-34
Social Credit, 174-76, 203-04
South Saskatchewan Dam, 260-61
Southesk, Earl of, 24
Stechishin, Michael, 102
Stevens, H. H., 163-64, 171, 190-91, 205, 254-55
Stirling, Grote, 198-200
Studer v. *Swain*, 183

Suez Crisis, 280-81
Sutherland, Countess of, 3

Taft, Robert A., 272
Thatcher, Ross, 49
Todmorden, 12-18
Topping, Ed, 182
Toronto, 12-21
Trotter, Bernard Freeman, 89
Trudeau, Pierre Elliott, 240, 255
Turgeon, W. F. A., 57
Tustin, George, 249

Ukrainian immigrants, 41, 43-44
Underwood, 9
Unionist Government, 7, 91
United Nations, 233-35, 281-82
University of Saskatchewan, 70, 77-85; *The Sheaf*, 83
Urquhart, 13
Uxbridge, 10, 12

Verigin, Peter "Lordly", 40
Veterans' Charter, 227-28
Victoria, Queen, 17

Wakaw, 97-98, 101-03, 132, 134-35
Walker, Bunty, 275
Walker, David J., 254, 275-76
War Measures Act, 219, 225
Wartime Elections Act (1917), 126-27, 148
Weir, Robert, 160-61
Western, Maurice, 181
Wheat, marketing, 52-54
Wheat Board, 243
Wheat Heart Public School, 81-82
White, Thomas, 74
Whitton, Charlotte, 238-39
Williams, George, 174
Wilson, James R., 91
Winnipeg, 21
Wood, Rev. Idell Hartson, 73
Woodsworth, J. S., 151, 203
Wright, Ed D., 137
Wright Brothers, 46-47

York Factory, 4

Zimmerman, Joe, 23